The
Catholic Mass Readings
For Liturgical Year B
2021

Part A
November 29, 2020 – May 31, 2021

Corpus Christi Publishing
4649 Parrish Avenue
Salina, CA 93901
California
USA

CONTENTS

SECTION A

SECTION B

SECTION A

PRINCIPAL CELEBRATIONS OF THE LITURGICAL YEAR B, 2021

First Sunday of Advent	Nov. 29, 2020
Ash Wednesday	February 17, 2021
Easter Sunday	April 4, 2021
The Ascension of the Lord [Thursday]	May 13, 2021
Pentecost Sunday	May 23, 2021
The Most Holy Body and Blood of Christ	June 6, 2021
First Sunday of Advent	Nov. 28, 2021

LITURGY OF THE HOURS

Nov. 29, 2020 – Jan. 10, 2021	Advent, Christmas
Jan. 11 – Feb. 16, 2021	Weeks 1 to 6, Ordinary Time
Feb. 17 – May 23, 2021	Lent, Triduum, Easter
May 24 – July 31, 2021	Weeks 8 to 17, Ordinary Time
Aug. 1 – Nov. 27, 2021	Weeks 18 to 34, Ordinary Time
Nov. 28, 2021 – Jan. 9, 2022	Advent, Christmas

SECTION B

DAILY AND SUNDAY MASS READINGS FOR LITURGICAL YEAR B, 2021 (Part A)

FIRST SUNDAY OF ADVENT

First Reading   **Isaiah 63:16b-17, 19b; 64:2-7**

You, LORD, are our father, our redeemer you are named forever. Why do you let us wander, O LORD, from your ways, and harden our hearts so that we fear you not? Return for the sake of your servants, the tribes of your heritage.

Oh, that you would rend the heavens and come down, with the mountains quaking before you, while you wrought awesome deeds we could not hope for, such as they had not heard of from of old. No ear has ever heard, no eye ever seen, any God but you doing such deeds for those who wait for him. Would that you might meet us doing right, that we were mindful of you in our ways!

Behold, you are angry, and we are sinful; all of us have become like unclean people, all our good deeds are like polluted rags; we have all withered like leaves, and our guilt carries us away like the wind. There is none who calls upon your name, who rouses himself to cling to you; for you have hidden your face from us and have delivered us up to our guilt. Yet, O LORD, you are our father; we are the clay and you the potter: we are all the work of your hands.

Responsorial Psalm   Psalm 80:2-3, 15-16, 18-19

R. (4) Lord, make us turn to you; let us see your face and we shall be saved.

O shepherd of Israel, hearken, from your throne upon the cherubim, shine forth. Rouse your power, and come to save us. **R.**

Once again, O LORD of hosts, look down from heaven, and see; take care of this vine, and protect what your right hand has planted the son of man whom you yourself made strong. **R.**

May your help be with the man of your right hand, with the son of man whom you yourself made strong. Then we will no more withdraw from you; give us new life, and we will call upon your name. **R.**

Second Reading   1 Corinthians 1:3-9

Brothers and sisters:

Grace to you and peace from God our Father and the Lord Jesus Christ. I give thanks to my God always on your account for the grace of God bestowed on you in Christ Jesus, that in him you were enriched in every way, with all discourse and all knowledge, as the testimony to Christ was confirmed among you, so that you are not lacking in any spiritual gift as you wait for the revelation of our Lord Jesus Christ. He will keep you firm to the end, irreproachable on the day of our Lord Jesus Christ. God is faithful, and by him you were called to fellowship with his Son, Jesus Christ our Lord.

Alleluia   Psalm 85:8

R. Alleluia, alleluia.

Show us Lord, your love; and grant us your salvation. **R.**

Gospel Mark 13:33-37

Jesus said to his disciples:

"Be watchful! Be alert! You do not know when the time will come. It is like a man traveling abroad. He leaves home and places his servants in charge, each with his own work, and orders the gatekeeper to be on the watch. Watch, therefore; you do not know when the Lord of the house is coming, whether in the evening, or at midnight, or at cockcrow, or in the morning. May he not come suddenly and find you sleeping. What I say to you, I say to all: Watch!'"

MONDAY, NOVEMBER 30, 2020

FEAST OF SAINT ANDREW, APOSTLE

First Reading Romans 10:9-18

Brothers and sisters:

If you confess with your mouth that Jesus is Lord and believe in your heart that God raised him from the dead, you will be saved. For one believes with the heart and so is justified, and one confesses with the mouth and so is saved.

The Scripture says, *No one who believes in him will be put to shame.* There is no distinction between Jew and Greek; the same Lord is Lord of all, enriching all who call upon him. *For everyone who calls on the name of the Lord will be saved.* But how can they call on him in whom they have not believed? And how can they believe in him of whom they have not heard? And how can they hear without someone to preach? And how can people preach unless they are sent? As it is written, *how beautiful are the feet of those who bring the good news!* But not everyone has heeded the good news; for Isaiah says, *Lord, who has believed what was heard from us?* Thus faith comes from what is heard, and what is heard comes through the word of Christ. But I ask, did they not hear? Certainly they did; for *their voice has gone forth to all the earth, and their words to the ends of the world.*

Responsorial Psalm · Psalm 19:8, 9, 10, 11

R. (10) The judgments of the Lord are true, and all of them are just.

Or:

R. (John 6:63) Your words, Lord, are Spirit and life.

The law of the LORD is perfect, refreshing the soul; the decree of the LORD is trustworthy, giving wisdom to the simple. **R.**

The precepts of the LORD are right, rejoicing the heart; the command of the LORD is clear, enlightening the eye. **R.**

The fear of the LORD is pure, enduring forever; the ordinances of the LORD are true, all of them just. **R.**

They are more precious than gold, than a heap of purest gold; Sweeter also than syrup or honey from the comb. **R.**

Alleluia · Matthew 4:19

R. Alleluia, alleluia.

Come after me, says the Lord, and I will make you fishers of men. **R.**

Gospel · Matthew 4:18-22

As Jesus was walking by the Sea of Galilee, he saw two brothers, Simon who is called Peter, and his brother Andrew, casting a net into the sea; they were fishermen. He said to them, "Come after me, and I will make you fishers of men." At once they left their nets and followed him. He walked along from there and saw two other brothers, James, the son of Zebedee, and his brother John. They were in a boat, with their father Zebedee, mending their nets. He called them, and immediately they left their boat and their father and followed him.

TUESDAY OF THE FIRST WEEK OF ADVENT

First Reading   **Isaiah 11:1-10**

On that day, a shoot shall sprout from the stump of Jesse, and from his roots a bud shall blossom. The Spirit of the LORD shall rest upon him: a Spirit of wisdom and of understanding, A Spirit of counsel and of strength, a Spirit of knowledge and of fear of the LORD, and his delight shall be the fear of the LORD. Not by appearance shall he judge, nor by hearsay shall he decide, but he shall judge the poor with justice, and decide aright for the land's afflicted. He shall strike the ruthless with the rod of his mouth, and with the breath of his lips he shall slay the wicked. Justice shall be the band around his waist, and faithfulness a belt upon his hips. Then the wolf shall be a guest of the lamb, and the leopard shall lie down with the kid; the calf and the young lion shall browse together, with a little child to guide them. The cow and the bear shall be neighbors, together their young shall rest; the lion shall eat hay like the ox. The baby shall play by the cobra's den, and the child lay his hand on the adder's lair. There shall be no harm or ruin on all my holy mountain; for the earth shall be filled with knowledge of the LORD, as water covers the sea. On that day, the root of Jesse, set up as a signal for the nations, The Gentiles shall seek out, for his dwelling shall be glorious.

Responsorial Psalm   **Psalm 72:1-2, 7-8, 12-13, 17**

R. (7) Justice shall flourish in his time, and fullness of peace forever.

O God, with your judgment endow the king, and with your justice, the king's son; He shall govern your people with justice and your afflicted ones with judgment.**R.**

Justice shall flower in his days, and profound peace, till the moon be no more. May he rule from sea to sea, and from the River to the ends of the earth. **R.**

He shall rescue the poor when he cries out, and the afflicted when he has no one to help him. He shall have pity for the lowly and the poor; the lives of the poor he shall save. **R.**

May his name be blessed forever; as long as the sun his name shall remain. In him shall all the tribes of the earth be blessed; all the nations shall proclaim his happiness. **R.**

Alleluia

R. Alleluia, alleluia.

Behold, our Lord shall come with power; he will enlighten the eyes of his servants. **R.**

Gospel   Luke 10:21-24

Jesus rejoiced in the Holy Spirit and said, "I give you praise, Father, Lord of heaven and earth, for although you have hidden these things from the wise and the learned you have revealed them to the childlike. Yes, Father, such has been your gracious will. All things have been handed over to me by my Father. No one knows who the Son is except the Father, and who the Father is except the Son and anyone to whom the Son wishes to reveal him." Turning to the disciples in private he said, "Blessed are the eyes that see what you see. For I say to you, many prophets and kings desired to see what you see, but did not see it, and to hear what you hear, but did not hear it."

WEDNESDAY OF THE FIRST WEEK OF ADVENT

First Reading   **Isaiah 25:6-10a**

On this mountain the LORD of hosts will provide for all peoples a feast of rich food and choice wines, juicy, rich food and pure, choice wines. On this mountain he will destroy the veil that veils all peoples, the web that is woven over all nations; he will destroy death forever. The Lord GOD will wipe away the tears from all faces; the reproach of his people he will remove from the whole earth; for the Lord has spoken. On that day it will be said: "Behold our God, to whom we looked to save us! This is the LORD for whom we looked; let us rejoice and be glad that he has saved us!" For the hand of the LORD will rest on this mountain.

Responsorial Psalm   **Psalm 23:1-3a, 3b-4, 5, 6**

R. (6cd) I shall live in the house of the Lord all the days of my life.

The LORD is my shepherd; I shall not want. In verdant pastures he gives me repose; beside restful waters he leads me; he refreshes my soul. **R.**

He guides me in right paths for his name's sake. Even though I walk in the dark valley I fear no evil; for you are at my side with your rod and your staff that give me courage. **R.**

You spread the table before me in the sight of my foes; you anoint my head with oil; my cup overflows. **R.**

Only goodness and kindness follow me all the days of my life; and I shall dwell in the house of the LORD for years to come. **R.**

Alleluia

R. Alleluia, alleluia.

Behold, the Lord comes to save his people; blessed are those prepared to meet him. **R.**

Gospel   Matthew 15:29-37

At that time: Jesus walked by the Sea of Galilee, went up on the mountain, and sat down there. Great crowds came to him, having with them the lame, the blind, the deformed, the mute, and many others. They placed them at his feet, and he cured them. The crowds were amazed when they saw the mute speaking, the deformed made whole, the lame walking, and the blind able to see, and they glorified the God of Israel.

Jesus summoned his disciples and said, "My heart is moved with pity for the crowd, for they have been with me now for three days and have nothing to eat. I do not want to send them away hungry, for fear they may collapse on the way." The disciples said to him, "Where could we ever get enough bread in this deserted place to satisfy such a crowd?" Jesus said to them, "How many loaves do you have?" "Seven," they replied, "and a few fish." He ordered the crowd to sit down on the ground.

Then he took the seven loaves and the fish, gave thanks, broke the loaves, and gave them to the disciples, who in turn gave them to the crowds. They all ate and were satisfied. They picked up the fragments left over–seven baskets full.

MEMORIAL OF SAINT FRANCIS XAVIER, PRIEST

First Reading   **Isaiah 26:1-6**

On that day they will sing this song in the land of Judah:

"A strong city have we; he sets up walls and ramparts to protect us. Open up the gates to let in a nation that is just, one that keeps faith. A nation of firm purpose you keep in peace; in peace, for its trust in you."

Trust in the LORD forever! For the LORD is an eternal Rock. He humbles those in high places, and the lofty city he brings down; He tumbles it to the ground, levels it with the dust. It is trampled underfoot by the needy, by the footsteps of the poor.

Responsorial Psalm   **Psalm 118:1 and 8-9, 19-21, 25-27a**

R. (26a) Blessed is he who comes in the name of the Lord.

Or:

R. Alleluia.

Give thanks to the LORD, for he is good, for his mercy endures forever. It is better to take refuge in the LORD than to trust in man. It is better to take refuge in the LORD than to trust in princes. **R.**

Open to me the gates of justice; I will enter them and give thanks to the LORD. This gate is the LORD's; the just shall enter it. I will give thanks to you, for you have answered me and have been my savior. **R.**

O LORD, grant salvation! O LORD, grant prosperity! Blessed is he who comes in the name of the LORD; we bless you from the house of the LORD. The LORD is God, and he has given us light. **R.**

Alleluia   **Isaiah 55:6**

R. Alleluia, alleluia.

Seek the LORD while he may be found; call him while he is near. **R.**

Gospel   **Matthew 7:21, 24-27**

Jesus said to his disciples:

"Not everyone who says to me, 'Lord, Lord,' will enter the Kingdom of heaven, but only the one who does the will of my Father in heaven. "Everyone who listens to these words of mine and acts on them will be like a wise man who built his house on rock. The rain fell, the floods came, and the winds blew and buffeted the house. But it did not collapse; it had been set solidly on rock. And everyone who listens to these words of mine but does not act on them will be like a fool who built his house on sand. The rain fell, the floods came, and the winds blew and buffeted the house. And it collapsed and was completely ruined."

FRIDAY, DECEMBER 4, 2020
FRIDAY OF THE FIRST WEEK OF ADVENT

First Reading   **Isaiah 29:17-24**

Thus says the Lord GOD:

But a very little while, and Lebanon shall be changed into an orchard, and the orchard be regarded as a forest! On that day the deaf shall hear the words of a book; And out of gloom and

13

darkness, the eyes of the blind shall see. The lowly will ever find joy in the LORD, and the poor rejoice in the Holy One of Israel. For the tyrant will be no more and the arrogant will have gone; All who are alert to do evil will be cut off, those whose mere word condemns a man, Who ensnare his defender at the gate, and leave the just man with an empty claim. Therefore thus says the LORD, the God of the house of Jacob, who redeemed Abraham: Now Jacob shall have nothing to be ashamed of, nor shall his face grow pale. When his children see the work of my hands in his midst, they shall keep my name holy; they shall reverence the Holy One of Jacob, and be in awe of the God of Israel. Those who err in spirit shall acquire understanding, and those who find fault shall receive instruction.

Responsorial Psalm   Psalm 27:1, 4, 13-14

R. (1a) The Lord is my light and my salvation.
The LORD is my light and my salvation; whom should I fear? The LORD is my life's refuge; of whom should I be afraid? **R.**
One thing I ask of the LORD; this I seek: To dwell in the house of the LORD all the days of my life, that I may gaze on the loveliness of the LORD and contemplate his temple. **R.**
I believe that I shall see the bounty of the LORD in the land of the living. Wait for the LORD with courage; be stouthearted, and wait for the LORD. **R.**

Alleluia

R. Alleluia, alleluia.
Behold, our Lord shall come with power; he will enlighten the eyes of his servants. **R.**

Gospel   Matthew 9:27-31

As Jesus passed by, two blind men followed him, crying out, "Son of David, have pity on us!" When he entered the house, the blind men approached him and Jesus said to them, "Do you believe that I can do this?" "Yes, Lord," they said to him. Then he touched their eyes and said, "Let it be done for you according to your faith." And their eyes were opened. Jesus warned them sternly, "See that no one knows about this." But they went out and spread word of him through all that land.

SATURDAY, DECEMBER 5, 2020

SATURDAY OF THE FIRST WEEK OF ADVENT

First Reading   Isaiah 30:19-21, 23-26

Thus says the Lord GOD, the Holy One of Israel:
O people of Zion, who dwell in Jerusalem, no more will you weep; He will be gracious to you when you cry out, as soon as he hears he will answer you. The Lord will give you the bread you need and the water for which you thirst. No longer will your Teacher hide himself, but with your own eyes you shall see your Teacher, While from behind, a voice shall sound in your ears: "This is the way; walk in it," when you would turn to the right or to the left. He will give rain for the seed that you sow in the ground, and the wheat that the soil produces will be rich and abundant. On that day your flock will be given pasture and the lamb will graze in spacious meadows; the oxen and the asses that till the ground will eat silage tossed to them with shovel and pitchfork. Upon every high mountain and lofty hill there will be streams of running water. On the day of the great slaughter, when the towers fall, the light of the

moon will be like that of the sun and the light of the sun will be seven times greater like the light of seven days. On the day the LORD binds up the wounds of his people, he will heal the bruises left by his blows.

Responsorial Psalm   Psalm 147:1-2, 3-4, 5-6

R. (Isaiah 30:18d) Blessed are all who wait for the Lord.
Praise the LORD, for he is good; sing praise to our God, for he is gracious; it is fitting to praise him. The LORD rebuilds Jerusalem; the dispersed of Israel he gathers. **R.**
He heals the brokenhearted and binds up their wounds. He tells the number of the stars; he calls each by name. **R.**
Great is our LORD and mighty in power: to his wisdom there is no limit. The LORD sustains the lowly; the wicked he casts to the ground. **R.**

Alleluia   Isaiah 33:22

R. Alleluia, alleluia.
The LORD is our Judge, our Lawgiver, our King; he it is who will save us. **R.**

Gospel   Matthew 9:35-10:1, 5a, 6-8

Jesus went around to all the towns and villages, teaching in their synagogues, proclaiming the Gospel of the Kingdom, and curing every disease and illness. At the sight of the crowds, his heart was moved with pity for them because they were troubled and abandoned, like sheep without a shepherd. Then he said to his disciples, "The harvest is abundant but the laborers are few; so ask the master of the harvest to send out laborers for his harvest."

Then he summoned his twelve disciples and gave them authority over unclean spirits to drive them out and to cure every disease and every illness. Jesus sent out these Twelve after instructing them thus, "Go to the lost sheep of the house of Israel. As you go, make this proclamation: 'The Kingdom of heaven is at hand.' Cure the sick, raise the dead, cleanse lepers, drive out demons. Without cost you have received; without cost you are to give."

SUNDAY, DECEMBER 6, 2020
SECOND SUNDAY OF ADVENT

First Reading   **Isaiah 40:1-5, 9-11**

Comfort, give comfort to my people, says your God. Speak tenderly to Jerusalem, and proclaim to her that her service is at an end, her guilt is expiated; indeed, she has received from the hand of the LORD double for all her sins. A voice cries out: In the desert prepare the way of the LORD! Make straight in the wasteland a highway for our God! Every valley shall be filled in, every mountain and hill shall be made low; the rugged land shall be made a plain, the rough country, a broad valley. Then the glory of the LORD shall be revealed, and all people shall see it together; for the mouth of the LORD has spoken.

Go up on to a high mountain, Zion, herald of glad tidings; cry out at the top of your voice, Jerusalem, herald of good news! Fear not to cry out and say to the cities of Judah: Here is your God! Here comes with power the Lord GOD, who rules by his strong arm; here is his reward with him, his recompense before him. Like a shepherd he feeds his flock; in his arms he gathers the lambs, carrying them in his bosom, and leading the ewes with care.

Responsorial Psalm   Psalm 85:9-10-11-12, 13-14

R. (8) Lord, let us see your kindness, and grant us your salvation.

I will hear what God proclaims; the LORD—for he proclaims peace to his people. Near indeed is his salvation to those who fear him, glory dwelling in our land. **R.**

Kindness and truth shall meet; justice and peace shall kiss. Truth shall spring out of the earth, and justice shall look down from heaven. **R.**

The LORD himself will give his benefits; our land shall yield its increase. Justice shall walk before him, and prepare the way of his steps. **R.**

Second Reading   2 Peter 3:8-14

Do not ignore this one fact, beloved, that with the Lord one day is like a thousand years and a thousand years like one day. The Lord does not delay his promise, as some regard "delay," but he is patient with you, not wishing that any should perish but that all should come to repentance. But the day of the Lord will come like a thief, and then the heavens will pass away with a mighty roar and the elements will be dissolved by fire, and the earth and everything done on it will be found out.

Since everything is to be dissolved in this way, what sort of persons ought you to be, conducting yourselves in holiness and devotion, waiting for and hastening the coming of the day of God, because of which the heavens will be dissolved in flames and the elements melted by fire. But according to his promise we await new heavens and a new earth in which righteousness dwells.

Therefore, beloved, since you await these things, be eager to be found without spot or blemish before him, at peace.

Alleluia   Luke 3:4, 6

R. Alleluia, alleluia.

Prepare the way of the Lord, make straight his paths: All flesh shall see the salvation of God. **R.**

Gospel   Mark 1:1-8

The beginning of the gospel of Jesus Christ the Son of God. As it is written in Isaiah the prophet:

Behold, I am sending my messenger ahead of you; he will prepare your way. A voice of one crying out in the desert: "Prepare the way of the Lord, make straight his paths."

John the Baptist appeared in the desert proclaiming a baptism of repentance for the forgiveness of sins. People of the whole Judean countryside and all the inhabitants of Jerusalem were going out to him and were being baptized by him in the Jordan River as they acknowledged their sins. John was clothed in camel's hair, with a leather belt around his waist. He fed on locusts and wild honey. And this is what he proclaimed:

"One mightier than I is coming after me. I am not worthy to stoop and loosen the thongs of his sandals. I have baptized you with water; he will baptize you with the Holy Spirit."

MEMORIAL OF SAINT AMBROSE, BISHOP AND DOCTOR OF THE CHURCH

First Reading   **Isaiah 35:1-10**

The desert and the parched land will exult; the steppe will rejoice and bloom. They will bloom with abundant flowers, and rejoice with joyful song. The glory of Lebanon will be given to them, the splendor of Carmel and Sharon; they will see the glory of the LORD, the splendor of our God. Strengthen the hands that are feeble, make firm the knees that are weak,

Say to those whose hearts are frightened: Be strong, fear not! Here is your God, he comes with vindication; with divine recompense he comes to save you. Then will the eyes of the blind be opened, the ears of the deaf be cleared; Then will the lame leap like a stag, then the tongue of the mute will sing.

Streams will burst forth in the desert, and rivers in the steppe. The burning sands will become pools, and the thirsty ground, springs of water; the abode where jackals lurk will be a marsh for the reed and papyrus. A highway will be there, called the holy way; No one unclean may pass over it, nor fools go astray on it. No lion will be there, nor beast of prey go up to be met upon it. It is for those with a journey to make, and on it the redeemed will walk. Those whom the LORD has ransomed will return and enter Zion singing, crowned with everlasting joy; they will meet with joy and gladness, sorrow and mourning will flee.

Responsorial Psalm   **Psalm 85:9ab and 10, 11-12, 13-14**

R. (Isaiah 35:4f) Our God will come to save us!

20

I will hear what God proclaims; the LORD –for he proclaims peace to his people. Near indeed is his salvation to those who fear him, glory dwelling in our land. **R.**

Kindness and truth shall meet; justice and peace shall kiss. Truth shall spring out of the earth, and justice shall look down from heaven. **R.**

The LORD himself will give his benefits; our land shall yield its increase. Justice shall walk before him, and salvation, along the way of his steps. **R.**

Alleluia

R. Alleluia, alleluia.

Behold the king will come, the Lord of the earth, and he himself will lift the yoke of our capacity. **R.**

Gospel   Luke 5:17-26

One day as Jesus was teaching, Pharisees and teachers of the law, who had come from every village of Galilee and Judea and Jerusalem, were sitting there, and the power of the Lord was with him for healing. And some men brought on a stretcher a man who was paralyzed; they were trying to bring him in and set him in his presence. But not finding a way to bring him in because of the crowd, they went up on the roof and lowered him on the stretcher through the tiles into the middle in front of Jesus. When Jesus saw their faith, he said, "As for you, your sins are forgiven." Then the scribes and Pharisees began to ask themselves, "Who is this who speaks blasphemies? Who but God alone can forgive sins?" Jesus knew their thoughts and said to them in reply, "What are you thinking in your hearts? Which is easier, to say, 'Your sins are forgiven,' or to say, 'Rise and walk'? But that you may know that the Son of Man has authority on earth to forgive sins"–he said to the one who was paralyzed, "I say to you, rise, pick up your stretcher, and go home." He stood up immediately before them, picked up what he had been lying on, and went home, glorifying God. Then astonishment seized them all and they glorified God, and, struck with awe, they said, "We have seen incredible things today."

TUESDAY, DECEMBER 8, 2020

SOLEMNITY OF THE IMMACULATE CONCEPTION OF THE BLESSED VIRGIN MARY

First Reading   **Genesis 3:9-15, 20**

After the man, Adam, had eaten of the tree, the LORD God called to the man and asked him, "Where are you?" He answered, "I heard you in the garden; but I was afraid, because I was naked, so I hid myself." Then he asked, "Who told you that you were naked? You have eaten, then, from the tree of which I had forbidden you to eat!" The man replied, "The woman whom you put here with me she gave me fruit from the tree, and so I ate it." The LORD God then asked the woman, "Why did you do such a thing?" The woman answered, "The serpent tricked me into it, so I ate it." Then the LORD God said to the serpent: "Because you have done this, you shall be banned from all the animals and from all the wild creatures; on your belly shall you crawl, and dirt shall you eat all the days of your life. I will put enmity between you and the woman, and between your offspring and hers; he will strike at your head, while you strike at his heel." The man called his wife Eve, because she became the mother of all the living.

Responsorial Psalm   Psalm 98:1, 2-3ab, 3cd-4

R. (1) Sing to the Lord a new song, for he has done marvelous deeds.

Sing to the LORD a new song, for he has done wondrous deeds;
His right hand has won victory for him, his holy arm. **R.**

The LORD has made his salvation known: in the sight of the
nations he has revealed his justice. He has remembered his
kindness and his faithfulness toward the house of Israel. **R.**

All the ends of the earth have seen the salvation by our God. Sing
joyfully to the LORD, all you lands; break into song; sing praise. **R.**

Second Reading   Ephesians 1:3-6, 11-12

Brothers and sisters:

Blessed be the God and Father of our Lord Jesus Christ, who has
blessed us in Christ with every spiritual blessing in the heavens, as
he chose us in him, before the foundation of the world, to be holy
and without blemish before him. In love he destined us for
adoption to himself through Jesus Christ, in accord with the favor
of his will, for the praise of the glory of his grace that he granted us
in the beloved. In him we were also chosen, destined in accord
with the purpose of the One who accomplishes all things according
to the intention of his will, so that we might exist for the praise of
his glory, we who first hoped in Christ.

Alleluia   Luke 1:28

R. Alleluia, alleluia.

Hail, Mary, full of grace, the Lord is with you; blessed are you
among women. **R.**

Gospel   Luke 1:26-38

The angel Gabriel was sent from God to a town of Galilee called Nazareth, to a virgin betrothed to a man named Joseph, of the house of David, and the virgin's name was Mary. And coming to her, he said, "Hail, full of grace! The Lord is with you." But she was greatly troubled at what was said and pondered what sort of greeting this might be. Then the angel said to her, "Do not be afraid, Mary, for you have found favor with God. Behold, you will conceive in your womb and bear a son, and you shall name him Jesus. He will be great and will be called Son of the Most High, and the Lord God will give him the throne of David his father, and he will rule over the house of Jacob forever, and of his Kingdom there will be no end." But Mary said to the angel, "How can this be, since I have no relations with a man?" And the angel said to her in reply, "The Holy Spirit will come upon you, and the power of the Most High will overshadow you. Therefore the child to be born will be called holy, the Son of God. And behold, Elizabeth, your relative, has also conceived a son in her old age, and this is the sixth month for her who was called barren; for nothing will be impossible for God." Mary said, "Behold, I am the handmaid of the Lord. May it be done to me according to your word." Then the angel departed from her.

WEDNESDAY OF THE SECOND WEEK OF ADVENT

First Reading   Isaiah 40:25-31

To whom can you liken me as an equal? Says the Holy One. Lift up your eyes on high and see who has created these things: He leads out their army and numbers them, calling them all by name. By his great might and the strength of his power not one of them is missing!

Why, O Jacob, do you say, and declare, O Israel, "My way is hidden from the LORD, and my right is disregarded by my God"? Do you not know or have you not heard? The LORD is the eternal God, creator of the ends of the earth. He does not faint nor grow weary, and his knowledge is beyond scrutiny. He gives strength to the fainting; for the weak he makes vigor abound. Though young men faint and grow weary, and youths stagger and fall, they that hope in the LORD will renew their strength, they will soar as with eagles' wings; they will run and not grow weary, walk and not grow faint.

Responsorial Psalm   Psalm 103:1-2, 3-4, 8 and 10

R. (1) O bless the Lord, my soul!

Bless the LORD, O my soul; and all my being, bless his holy name. Bless the LORD, O my soul, and forget not all his benefits. **R.**

He pardons all your iniquities, he heals all your ills. He redeems your life from destruction, he crowns you with kindness and compassion. **R.**

Merciful and gracious is the LORD, slow to anger and abounding in kindness. Not according to our sins does he deal with us, nor does he requite us according to our crimes. **R.**

Alleluia

R. Alleluia, alleluia.

Behold, the Lord comes to save his people; blessed are those prepared to meet him. **R.**

Gospel   Matthew 11:28-30

Jesus said to the crowds:

"Come to me, all you who labor and are burdened, and I will give you rest. Take my yoke upon you and learn from me, for I am meek and humble of heart; and you will find rest for yourselves. For my yoke is easy, and my burden light."

THURSDAY, DECEMBER 10, 2020

THURSDAY OF THE SECOND WEEK OF ADVENT

First Reading   Isaiah 41:13-20

I am the LORD, your God, who grasp your right hand; it is I who say to you, "Fear not, I will help you." Fear not, O worm Jacob, O maggot Israel; I will help you, says the LORD; your redeemer is the Holy One of Israel. I will make of you a threshing sledge, sharp, new, and double-edged, to thresh the mountains and crush them, to make the hills like chaff. When you winnow them, the wind shall carry them off and the storm shall scatter them. But you shall rejoice in the LORD, and glory in the Holy One of Israel. The afflicted and the needy seek water in vain, their tongues are parched with thirst. I, the LORD, will answer them; I, the God of Israel, will not forsake them. I will open up rivers on the bare heights, and fountains in the broad valleys; I will turn the desert into a marshland, and the dry ground into springs of water. I will plant in the desert the cedar, acacia, myrtle, and olive; I will set in the wasteland the cypress, together with the plane tree and the pine, that all may see and know, observe and understand, that the hand of the LORD has done this, the Holy One of Israel has created it.

Responsorial Psalm
Psalm 145:1 and 9, 10-11, 12-13ab

R. (8) The Lord is gracious and merciful; slow to anger, and of great kindness.

I will extol you, O my God and King, and I will bless your name forever and ever. The LORD is good to all and compassionate toward all his works. **R.**

Let all your works give you thanks, O LORD, and let your faithful ones bless you. Let them discourse of the glory of your Kingdom and speak of your might. **R.**

Let them make known to men your might and the glorious splendor of your Kingdom. Your Kingdom is a Kingdom for all ages, and your dominion endures through all generations. **R.**

Alleluia
Isaiah 45:8

R. Alleluia, alleluia.

Let the clouds rain down the Just One, and the earth bring forth a Savior. **R.**

Gospel
Matthew 11:11-15

Jesus said to the crowds:

"Amen, I say to you, among those born of women there has been none greater than John the Baptist; yet the least in the Kingdom of heaven is greater than he. From the days of John the Baptist until now, the Kingdom of heaven suffers violence, and the violent are taking it by force. All the prophets and the law prophesied up to the time of John. And if you are willing to accept it, he is Elijah, the one who is to come. Whoever has ears ought to hear."

FRIDAY OF THE SECOND WEEK OF ADVENT

First Reading   **Isaiah 48:17-19**

Thus says the LORD, your redeemer, the Holy One of Israel:
I, the LORD, your God, teach you what is for your good, and lead you on the way you should go. If you would hearken to my commandments, your prosperity would be like a river, and your vindication like the waves of the sea; your descendants would be like the sand, and those born of your stock like its grains, their name never cut off or blotted out from my presence.

Responsorial Psalm   **Psalm 1:1-2, 3, 4 and 6**

R. (John 8:12) Those who follow you, Lord, will have the light of life.

Blessed the man who follows not the counsel of the wicked nor walks in the way of sinners, nor sits in the company of the insolent, but delights in the law of the LORD and meditates on his law day and night. **R.**

He is like a tree planted near running water, that yields its fruit in due season, and whose leaves never fade. Whatever he does, prospers. **R.**

Not so the wicked, not so; they are like chaff which the wind drives away. For the LORD watches over the way of the just, but the way of the wicked vanishes. **R.**

Alleluia

R. Alleluia, alleluia.

The Lord will come; go out to meet him! He is the prince of peace.
R.

Gospel   Matthew 11:16-19

Jesus said to the crowds:

"To what shall I compare this generation? It is like children who sit in marketplaces and call to one another, 'We played the flute for you, but you did not dance, we sang a dirge but you did not mourn.' For John came neither eating nor drinking, and they said, 'He is possessed by a demon.' The Son of Man came eating and drinking and they said, 'Look, he is a glutton and a drunkard, a friend of tax collectors and sinners.' But wisdom is vindicated by her works."

SATURDAY, DECEMBER 12, 2020
FEAST OF OUR LADY OF GUADALUPE
First Reading   **Zechariah 2:14-17 or Revelation 11:19a; 12:1-6a, 10ab**

Zechariah 2:14-17

Sing and rejoice, O daughter Zion! See, I am coming to dwell among you, says the LORD. Many nations shall join themselves to the LORD on that day, and they shall be his people, and he will dwell among you, and you shall know that the LORD of hosts has sent me to you. The LORD will possess Judah as his portion in the holy land, and he will again choose Jerusalem. Silence, all mankind, in the presence of the LORD! For he stirs forth from his holy dwelling.

Or:

Revelation 11:19a; 12:1-6a, 10ab

God's temple in heaven was opened, and the ark of his covenant could be seen in the temple. A great sign appeared in the sky, a woman clothed with the sun, with the moon under her feet, and on her head a crown of twelve stars. She was with child and wailed aloud in pain as she labored to give birth. Then another sign appeared in the sky; it was a huge red dragon, with seven heads and ten horns, and on its heads were seven diadems. Its tail swept away a third of the stars in the sky and hurled them down to the earth. Then the dragon stood before the woman about to give birth, to devour her child when she gave birth. She gave birth to a son, a male child, destined to rule all the nations with an iron rod. Her child was caught up to God and his throne. The woman herself fled into the desert where she had a place prepared by God. Then I heard a loud voice in heaven say: "Now have salvation and power come, and the Kingdom of our God and the authority of his Anointed."

Responsorial Psalm   Judith 13:18bcde, 19

R. (15:9d) You are the highest honor of our race.

Blessed are you, daughter, by the Most High God, above all the women on earth; and blessed be the LORD God, the creator of heaven and earth. **R.**

Your deed of hope will never be forgotten by those who tell of the might of God. **R.**

Alleluia

R. Alleluia, alleluia.

Blessed are you, holy Virgin Mary, deserving of all praise; from you rose the sun of justice, Christ our God. **R.**

Gospel   Luke 1:26-38 or Luke 1:39-47

Luke 1:26-38

The angel Gabriel was sent from God to a town of Galilee called Nazareth, to a virgin betrothed to a man named Joseph, of the house of David, and the virgin's name was Mary. And coming to her, he said, "Hail, full of grace! The Lord is with you." But she was greatly troubled at what was said and pondered what sort of greeting this might be. Then the angel said to her, "Do not be afraid, Mary, for you have found favor with God. Behold, you will conceive in your womb and bear a son, and you shall name him Jesus. He will be great and will be called Son of the Most High, and the Lord God will give him the throne of David his father, and he will rule over the house of Jacob forever, and of his Kingdom there will be no end." But Mary said to the angel, "How can this be, since I have no relations with a man?" And the angel said to her in reply, "The Holy Spirit will come upon you, and the power of the Most High will overshadow you. Therefore the child to be born will be called holy, the Son of God. And behold, Elizabeth, your relative, has also conceived a son in her old age, and this is the sixth month for her who was called barren; for nothing will be impossible for God." Mary said, "Behold, I am the handmaid of the Lord. May it be done to me according to your word." Then the angel departed from her.

Or:

Luke 1:39-47

Mary set out and traveled to the hill country in haste to a town of Judah, where she entered the house of Zechariah and greeted Elizabeth. When Elizabeth heard Mary's greeting, the infant leaped in her womb, and Elizabeth, filled with the Holy Spirit, cried out in a loud voice and said, "Most blessed are you among women, and blessed is the fruit of your womb. And how does this happen to me, that the mother of my Lord should come to me? For at the moment the sound of your greeting reached my ears, the infant in my womb leaped for joy. Blessed are you who believed that what was spoken to you by the Lord would be fulfilled." And Mary said: "My soul proclaims the greatness of the Lord; my spirit rejoices in God my savior."

SUNDAY, DECEMBER 13, 2020
THIRD SUNDAY OF ADVENT

First Reading   **Isaiah 61:1-2a, 10-11**

The spirit of the Lord GOD is upon me, because the LORD has anointed me; he has sent me to bring glad tidings to the poor, to heal the brokenhearted, to proclaim liberty to the captives and release to the prisoners, to announce a year of favor from the LORD and a day of vindication by our God. I rejoice heartily in the LORD, in my God is the joy of my soul; for he has clothed me with a robe of salvation and wrapped me in a mantle of justice, like a bridegroom adorned with a diadem, like a bride bedecked with her jewels. As the earth brings forth its plants, and a garden makes its growth spring up, so will the Lord GOD make justice and praise spring up before all the nations.

Responsorial Psalm   Luke 1:46-48, 49-50, 53-54

R. (Is 61:10b) My soul rejoices in my God.

My soul proclaims the greatness of the Lord; my spirit rejoices in God my Savior, for he has looked upon his lowly servant. From this day all generations will call me blessed. **R.**

The Almighty has done great things for me, and holy is his Name. He has mercy on those who fear him in every generation. **R.**

He has filled the hungry with good things, and the rich he has sent away empty. He has come to the help of his servant Israel for he has remembered his promise of mercy, **R.**

Second Reading   1 Thessalonians 5:16-24

Rejoice always. Pray without ceasing. In all circumstances give thanks, for this is the will of God for you in Christ Jesus. Do not quench the Spirit. Do not despise prophetic utterances. Test everything; retain what is good. Refrain from every kind of evil. May the God of peace make you perfectly holy and may you entirely, spirit, soul, and body, be preserved blameless for the coming of our Lord Jesus Christ. The one who calls you is faithful, and he will also accomplish it.

Alleluia   Isaiah 61:1

R. Alleluia, alleluia.

The Spirit of the Lord is upon me, because he has anointed me to bring glad tidings to the poor. **R.**

Gospel   John 1:6-8, 19-28

A man named John was sent from God. He came for testimony, to testify to the light, so that all might believe through him. He was not the light, but came to testify to the light. And this is the testimony of John. When the Jews from Jerusalem sent priests and Levites to him to ask him, "Who are you?" He admitted and did not deny it, but admitted, "I am not the Christ." So they asked him, "What are you then? Are you Elijah?" And he said, "I am not." "Are you the Prophet?" He answered, "No." So they said to him, "Who are you, so we can give an answer to those who sent us? What do you have to say for yourself?" He said: "I am *the voice of one crying out in the desert, 'make straight the way of the Lord,'*" as Isaiah the prophet said." Some Pharisees were also sent. They asked him, "Why then do you baptize if you are not the Christ or Elijah or the Prophet?" John answered them, "I baptize with water; but there is one among you whom you do not recognize, the one who is coming after me, whose sandal strap I am not worthy to untie." This happened in Bethany across the Jordan, where John was baptizing.

MONDAY, DECEMBER 14, 2020

MEMORIAL OF SAINT JOHN OF THE CROSS, PRIEST AND DOCTOR OF THE CHURCH

First Reading   **Numbers 24:2-7, 15-17a**

When Balaam raised his eyes and saw Israel encamped, tribe by tribe, the spirit of God came upon him, and he gave voice to his oracle: The utterance of Balaam, son of Beor, the utterance of a man whose eye is true, The utterance of one who hears what God says, and knows what the Most High knows, Of one who sees what the Almighty sees, enraptured, and with eyes unveiled: How goodly are your tents, O Jacob; your encampments, O Israel! They are like gardens beside a stream, like the cedars planted by the

LORD. His wells shall yield free-flowing waters, he shall have the sea within reach; His king shall rise higher, and his royalty shall be exalted. Then Balaam gave voice to his oracle: The utterance of Balaam, son of Beor, the utterance of the man whose eye is true, The utterance of one who hears what God says, and knows what the Most High knows, Of one who sees what the Almighty sees, enraptured, and with eyes unveiled. I see him, though not now; I behold him, though not near: A star shall advance from Jacob, and a staff shall rise from Israel.

Responsorial Psalm   Psalm 25:4-5ab, 6 and 7bc, 8-9

R. (4) Teach me your ways, O Lord.

Your ways, O LORD, make known to me; teach me your paths,
Guide me in your truth and teach me, for you are God my savior.
R.

Remember that your compassion, O LORD, and your kindness are from of old. In your kindness remember me, because of your goodness, O LORD. **R.**

Good and upright is the LORD; thus he shows sinners the way. He guides the humble to justice, he teaches the humble his way. **R.**

Alleluia   Psalm 85:8

R. Alleluia, alleluia.

Show us, LORD, your love, and grant us your salvation. **R.**

Gospel   Matthew 21:23-27

When Jesus had come into the temple area, the chief priests and the elders of the people approached him as he was teaching and said, "By what authority are you doing these things? And who gave you this authority?" Jesus said to them in reply, "I shall ask you one question, and if you answer it for me, then I shall tell you by what authority I do these things. Where was John's baptism from? Was it of heavenly or of human origin?" They discussed this among themselves and said, "If we say 'Of heavenly origin,' he will say to us, 'Then why did you not believe him?' But if we say, 'Of human origin,' we fear the crowd, for they all regard John as a prophet." So they said to Jesus in reply, "We do not know." He himself said to them, "Neither shall I tell you by what authority I do these things."

TUESDAY, DECEMBER 15, 2020

TUESDAY OF THE THIRD WEEK OF ADVENT

First Reading   **Zephaniah 3:1-2, 9-13**

Thus says the Lord:

Woe to the city, rebellious and polluted, to the tyrannical city! She hears no voice, accepts no correction; In the Lord she has not trusted, to her God she has not drawn near. For then I will change and purify the lips of the peoples, That they all may call upon the name of the Lord, to serve him with one accord; From beyond the rivers of Ethiopia and as far as the recesses of the North, they shall bring me offerings. On that day you need not be ashamed of all your deeds, your rebellious actions against me; for then will I remove from your midst the proud braggarts, and you shall no longer exalt yourself on my holy mountain. But I will leave as a remnant in your midst a people humble and lowly, who shall take refuge in the name of the Lord: the remnant of Israel. They shall do no wrong and speak no lies; nor shall there be found in their

36

mouths a deceitful tongue; they shall pasture and couch their flocks with none to disturb them. The word of the Lord.

Responsorial Psalm
Psalm 34:2-3, 6-7, 17-18, 19 and 23

R. (7a) The Lord hears the cry of the poor.

I will bless the Lord at all times; his praise shall be ever in my mouth. Let my soul glory in the Lord; the lowly will hear me and be glad. **R.**

Look to him that you may be radiant with joy, and your faces may not blush with shame. When the poor one called out, the Lord heard, and from all his distress he saved him. **R.**

The Lord confronts the evildoers, to destroy remembrance of them from the earth. When the just cry out, the Lord hears them, and from all their distress he rescues them. **R.**

The Lord is close to the brokenhearted; and those who are crushed in spirit he saves. The Lord redeems the lives of his servants; no one incurs guilt who takes refuge in him. **R.**

Alleluia

R. Alleluia, alleluia.

Come, O Lord, do not delay; forgive the sins of your people. **R.**

Gospel
Matthew 21:28-32

Jesus said to the chief priests and the elders of the people:
"What is your opinion? A man had two sons. He came to the first and said, 'Son, go out and work in the vineyard today.' The son said in reply, 'I will not,' but afterwards he changed his mind and went. The man came to the other son and gave the same order. He

said in reply, 'Yes, sir,' but did not go. Which of the two did his father's will?" They answered, "The first." Jesus said to them, "Amen, I say to you, tax collectors and prostitutes are entering the Kingdom of God before you. When John came to you in the way of righteousness, you did not believe him; but tax collectors and prostitutes did. Yet even when you saw that, you did not later change your minds and believe him."

WEDNESDAY OF THE THIRD WEEK OF ADVENT

First Reading   **Isaiah 45:6c-8, 18, 21c-25**

I am the Lord, there is no other; I form the light, and create the darkness, I make well-being and create woe; I, the Lord, do all these things. Let justice descend, O heavens, like dew from above, like gentle rain let the skies drop it down. Let the earth open and salvation bud forth; let justice also spring up! I, the Lord, have created this. For thus says the Lord, The creator of the heavens, who is God, The designer and maker of the earth who established it, Not creating it to be a waste, but designing it be lived in: I am the Lord, and there is no other. Who announced this from the beginning and foretold it from of old? Was it not I, the Lord, besides whom there is no other God? There is no just and saving God but me. Turn to me and be safe, all you ends of the earth, for I am God; there is no other! By myself I swear, uttering my just decree and my unalterable word: To me every knee shall bend; by me every tongue shall swear, saying, "Only in the Lord are just deeds and power. Before him in shame shall come all who vent their anger against him. In the Lord shall be the vindication and the glory of all the descendants of Israel."

Responsorial Psalm
Psalm 85:9ab and 10, 11-12, 13-14

R. (Isaiah 45:8) Let the clouds rain down the Just One, and the earth bring forth a Savior.

I will hear what God proclaims; the Lord–for he proclaims peace to his people. Near indeed is his salvation to those who fear him, glory dwelling in our land. **R.**

Kindness and truth shall meet; justice and peace shall kiss. Truth shall spring out of the earth, and justice shall look down from heaven. **R.**

The Lord himself will give his benefits; our land shall yield its increase. Justice shall walk before him, and salvation, along the way of his steps. **R.**

Alleluia
Isaiah 40:9-10

R. Alleluia, alleluia.

Raise your voice and tell the Good News: Behold, the Lord God comes with power. **R.**

Gospel
Luke 7:18b-23

At that time, John summoned two of his disciples and sent them to the Lord to ask, "Are you the one who is to come, or should we look for another?" When the men came to the Lord, they said, "John the Baptist has sent us to you to ask, 'Are you the one who is to come, or should we look for another?'"

At that time Jesus cured many of their diseases, sufferings, and evil spirits; he also granted sight to many who were blind. And Jesus said to them in reply, "Go and tell John what you have seen and heard: the blind regain their sight, the lame walk, lepers are cleansed, the deaf hear, the dead are raised, the poor have the good news proclaimed to them. And blessed is the one who takes no offense at me."

THURSDAY OF THE THIRD WEEK OF ADVENT

First Reading   **Genesis 49:2, 8-10**

Jacob called his sons and said to them:

"Assemble and listen, sons of Jacob, listen to Israel, your father.

"You, Judah, shall your brothers praise—your hand on the neck of your enemies; the sons of your father shall bow down to you. Judah, like a lion's whelp, you have grown up on prey, my son. He crouches like a lion recumbent, the king of beasts—who would dare rouse him? The scepter shall never depart from Judah, or the mace from between his legs, while tribute is brought to him, and he receives the people's homage."

Responsorial Psalm   **Psalm 72:1-2, 3-4ab, 7-8, 17**

R. (7) Justice shall flourish in his time, and fullness of peace forever.

O God, with your judgment endow the king, and with your justice, the king's son; He shall govern your people with justice and your afflicted ones with judgment. **R.**

The mountains shall yield peace for the people, and the hills justice. He shall defend the afflicted among the people, save the children of the poor. **R.**

Justice shall flower in his days, and profound peace, till the moon be no more. May he rule from sea to sea, and from the River to the ends of the earth. **R.**

May his name be blessed forever; as long as the sun his name shall remain. In him shall all the tribes of the earth be blessed; all the nations shall proclaim his happiness. **R.**

Alleluia

R. Alleluia, alleluia.

O Wisdom of our God Most High, guiding creation with power and love: come to teach us the path of knowledge! **R.**

Gospel   Matthew 1:1-17

The book of the genealogy of Jesus Christ, the son of David, the son of Abraham.

Abraham became the father of Isaac, Isaac the father of Jacob, Jacob the father of Judah and his brothers. Judah became the father of Perez and Zerah, whose mother was Tamar. Perez became the father of Hezron, Hezron the father of Ram, Ram the father of Amminadab. Amminadab became the father of Nahshon, Nahshon the father of Salmon, Salmon the father of Boaz, whose mother was Rahab. Boaz became the father of Obed, whose mother was Ruth. Obed became the father of Jesse, Jesse the father of David the king. David became the father of Solomon, whose mother had been the wife of Uriah. Solomon became the father of Rehoboam, Rehoboam the father of Abijah, Abijah the father of Asaph. Asaph became the father of Jehoshaphat, Jehoshaphat the father of Joram, Joram the father of Uzziah. Uzziah became the father of Jotham, Jotham the father of Ahaz,

Ahaz the father of Hezekiah. Hezekiah became the father of Manasseh, Manasseh the father of Amos, Amos the father of Josiah. Josiah became the father of Jechoniah and his brothers at the time of the Babylonian exile. After the Babylonian exile, Jechoniah became the father of Shealtiel, Shealtiel the father of Zerubbabel, Zerubbabel the father of Abiud. Abiud became the father of Eliakim, Eliakim the father of Azor, Azor the father of Zadok. Zadok became the father of Achim, Achim the father of Eliud, Eliud the father of Eleazar. Eleazar became the father of Matthan, Matthan the father of Jacob, Jacob the father of Joseph, the husband of Mary. Of her was born Jesus who is called the Christ. Thus the total number of generations from Abraham to David is fourteen generations; from David to the Babylonian exile, fourteen generations; from the Babylonian exile to the Christ, fourteen generations.

FRIDAY OF THE THIRD WEEK OF ADVENT

First Reading   **Jeremiah 23:5-8**

Behold, the days are coming, says the LORD, when I will raise up a righteous shoot to David; As king he shall reign and govern wisely, he shall do what is just and right in the land. In his days Judah shall be saved, Israel shall dwell in security. This is the name they give him: "The LORD our justice." Therefore, the days will come, says the LORD, when they shall no longer say, "As the LORD lives, who brought the children of Israel out of the land of Egypt"; but rather, "As the LORD lives, who brought the descendants of the house of Israel up from the land of the north"–and from all the lands to which I banished them; they shall again live on their own land.

Responsorial Psalm — Psalm 72:1-2, 12-13, 18-19

R. (7) Justice shall flourish in his time, and fullness of peace forever.

O God, with your judgment endow the king, and with your justice, the king's son; He shall govern your people with justice and your afflicted ones with judgment. **R.**

For he shall rescue the poor when he cries out, and the afflicted when he has no one to help him. He shall have pity for the lowly and the poor; the lives of the poor he shall save. **R.**

Blessed be the LORD, the God of Israel, who alone does wondrous deeds. And blessed forever be his glorious name; may the whole earth be filled with his glory. **R.**

Alleluia

R. Alleluia, alleluia.

O Leader of the House of Israel, giver of the Law to Moses on Sinai: come to rescue us with your mighty power! **R.**

Gospel — Matthew 1:18-25

This is how the birth of Jesus Christ came about. When his mother Mary was betrothed to Joseph, but before they lived together, she was found with child through the Holy Spirit. Joseph her husband, since he was a righteous man, yet unwilling to expose her to shame, decided to divorce her quietly. Such was his intention when, behold, the angel of the Lord appeared to him in a dream and said, "Joseph, son of David, do not be afraid to take Mary your wife into your home. For it is through the Holy Spirit that this child has been conceived in her. She will bear a son and you are to name him Jesus, because he will save his people from their sins."

All this took place to fulfill what the Lord had said through the prophet: *Behold, the virgin shall be with child and bear a son, and they shall name him Emmanuel,* which means "God is with us."

When Joseph awoke, he did as the angel of the Lord had commanded him and took his wife into his home. He had no relations with her until she bore a son, and he named him Jesus.

SATURDAY OF THE THIRD WEEK OF ADVENT

First Reading   **Judges 13:2-7, 24-25a**

There was a certain man from Zorah, of the clan of the Danites, whose name was Manoah. His wife was barren and had borne no children. An angel of the LORD appeared to the woman and said to her, "Though you are barren and have had no children, yet you will conceive and bear a son. Now, then, be careful to take no wine or strong drink and to eat nothing unclean. As for the son you will conceive and bear, no razor shall touch his head, for this boy is to be consecrated to God from the womb. It is he who will begin the deliverance of Israel from the power of the Philistines." The woman went and told her husband, "A man of God came to me; he had the appearance of an angel of God, terrible indeed. I did not ask him where he came from, nor did he tell me his name. But he said to me, 'You will be with child and will bear a son. So take neither wine nor strong drink, and eat nothing unclean. For the boy shall be consecrated to God from the womb, until the day of his death.'" The woman bore a son and named him Samson. The boy grew up and the LORD blessed him; the Spirit of the LORD stirred him.

Responsorial Psalm   Psalm 71:3-4a, 5-6ab, 16-17

R. (8) My mouth shall be filled with your praise, and I will sing your glory!

Be my rock of refuge, a stronghold to give me safety, for you are my rock and my fortress. O my God, rescue me from the hand of the wicked. **R.**

For you are my hope, O LORD; my trust, O God, from my youth. On you I depend from birth; from my mother's womb you are my strength. **R.**

I will treat of the mighty works of the LORD; O God, I will tell of your singular justice. O God, you have taught me from my youth, and till the present I proclaim your wondrous deeds. **R.**

Alleluia

R. Alleluia, alleluia.

O Root of Jesse's stem, sign of God's love for all his people; come to save us without delay! **R.**

Gospel   Luke 1:5-25

In the days of Herod, King of Judea, there was a priest named Zechariah of the priestly division of Abijah; his wife was from the daughters of Aaron, and her name was Elizabeth. Both were righteous in the eyes of God, observing all the commandments and ordinances of the Lord blamelessly. But they had no child, because

Elizabeth was barren and both were advanced in years. Once when he was serving as priest in his division's turn before God, according to the practice of the priestly service, he was chosen by lot to enter the sanctuary of the Lord to burn incense.

Then, when the whole assembly of the people was praying outside at the hour of the incense offering, the angel of the Lord appeared to him, standing at the right of the altar of incense. Zechariah was troubled by what he saw, and fear came upon him. But the angel said to him, "Do not be afraid, Zechariah, because your prayer has been heard. Your wife Elizabeth will bear you a son, and you shall name him John. And you will have joy and gladness, and many will rejoice at his birth, for he will be great in the sight of the Lord. He will drink neither wine nor strong drink. He will be filled with the Holy Spirit even from his mother's womb, and he will turn many of the children of Israel to the Lord their God. He will go before him in the spirit and power of Elijah to turn the hearts of fathers toward children and the disobedient to the understanding of the righteous, to prepare a people fit for the Lord." Then Zechariah said to the angel, "How shall I know this? For I am an old man, and my wife is advanced in years." And the angel said to him in reply, "I am Gabriel, who stand before God. I was sent to speak to you and to announce to you this good news. But now you will be speechless and unable to talk until the day these things take place, because you did not believe my words, which will be fulfilled at their proper time."

Meanwhile the people were waiting for Zechariah and were amazed that he stayed so long in the sanctuary. But when he came out, he was unable to speak to them, and they realized that he had seen a vision in the sanctuary. He was gesturing to them but remained mute. Then, when his days of ministry were completed, he went home.

After this time his wife Elizabeth conceived, and she went into seclusion for five months, saying, "So has the Lord done for me at a time when he has seen fit to take away my disgrace before others."

SUNDAY, DECEMBER 20, 2020

FOURTH SUNDAY OF ADVENT

First Reading   **2 Samuel 7:1-5, 8b-12, 14a, 16**

When King David was settled in his palace, and the LORD had given him rest from his enemies on every side, he said to Nathan the prophet, "Here I am living in a house of cedar, while the ark of God dwells in a tent!" Nathan answered the king, "Go, do whatever you have in mind, for the LORD is with you." But that night the LORD spoke to Nathan and said: "Go, tell my servant David, 'thus says the LORD: Should you build me a house to dwell in?' "It was I who took you from the pasture and from the care of the flock to be commander of my people Israel. I have been with you wherever you went, and I have destroyed all your enemies before you. And I will make you famous like the great ones of the earth. I will fix a place for my people Israel; I will plant them so that they may dwell in their place without further disturbance. Neither shall the wicked continue to afflict them as they did of old, since the time I first appointed judges over my people Israel. I will give you rest from all your enemies. The LORD also reveals to you that he will establish a house for you. And when your time comes and you rest with your ancestors, I will raise up your heir after you, sprung from your loins, and I will make his kingdom firm. I will be a father to him, and he shall be a son to me. Your house and your kingdom shall endure forever before me; your throne shall stand firm forever."

Responsorial Psalm   Psalm 89:2-3, 4-5, 27, 29

R. (2a) For ever I will sing the goodness of the Lord.

The promises of the LORD I will sing forever; through all generations my mouth shall proclaim your faithfulness. For you have said, "My kindness is established forever"; in heaven you have confirmed your faithfulness. **R.**

"I have made a covenant with my chosen one, I have sworn to David my servant: Forever will I confirm your posterity and establish your throne for all generations." **R.**

"He shall say of me, 'You are my father, my God, the Rock, my savior.' Forever I will maintain my kindness toward him, and my covenant with him stands firm." **R.**

Second Reading   Romans 16:25-27

Brothers and sisters:

To him who can strengthen you, according to my gospel and the proclamation of Jesus Christ, according to the revelation of the mystery kept secret for long ages but now manifested through the prophetic writings and, according to the command of the eternal God, made known to all nations to bring about the obedience of faith, to the only wise God, through Jesus Christ be glory forever and ever. Amen.

Alleluia   Luke 1:38

R. Alleluia, alleluia.

Behold, I am the handmaid of the Lord. May it be done to me according to your word. **R.**

Gospel _____ Luke 1:26-38

The angel Gabriel was sent from God to a town of Galilee called Nazareth, to a virgin betrothed to a man named Joseph, of the house of David, and the virgin's name was Mary. And coming to her, he said, "Hail, full of grace! The Lord is with you." But she was greatly troubled at what was said and pondered what sort of greeting this might be. Then the angel said to her, "Do not be afraid, Mary, for you have found favor with God. "Behold, you will conceive in your womb and bear a son, and you shall name him Jesus. He will be great and will be called Son of the Most High, and the Lord God will give him the throne of David his father, and he will rule over the house of Jacob forever, and of his kingdom there will be no end." But Mary said to the angel, "How can this be, since I have no relations with a man?" And the angel said to her in reply, "The Holy Spirit will come upon you, and the power of the Most High will overshadow you. Therefore the child to be born will be called holy, the Son of God. And behold, Elizabeth, your relative, has also conceived a son in her old age, and this is the sixth month for her who was called barren; for nothing will be impossible for God." Mary said, "Behold, I am the handmaid of the Lord. May it be done to me according to your word." Then the angel departed from her.

MONDAY OF THE FOURTH WEEK OF ADVENT

First Reading   **Song of Songs 2:8-14 or**
                                     Zephaniah 3:14-18a

Song of Songs 2:8-14

Hark! My lover–here he comes springing across the mountains, leaping across the hills. My lover is like a gazelle or a young stag. Here he stands behind our wall, gazing through the windows, peering through the lattices. My lover speaks; he says to me, "Arise, my beloved, my dove, my beautiful one, and come! "For see, the winter is past, the rains are over and gone. The flowers appear on the earth, the time of pruning the vines has come, and the song of the dove is heard in our land. The fig tree puts forth its figs, and the vines, in bloom, give forth fragrance. Arise, my beloved, my beautiful one, and come! "O my dove in the clefts of the rock, in the secret recesses of the cliff, let me see you, let me hear your voice, for your voice is sweet, and you are lovely."

Or:

Zephaniah 3:14-18a

Shout for joy, O daughter Zion! Sing joyfully, O Israel! Be glad and exult with all your heart, O daughter Jerusalem! The LORD has removed the judgment against you, he has turned away your enemies; The King of Israel, the LORD, is in your midst, you have no further misfortune to fear. On that day, it shall be said to Jerusalem: Fear not, O Zion, be not discouraged! The LORD, your God, is in your midst, a mighty savior; He will rejoice over you with gladness, and renew you in his love, He will sing joyfully because of you, as one sings at festivals.

50

Responsorial Psalm   Psalm 33:2-3, 11-12, 20-21

R. (1a; 3a) Exult, you just, in the Lord! Sing to him a new song.

Give thanks to the LORD on the harp; with the ten-stringed lyre chant his praises. Sing to him a new song; pluck the strings skillfully, with shouts of gladness. **R.**

But the plan of the LORD stands forever; the design of his heart, through all generations. Blessed the nation whose God is the LORD, the people he has chosen for his own inheritance. **R.**

Our soul waits for the LORD, who is our help and our shield, for in him our hearts rejoice; in his holy name we trust. **R.**

Alleluia

R. Alleluia, alleluia.

O Emmanuel, our King and Giver of Law: come to save us, Lord our God! **R.**

Gospel   Luke 1:39-45

Mary set out in those days and traveled to the hill country in haste to a town of Judah, where she entered the house of Zechariah and greeted Elizabeth. When Elizabeth heard Mary's greeting, the infant leaped in her womb, and Elizabeth, filled with the Holy Spirit, cried out in a loud voice and said, "Most blessed are you among women, and blessed is the fruit of your womb. And how does this happen to me, that the mother of my Lord should come to me? For at the moment the sound of your greeting reached my ears, the infant in my womb leaped for joy. Blessed are you who believed that what was spoken to you by the Lord would be fulfilled."

TUESDAY OF THE FOURTH WEEK OF ADVENT

First Reading   **1 Samuel 1:24-28**

In those days, Hannah brought Samuel with her, along with a three-year-old bull, an ephah of flour, and a skin of wine, and presented him at the temple of the LORD in Shiloh.

After the boy's father had sacrificed the young bull, Hannah, his mother, approached Eli and said: "Pardon, my lord! As you live, my lord, I am the woman who stood near you here, praying to the LORD. I prayed for this child, and the LORD granted my request. Now I, in turn, give him to the LORD; as long as he lives, he shall be dedicated to the LORD." She left Samuel there.

Responsorial Psalm   **1 Samuel 2:1, 4-5, 6-7, 8abcd**

R. (1a) My heart exults in the Lord, my Savior.

"My heart exults in the LORD, my horn is exalted in my God. I have swallowed up my enemies; I rejoice in my victory." **R.**

"The bows of the mighty are broken, while the tottering gird on strength. The well-fed hire themselves out for bread, while the hungry batten on spoil. The barren wife bears seven sons, while the mother of many languishes." **R.**

"The LORD puts to death and gives life; he casts down to the nether world; he raises up again. The LORD makes poor and makes rich, he humbles, he also exalts." **R.**

"He raises the needy from the dust; from the dung heap he lifts up the poor, to seat them with nobles and make a glorious throne their heritage." **R.**

Alleluia

R. Alleluia, alleluia.

O King of all nations and keystone of the Church: come and save man, whom you formed from the dust! **R.**

Gospel   Luke 1:46-56

Mary said:

"My soul proclaims the greatness of the Lord; my spirit rejoices in God my savior. For he has looked upon his lowly servant. From this day all generations will call me blessed: the Almighty has done great things for me, and holy is his Name. He has mercy on those who fear him in every generation. He has shown the strength of his arm, and has scattered the proud in their conceit. He has cast down the mighty from their thrones and has lifted up the lowly. He has filled the hungry with good things, and the rich he has sent away empty. He has come to the help of his servant Israel for he remembered his promise of mercy, the promise he made to our fathers, to Abraham and his children forever." Mary remained with Elizabeth about three months and then returned to her home.

WEDNESDAY, DECEMBER 23, 2020
WEDNESDAY OF THE FOURTH WEEK OF ADVENT

First Reading   Malachi 3:1-4, 23-24

Thus says the Lord GOD:

Lo, I am sending my messenger to prepare the way before me; and suddenly there will come to the temple the LORD whom you seek, and the messenger of the covenant whom you desire. Yes, he is coming, says the LORD of hosts. But who will endure the day of his coming? And who can stand when he appears? For he is like the refiner's fire, or like the fuller's lye. He will sit refining and purifying silver, and he will purify the sons of Levi, refining them like gold or like silver that they may offer due sacrifice to the LORD. Then the sacrifice of Judah and Jerusalem will please the LORD, as in the days of old, as in years gone by. Lo, I will send you Elijah, the prophet, before the day of the LORD comes, the great and terrible day, to turn the hearts of the fathers to their children, and the hearts of the children to their fathers, lest I come and strike the land with doom.

Responsorial Psalm   Psalm 25:4-5ab, 8-9, 10 and 14
R. (Luke 21:28) Lift up your heads and see; your redemption is near at hand.

Your ways, O LORD, make known to me; teach me your paths,
Guide me in your truth and teach me, for you are God my savior.
R.
Good and upright is the LORD; thus he shows sinners the way. He guides the humble to justice, he teaches the humble his way. **R.**
All the paths of the LORD are kindness and constancy toward those who keep his covenant and his decrees. The friendship of the LORD is with those who fear him, and his covenant, for their instruction. **R.**

Alleluia
R. Alleluia, alleluia.
O King of all nations and keystone of the Church; come and save man, whom you formed from the dust! **R.**

Gospel   Luke 1:57-66

When the time arrived for Elizabeth to have her child she gave birth to a son. Her neighbors and relatives heard that the Lord had shown his great mercy toward her, and they rejoiced with her.

When they came on the eighth day to circumcise the child, they were going to call him Zechariah after his father, but his mother said in reply, "No. He will be called John." But they answered her, "There is no one among your relatives who has this name." So they made signs, asking his father what he wished him to be called. He asked for a tablet and wrote, "John is his name," and all were amazed. Immediately his mouth was opened, his tongue freed, and he spoke blessing God.

Then fear came upon all their neighbors, and all these matters were discussed throughout the hill country of Judea. All who heard these things took them to heart, saying, "What, then, will this child be? For surely the hand of the Lord was with him."

THURSDAY OF THE FOURTH WEEK OF ADVENT

(Mass in the Morning)

First Reading   **2 Samuel 7:1-5, 8b-12, 14a, 16**

When King David was settled in his palace, and the LORD had given him rest from his enemies on every side, he said to Nathan the prophet, "Here I am living in a house of cedar, while the ark of God dwells in a tent!" Nathan answered the king, "Go, do whatever you have in mind, for the LORD is with you." But that night the LORD spoke to Nathan and said: "Go, tell my servant David, 'thus says the LORD: Should you build me a house to dwell in? "'It was I who took you from the pasture and from the care of the flock to be commander of my people Israel. I have been with you wherever you went, and I have destroyed all your enemies before you. And I will make you famous like the great ones of the earth. I will fix a place for my people Israel; I will plant them so that they may dwell in their place without further disturbance. Neither shall the wicked continue to afflict them as they did of old, since the time I first appointed judges over my people Israel. I will give you rest from all your enemies.

The LORD also reveals to you that he will establish a house for you. And when your time comes and you rest with your ancestors, I will raise up your heir after you, sprung from your loins, and I will make his Kingdom firm. I will be a father to him, and he shall be a son to me. Your house and your Kingdom shall endure forever before me; your throne shall stand firm forever.'"

Responsorial Psalm   **Psalm 89:2-3, 4-5, 27 and 29**

R. (2) For ever I will sing the goodness of the Lord.

The favors of the LORD I will sing forever; through all generations my mouth shall proclaim your faithfulness. For you have said, "My kindness is established forever"; in heaven you have confirmed your faithfulness. **R.**

"I have made a covenant with my chosen one, I have sworn to David my servant: Forever will I confirm your posterity and establish your throne for all generations." **R.**

"He shall say of me, 'You are my father, my God, the rock, my savior.' Forever I will maintain my kindness toward him, and my covenant with him stands firm." **R.**

Alleluia

R. Alleluia, alleluia.

O Radiant Dawn, splendor of eternal light, sun of justice: come and shine on those who dwell in darkness and in the shadow of death. **R.**

Gospel   Luke 1:67-79

Zechariah his father, filled with the Holy Spirit, prophesied, saying: "Blessed be the Lord, the God of Israel; for he has come to his people and set them free. He has raised up for us a mighty Savior, born of the house of his servant David. Through his prophets he promised of old that he would save us from our enemies, from the hands of all who hate us. He promised to show mercy to our fathers and to remember his holy covenant. This was the oath he swore to our father Abraham: to set us free from the hand of our enemies, free to worship him without fear, holy and righteous in his sight all the days of our life. You, my child, shall be called the prophet of the Most High, for you will go before the

Lord to prepare his way, to give his people knowledge of salvation by the forgiveness of their sins. In the tender compassion of our God the dawn from on high shall break upon us, to shine on those who dwell in darkness and the shadow of death, and to guide our feet into the way of peace."

THE NATIVITY OF THE LORD (CHRISTMAS)

(At the Vigil Mass)

First Reading   Isaiah 62:1-5

For Zion's sake I will not be silent, for Jerusalem's sake I will not be quiet, until her vindication shines forth like the dawn and her victory like a burning torch. Nations shall behold your vindication, and all the kings your glory; you shall be called by a new name pronounced by the mouth of the LORD. You shall be a glorious crown in the hand of the LORD, a royal diadem held by your God. No more shall people call you "Forsaken," or your land "Desolate," but you shall be called "My Delight," and your land "Espoused." For the LORD delights in you and makes your land his spouse. As a young man marries a virgin, your Builder shall marry you; and as a bridegroom rejoices in his bride so shall your God rejoice in you.

Responsorial Psalm   Psalm 89:4-5, 16-17, 27, 29

R. (2a) For ever I will sing the goodness of the Lord.

I have made a covenant with my chosen one, I have sworn to David my servant: Forever will I confirm your posterity and establish your throne for all generations. **R.**

Blessed the people who know the joyful shout; in the light of your countenance, O LORD, they walk. At your name they rejoice all the day, and through your justice they are exalted. **R.**

He shall say of me, "You are my father, my God, the rock, my savior." Forever I will maintain my kindness toward him, and my covenant with him stands firm. **R.**

Second Reading   Acts 13:16-17, 22-25

When Paul reached Antioch in Pisidia and entered the synagogue, he stood up, motioned with his hand, and said, "Fellow Israelites and you others who are God-fearing, listen.

The God of this people Israel chose our ancestors and exalted the people during their sojourn in the land of Egypt. With uplifted arm he led them out of it. Then he removed Saul and raised up David as king; of him he testified, 'I have found David, son of Jesse, a man after my own heart; he will carry out my every wish.' From this man's descendants God, according to his promise, has brought to Israel a savior, Jesus. John heralded his coming by proclaiming a baptism of repentance to all the people of Israel; and as John was completing his course, he would say, 'What do you suppose that I am? I am not he. Behold, one is coming after me; I am not worthy to unfasten the sandals of his feet.'"

Alleluia

R. Alleluia, alleluia.

Tomorrow the wickedness of the earth will be destroyed: the Savior of the world will reign over us. **R.**

Gospel   Matthew 1:1-25 or Matthew 1:18-25

Matthew 1:1-25

The book of the genealogy of Jesus Christ, the son of David, the son of Abraham. Abraham became the father of Isaac, Isaac the father of Jacob, Jacob the father of Judah and his brothers. Judah became the father of Perez and Zerah, whose mother was Tamar. Perez became the father of Hezron, Hezron the father of Ram, Ram the father of Amminadab. Amminadab became the father of Nahshon, Nahshon the father of Salmon, Salmon the father of Boaz, whose mother was Rahab. Boaz became the father of Obed, whose mother was Ruth. Obed became the father of Jesse, Jesse the father of David the king. David became the father of Solomon, whose mother had been the wife of Uriah. Solomon became the father of Rehoboam, Rehoboam the father of Abijah, Abijah the father of Asaph. Asaph became the father of Jehoshaphat, Jehoshaphat the father of Joram, Joram the father of Uzziah. Uzziah became the father of Jotham, Jotham the father of Ahaz, Ahaz the father of Hezekiah. Hezekiah became the father of Manasseh, Manasseh the father of Amos, Amos the father of Josiah. Josiah became the father of Jechoniah and his brothers at the time of the Babylonian exile. After the Babylonian exile, Jechoniah became the father of Shealtiel, Shealtiel the father of Zerubbabel, Zerubbabel the father of Abiud. Abiud became the father of Eliakim, Eliakim the father of Azor, Azor the father of Zadok. Zadok became the father of Achim, Achim the father of Eliud, Eliud the father of Eleazar. Eleazar became the father of Matthan, Matthan the father of Jacob, Jacob the father of Joseph, the husband of Mary. Of her was born Jesus who is called the Christ. Thus the total number of generations from Abraham to David is fourteen generations; from David to the Babylonian exile, fourteen generations; from the Babylonian exile to the Christ, fourteen generations. Now this is how the birth of Jesus Christ came about. When his mother Mary was betrothed to Joseph, but before they lived together, she was found with child through the Holy Spirit. Joseph her husband, since he was a righteous man, yet unwilling to expose her to shame, decided to divorce her quietly. Such was his intention when, behold, the angel of the Lord appeared to him in a dream and said, "Joseph, son of David, do not be afraid to take Mary your wife into your home. For it is through the Holy Spirit that this child has been conceived in her. She will bear a son and you are to name him Jesus, because he will save his people from their sins." All this took place to fulfill what the Lord had said through the prophet:

Behold, the virgin shall conceive and bear a son, and they shall name him Emmanuel, which means "God is with us."

When Joseph awoke, he did as the angel of the Lord had commanded him and took his wife into his home. He had no relations with her until she bore a son, and he named him Jesus.

Or:

Matthew 1:18-25

Now this is how the birth of Jesus Christ came about. When his mother Mary was betrothed to Joseph, but before they lived together, she was found with child through the Holy Spirit. Joseph her husband, since he was a righteous man, yet unwilling to expose her to shame, decided to divorce her quietly. Such was his intention when, behold, the angel of the Lord appeared to him in a dream and said, "Joseph, son of David, do not be afraid to take Mary your wife into your home. For it is through the Holy Spirit that this child has been conceived in her. She will bear a son and you are to name him Jesus, because he will save his people from their sins." All this took place to fulfill what the Lord had said through the prophet:

Behold, the virgin shall conceive and bear a son, and they shall name him Emmanuel, which means "God is with us."

When Joseph awoke, he did as the angel of the Lord had commanded him and took his wife into his home. He had no relations with her until she bore a son, and he named him Jesus.

THE NATIVITY OF THE LORD (CHRISTMAS)
(Mass during the Night)

First Reading   **Isaiah 9:1-6**

The people who walked in darkness have seen a great light; upon those who dwelt in the land of gloom a light has shone. You have brought them abundant joy and great rejoicing, as they rejoice before you as at the harvest, as people make merry when dividing spoils. For the yoke that burdened them, the pole on their shoulder, and the rod of their taskmaster you have smashed, as on the day of Midian. For every boot that tramped in battle, every cloak rolled in blood, will be burned as fuel for flames. For a child is born to us, a son is given us; upon his shoulder dominion rests. They name him Wonder-Counselor, God-Hero, Father-Forever, Prince of Peace. His dominion is vast and forever peaceful, from David's throne, and over his kingdom, which he confirms and sustains by judgment and justice, both now and forever. The zeal of the LORD of hosts will do this!

Responsorial Psalm   **Psalm 96: 1-2, 2-3, 11-12, 13**

R. (Luke 2:11) Today is born our Savior, Christ the Lord.

Sing to the LORD a new song; sing to the LORD, all you lands.
Sing to the LORD; bless his name. **R.**

Announce his salvation, day after day. Tell his glory among the
nations; among all peoples, his wondrous deeds. **R.**

Let the heavens be glad and the earth rejoice; let the sea and what
fills it resound; let the plains be joyful and all that is in them! Then
shall all the trees of the forest exult. **R.**

They shall exult before the LORD, for he comes; for he comes to
rule the earth. He shall rule the world with justice and the peoples
with his constancy. **R.**

Second Reading   Titus 2:11-14

Beloved:

The grace of God has appeared, saving all and training us to reject
godless ways and worldly desires and to live temperately, justly,
and devoutly in this age, as we await the blessed hope, the
appearance of the glory of our great God and savior Jesus Christ,
who gave himself for us to deliver us from all lawlessness and to
cleanse for himself a people as his own, eager to do what is good.

Alleluia   Luke 2:10-11

R. Alleluia, alleluia.

I proclaim to you good news of great joy: today a Savior is born for
us, Christ the Lord. **R.**

Gospel   Luke 2:1-14

In those days a decree went out from Caesar Augustus that the
whole world should be enrolled. This was the first enrollment,

when Quirinius was governor of Syria. So all went to be enrolled, each to his own town. And Joseph too went up from Galilee from the town of Nazareth to Judea, to the city of David that is called Bethlehem, because he was of the house and family of David, to be enrolled with Mary, his betrothed, who was with child. While they were there, the time came for her to have her child, and she gave birth to her firstborn son. She wrapped him in swaddling clothes and laid him in a manger, because there was no room for them in the inn. Now there were shepherds in that region living in the fields and keeping the night watch over their flock. The angel of the Lord appeared to them and the glory of the Lord shone around them, and they were struck with great fear. The angel said to them, "Do not be afraid; for behold, I proclaim to you good news of great joy that will be for all the people. For today in the city of David a savior has been born for you who is Christ and Lord. And this will be a sign for you: you will find an infant wrapped in swaddling clothes and lying in a manger." And suddenly there was a multitude of the heavenly host with the angel, praising God and saying: "Glory to God in the highest and on earth peace to those on whom his favor rests."

THE NATIVITY OF THE LORD (CHRISTMAS)

(Mass at Dawn)

First Reading   Isaiah 62:11-12

See, the LORD proclaims to the ends of the earth: say to daughter Zion, your savior comes! Here is his reward with him, his recompense before him. They shall be called the holy people, the redeemed of the LORD, and you shall be called "Frequented," a city that is not forsaken.

Responsorial Psalm   Psalm 97:1, 6, 11-12

R. A light will shine on us this day: the Lord is born for us.

The LORD is king; let the earth rejoice; let the many isles be glad.
The heavens proclaim his justice, and all peoples see his glory. **R.**
Light dawns for the just; and gladness, for the upright of heart. Be
glad in the LORD, you just, and give thanks to his holy name. **R.**

Second Reading   Titus 3:4-7

Beloved:

When the kindness and generous love of God our savior appeared,
not because of any righteous deeds we had done but because of his
mercy, He saved us through the bath of rebirth and renewal by the
Holy Spirit, whom he richly poured out on us through Jesus Christ
our savior, so that we might be justified by his grace and become
heirs in hope of eternal life.

Alleluia   Luke 2:14

R. Alleluia, alleluia.

Glory to God in the highest, and on earth peace to those on whom
his favor rests. **R.**

Gospel   Luke 2:15-20

When the angels went away from them to heaven, the shepherds
said to one another, "Let us go, then, to Bethlehem to see this
thing that has taken place, which the Lord has made known to us."
So they went in haste and found Mary and Joseph, and the infant
lying in the manger. When they saw this, they made known the

message that had been told them about this child. All who heard it were amazed by what had been told them by the shepherds. And Mary kept all these things, reflecting on them in her heart. Then the shepherds returned, glorifying and praising God for all they had heard and seen, just as it had been told to them.

THE NATIVITY OF THE LORD (CHRISTMAS)
(Mass during the Day)

First Reading   **Isaiah 52:7-10**

How beautiful upon the mountains are the feet of him who brings glad tidings, announcing peace, bearing good news, announcing salvation, and saying to Zion, "Your God is King!" Hark! Your sentinels raise a cry, together they shout for joy, for they see directly, before their eyes, the LORD restoring Zion. Break out together in song, O ruins of Jerusalem! For the LORD comforts his people, he redeems Jerusalem. The LORD has bared his holy arm in the sight of all the nations; all the ends of the earth will behold the salvation of our God.

Responsorial Psalm   **Psalm 98:1, 2-3, 3-4, 5-6**

R. (3c) All the ends of the earth have seen the saving power of God.

Sing to the LORD a new song, for he has done wondrous deeds; his right hand has won victory for him, his holy arm. **R.**

The LORD has made his salvation known: in the sight of the nations he has revealed his justice. He has remembered his kindness and his faithfulness toward the house of Israel. **R.**

All the ends of the earth have seen the salvation by our God. Sing joyfully to the LORD, all you lands; break into song; sing praise. **R.**

Sing praise to the LORD with the harp, with the harp and melodious song. With trumpets and the sound of the horn sing joyfully before the King, the LORD. **R.**

Second Reading   Hebrews 1:1-6

Brothers and sisters:

In times past, God spoke in partial and various ways to our ancestors through the prophets; in these last days, he has spoken to us through the Son, whom he made heir of all things and through whom he created the universe, who is the refulgence of his glory, the very imprint of his being, and who sustains all things by his mighty word. When he had accomplished purification from sins, he took his seat at the right hand of the Majesty on high, as far superior to the angels as the name he has inherited is more excellent than theirs. For to which of the angels did God ever say: *You are my son; this day I have begotten you?* Or again: *I will be a father to him, and he shall be a son to me?* And again, when he leads the firstborn into the world, he says: *Let all the angels of God worship him.*

Alleluia

R. Alleluia, alleluia.

A holy day has dawned upon us. Come, you nations, and adore the Lord. For today a great light has come upon the earth. **R.**

Gospel   John 1:1-18 or John 1:1-5,9-14

John 1:1-18

In the beginning was the Word, and the Word was with God, and the Word was God. He was in the beginning with God. All things came to be through him, and without him nothing came to be. What came to be through him was life, and this life was the light of the human race; the light shines in the darkness, and the darkness has not overcome it. A man named John was sent from God. He came for testimony, to testify to the light, so that all might believe through him. He was not the light, but came to testify to the light. The true light, which enlightens everyone, was coming into the world. He was in the world, and the world came to be through him, but the world did not know him. He came to what was his own, but his own people did not accept him. But to those who did accept him he gave power to become children of God, to those who believe in his name, who were born not by natural generation nor by human choice nor by a man's decision but of God. And the Word became flesh and made his dwelling among us, and we saw his glory, the glory as of the Father's only Son, full of grace and truth. John testified to him and cried out, saying, "This was he of whom I said, 'The one who is coming after me ranks ahead of me because he existed before me.'" From his fullness we have all received, grace in place of grace, because while the law was given through Moses, grace and truth came through Jesus Christ. No one has ever seen God. The only Son, God, who is at the Father's side, has revealed him.

Or:

John 1:1-5, 9-14

In the beginning was the Word, and the Word was with God, and the Word was God. He was in the beginning with God. All things came to be through him, and without him nothing came to be. What came to be through him was life, and this life was the light of the human race; the light shines in the darkness, and the darkness has not overcome it. The true light, which enlightens everyone, was coming into the world. He was in the world, and the world came to be through him, but the world did not know him. He came to what was his own, but his own people did not accept him. But to those who did accept him he gave power to become children of God, to those who believe in his name, who were born not by natural generation nor by human choice nor by a man's decision but of God. And the Word became flesh and made his dwelling among us, and we saw his glory, the glory as of the Father's only Son, full of grace and truth.

SATURDAY, DECEMBER 26, 2020
FEAST OF SAINT STEPHEN, FIRST MARTYR
First Reading   **Acts 6:8-10; 7:54-59**

Stephen, filled with grace and power, was working great wonders and signs among the people. Certain members of the so-called Synagogue of Freedmen, Cyrenians, and Alexandrians, and people from Cilicia and Asia, came forward and debated with Stephen, but they could not withstand the wisdom and the spirit with which he spoke.

When they heard this, they were infuriated, and they ground their teeth at him. But he, filled with the Holy Spirit, looked up intently to heaven and saw the glory of God and Jesus standing at the right hand of God, and he said, "Behold, I see the heavens opened and the Son of Man standing at the right hand of God." But they cried out in a loud voice, covered their ears, and rushed upon him together. They threw him out of the city, and began to stone him. The witnesses laid down their cloaks at the feet of a young man named Saul. As they were stoning Stephen, he called out "Lord Jesus, receive my spirit."

Responsorial Psalm   Psalm 31:3cd-4, 6 and 8ab, 16bc and 17

R. (6) Into your hands, O Lord, I commend my spirit.

Be my rock of refuge, a stronghold to give me safety. You are my rock and my fortress; for your name's sake you will lead and guide me. **R.**

Into your hands I commend my spirit; you will redeem me, O LORD, O faithful God. I will rejoice and be glad because of your mercy. **R.**

Rescue me from the clutches of my enemies and my persecutors. Let your face shine upon your servant; save me in your kindness. **R.**

Alleluia   Psalm 118:26a, 27a

R. Alleluia, alleluia.

Blessed is he who comes in the name of the LORD: the LORD is God and has given us light. **R.**

Gospel   Matthew 10:17-22

Jesus said to his disciples:

"Beware of men, for they will hand you over to courts and scourge you in their synagogues, and you will be led before governors and kings for my sake as a witness before them and the pagans. When they hand you over, do not worry about how you are to speak or what you are to say. You will be given at that moment what you are to say. For it will not be you who speak but the Spirit of your Father speaking through you. Brother will hand over brother to death, and the father his child; children will rise up against parents and have them put to death. You will be hated by all because of my name, but whoever endures to the end will be saved."

THE HOLY FAMILY OF JESUS, MARY AND JOSEPH

First Reading   **Sirach 3:2-6, 12-14 or Genesis 15:1-6;21:1-3**

Sirach 3:2-6

God sets a father in honor over his children; a mother's authority he confirms over her sons. Whoever honors his father atones for sins, and preserves himself from them. When he prays, he is heard; he stores up riches who reveres his mother. Whoever honors his father is gladdened by children, and, when he prays, is heard. Whoever reveres his father will live a long life; he who obeys his father brings comfort to his mother. My son, take care of your father when he is old; grieve him not as long as he lives. Even if his mind fail, be considerate of him; revile him not all the days of his life; kindness to a father will not be forgotten, firmly planted against the debt of your sins—a house raised in justice to you.

Or:

Genesis 15:1-6; 21:1-3

The word of the LORD came to Abram in a vision, saying: "Fear not, Abram! I am your shield; I will make your reward very great." But Abram said, "O Lord GOD, what good will your gifts be, if I keep on being childless and have as my heir the steward of my house, Eliezer?" Abram continued, "See, you have given me no offspring, and so one of my servants will be my heir." Then the word of the LORD came to him: "No, that one shall not be your heir; your own issue shall be your heir." The Lord took Abram outside and said, "Look up at the sky and count the stars, if you can. Just so," he added, "shall your descendants be." Abram put his faith in the LORD, who credited it to him as an act of righteousness. The LORD took note of Sarah as he had said he would; he did for her as he had promised. Sarah became pregnant and bore Abraham a son in his old age, at the set time that God had stated. Abraham gave the name Isaac to this son of his whom Sarah bore him.

Responsorial Psalm   Psalm 128:1-2, 3, 4-5

R. (1) Blessed are those who fear the Lord and walk in his ways.

Blessed is everyone who fears the LORD, who walks in his ways!
For you shall eat the fruit of your handiwork; blessed shall you be,
and favored. **R.**

Your wife shall be like a fruitful vine in the recesses of your home;
your children like olive plants around your table. **R.**

Behold, thus is the man blessed who fears the LORD. The LORD
bless you from Zion: may you see the prosperity of Jerusalem all
the days of your life. **R.**

Or:

Psalm 105:1-2, 3-4, 5-6, 8-9

R. (7a, 8a) The Lord remembers his covenant forever.

Give thanks to the LORD, invoke his name; make known among the nations his deeds. Sing to him, sing his praise, proclaim all his wondrous deeds. **R.**

Glory in his holy name; rejoice, O hearts that seek the LORD! Look to the LORD in his strength; constantly seek his face. **R.**

You descendants of Abraham, his servants, sons of Jacob, his chosen ones! He, the LORD, is our God; throughout the earth his judgments prevail. **R.**

He remembers forever his covenant which he made binding for a thousand generations which he entered into with Abraham and by his oath to Isaac. **R.**

Second Reading   Colossians 3:12-21
or Colossians 3:12-17 or Hebrew 11:8, 11-12, 17-19
Colossians 3:12-21

Brothers and sisters:

Put on, as God's chosen ones, holy and beloved, heartfelt compassion, kindness, humility, gentleness, and patience, bearing with one another and forgiving one another, if one has a grievance against another; as the Lord has forgiven you, so must you also do. And over all these put on love, that is, the bond of perfection. And let the peace of Christ control your hearts, the peace into which you were also called in one body. And be thankful. Let the word of Christ dwell in you richly, as in all wisdom you teach and admonish one another, singing psalms, hymns, and spiritual songs with gratitude in your hearts to God. And whatever you do, in word or in deed, do everything in the name of the Lord Jesus, giving thanks to God the Father through him. Wives, be subordinate to your husbands, as is proper in the Lord. Husbands, love your wives, and avoid any bitterness toward them. Children, obey your parents in everything, for this is pleasing to the Lord. Fathers, do not provoke your children, so they may not become discouraged.

Or:

Colossians 3:12-17

Brothers and sisters:

Put on, as God's chosen ones, holy and beloved, heartfelt compassion, kindness, humility, gentleness, and patience, bearing with one another and forgiving one another, if one has a grievance against another; as the Lord has forgiven you, so must you also do. And over all these put on love, that is, the bond of perfection. And let the peace of Christ control your hearts, the peace into which you were also called in one body. And be thankful. Let the word of Christ dwell in you richly, as in all wisdom you teach and admonish one another, singing psalms, hymns, and spiritual songs with gratitude in your hearts to God. And whatever you do, in word or in deed, do everything in the name of the Lord Jesus, giving thanks to God the Father through him.

Or:

Hebrews 11:8, 11-12, 17-19

Brothers and sisters:

By faith Abraham obeyed when he was called to go out to a place that he was to receive as an inheritance; he went out, not knowing where he was to go. By faith he received power to generate, even though he was past the normal age and Sarah herself was sterile for he thought that the one who had made the promise was trustworthy. So it was that there came forth from one man, himself as good as dead, descendants as numerous as the stars in the sky and as countless as the sands on the seashore. By faith Abraham, when put to the test, offered up Isaac, and he who had received the promises was ready to offer his only son, of whom it was said, "Through Isaac descendants shall bear your name." He reasoned that God was able to raise even from the dead, and he received Isaac back as a symbol.

Alleluia   Colossians 3:15a, 16a or Hebrew 1:1-2

Colossians 3:15a
R. Alleluia, alleluia.

Let the peace of Christ control your hearts; let the word of Christ dwell in you richly. **R.**

Or:
Hebrews 1:1-2
R. Alleluia, alleluia.

In the past God spoke to our ancestors through the prophets; in these last days, he has spoken to us through the Son. **R.**

Gospel   Luke 2:22-40 or Luke 2:22, 39-40

Luke 2:22-40

When the days were completed for their purification according to the Law of Moses, They took him up to Jerusalem to present him to the Lord, just as it is written in the law of the Lord,

Every male that opens the womb shall be consecrated to the Lord, and to offer the sacrifice of *a pair of turtledoves or two young pigeons,* in accordance with the dictate in the law of the Lord.

Now there was a man in Jerusalem whose name was Simeon. This man was righteous and devout, awaiting the consolation of Israel, and the Holy Spirit was upon him. It had been revealed to him by the Holy Spirit that he should not see death before he had seen the Christ of the Lord. He came in the Spirit into the temple; and when the parents brought in the child Jesus to perform the custom of the law in regard to him, He took him into his arms and blessed God, saying: "Now, Master, you may let your servant go in peace, according to your word, for my eyes have seen your salvation, which you prepared in sight of all the peoples, a light for revelation to the Gentiles, and glory for your people Israel." The child's father and mother were amazed at what was said about him; and Simeon blessed them and said to Mary his mother, "Behold, this child is destined for the fall and rise of many in Israel, and to be a sign that will be contradicted—and you yourself a sword will pierce—so that the thoughts of many hearts may be revealed."

There was also a prophetess, Anna, the daughter of Phanuel, of the tribe of Asher. She was advanced in years, having lived seven years with her husband after her marriage, and then as a widow until she was eighty-four. She never left the temple, but worshiped night and day with fasting and prayer. And coming forward at that very time, she gave thanks to God and spoke about the child to all who were awaiting the redemption of Jerusalem. When they had fulfilled all the prescriptions of the law of the Lord, they returned to Galilee, to their own town of Nazareth. The child grew and became strong, filled with wisdom; and the favor of God was upon him.

Or:

Luke 2:22, 39-40

When the days were completed for their purification according to the Law of Moses, they took him up to Jerusalem to present him to the Lord. When they had fulfilled all the prescriptions of the law of the Lord, they returned to Galilee, to their own town of Nazareth. The child grew and became strong, filled with wisdom; and the favor of God was upon him.

MONDAY, DECEMBER 28, 2020

FEAST OF THE HOLY INNOCENTS, MARTYRS

First Reading   **1 John 1:5-2:2**

Beloved:

This is the message that we have heard from Jesus Christ and proclaim to you: God is light, and in him there is no darkness at all. If we say, "We have fellowship with him," while we continue to walk in darkness, we lie and do not act in truth. But if we walk in the light as he is in the light, then we have fellowship with one another, and the Blood of his Son Jesus cleanses us from all sin. If we say, "We are without sin," we deceive ourselves, and the truth is not in us. If we acknowledge our sins, he is faithful and just and will forgive our sins and cleanse us from every wrongdoing. If we say, "We have not sinned," we make him a liar, and his word is not in us. My children, I am writing this to you so that you may not commit sin. But if anyone does sin, we have an Advocate with the

Father, Jesus Christ the righteous one. He is expiation for our sins, and not for our sins only but for those of the whole world.

Responsorial Psalm   Psalm 124:2-3, 4-5, 7cd-8

R. (7) Our soul has been rescued like a bird from the fowler's snare.

Had not the LORD been with us—when men rose up against us, then would they have swallowed us alive, when their fury was inflamed against us. **R.**

Then would the waters have overwhelmed us; the torrent would have swept over us; over us then would have swept the raging waters. **R.**

Broken was the snare, and we were freed. Our help is in the name of the LORD, who made heaven and earth. **R.**

Alleluia

R. Alleluia, alleluia.

We praise you, O God, we acclaim you as Lord; the white-robed army of martyrs praise you. **R.**

Gospel   Matthew 2:13-18

When the magi had departed, behold, the angel of the Lord appeared to Joseph in a dream and said,

"Rise, take the child and his mother, flee to Egypt, and stay there until I tell you. Herod is going to search for the child to destroy him." Joseph rose and took the child and his mother by night and departed for Egypt. He stayed there until the death of Herod, that what the Lord had said through the prophet might be fulfilled, *Out of Egypt I called my son.*

When Herod realized that he had been deceived by the magi, he became furious. He ordered the massacre of all the boys in Bethlehem and its vicinity two years old and under, in accordance with the time he had ascertained from the magi. Then was fulfilled what had been said through Jeremiah the prophet:

A voice was heard in Ramah, sobbing and loud lamentation; Rachel weeping for her children, and she would not be consoled, since they were no more.

TUESDAY, DECEMBER 29, 2020
THE FIFTH DAY IN THE OCTAVE OF CHRISTMAS

First Reading   **1 John 2:3-11**

Beloved:

The way we may be sure that we know Jesus is to keep his commandments. Whoever says, "I know him," but does not keep his commandments is a liar, and the truth is not in him. But whoever keeps his word, the love of God is truly perfected in him. This is the way we may know that we are in union with him: whoever claims to abide in him ought to walk just as he walked. Beloved, I am writing no new commandment to you but an old commandment that you had from the beginning. The old commandment is the word that you have heard. And yet I do write a new commandment to you, which holds true in him and among you, for the darkness is passing away, and the true light is already shining. Whoever says he is in the light, yet hates his brother, is still in the darkness. Whoever loves his brother remains in the light, and there is nothing in him to cause a fall. Whoever hates his brother is in darkness; he walks in darkness and does not know where he is going because the darkness has blinded his eyes.

Responsorial Psalm   Psalm 96:1-2a, 2b-3, 5b-6

R. (11a) Let the heavens be glad and the earth rejoice!
Sing to the LORD a new song; sing to the LORD, all you lands.
Sing to the LORD; bless his name. **R.**
Announce his salvation, day after day. Tell his glory among the nations; among all peoples, his wondrous deeds. **R.**
The LORD made the heavens. Splendor and majesty go before him; praise and grandeur are in his sanctuary. **R.**

Alleluia   Luke 2:32

R. Alleluia, alleluia.
A light of revelation to the Gentiles and glory for your people Israel. **R.**

Gospel   Luke 2:22-35

When the days were completed for their purification according to the law of Moses, the parents of Jesus took him up to Jerusalem to present him to the Lord, just as it is written in the law of the Lord, *Every male that opens the womb shall be consecrated to the Lord,* and to offer the sacrifice of *a pair of turtledoves or two young pigeons,* in accordance with the dictate in the law of the Lord.

Now there was a man in Jerusalem whose name was Simeon. This man was righteous and devout, awaiting the consolation of Israel, and the Holy Spirit was upon him. It had been revealed to him by the Holy Spirit that he should not see death before he had seen the Christ of the Lord. He came in the Spirit into the temple; and when the parents brought in the child Jesus to perform the custom of the law in regard to him, he took him into his arms and blessed God, saying: "Lord, now let your servant go in peace; your word has been fulfilled: my own eyes have seen the salvation which you prepared in the sight of every people, a light to reveal you to the nations and the glory of your people Israel."

The child's father and mother were amazed at what was said about him; and Simeon blessed them and said to Mary his mother, "Behold, this child is destined for the fall and rise of many in Israel, and to be a sign that will be contradicted (and you yourself a sword will pierce) so that the thoughts of many hearts may be revealed."

WEDNESDAY, DECEMBER 30, 2020
THE SIXTH DAY IN THE OCTAVE OF CHRISTMAS
First Reading   1 John 2:12-17

I am writing to you, children, because your sins have been forgiven for his name's sake. I am writing to you, fathers, because you know him who is from the beginning. I am writing to you, young men, because you have conquered the Evil One. I write to you, children, because you know the Father. I write to you, fathers, because you know him who is from the beginning. I write to you, young men, because you are strong and the word of God remains in you, and you have conquered the Evil One. Do not love the world or the things of the world. If anyone loves the world, the love of the Father is not in him. For all that is in the world, sensual lust, enticement for the eyes, and a retentious life, is not from the Father but is from the world. Yet the world and its enticement are passing away. But whoever does the will of God remains forever.

Responsorial Psalm   Psalm 96:7-8a, 8b-9, 10

R. (11a) Let the heavens be glad and the earth rejoice!

Give to the LORD, you families of nations, give to the LORD glory
and praise; give to the LORD the glory due his name! **R.**

Bring gifts, and enter his courts; worship the LORD in holy attire.
Tremble before him, all the earth. **R.**

Say among the nations: The LORD is king. He has made the world
firm, not to be moved; he governs the peoples with equity. **R.**

Alleluia

R. Alleluia, alleluia.

A holy day has dawned upon us. Come, you nations, and adore the
Lord. Today a great light has come upon the earth. **R.**

Gospel   Luke 2:36-40

There was a prophetess, Anna, the daughter of Phanuel, of the
tribe of Asher. She was advanced in years, having lived seven years
with her husband after her marriage, and then as a widow until
she was eighty-four. She never left the temple, but worshiped
night and day with fasting and prayer. And coming forward at that
very time, she gave thanks to God and spoke about the child to all
who were awaiting the redemption of Jerusalem. When they had
fulfilled all the prescriptions of the law of the Lord, they returned
to Galilee, to their own town of Nazareth. The child grew and
became strong, filled with wisdom; and the favor of God was upon
him.

THE SEVENTH DAY IN THE OCTAVE OF CHRISTMAS

First Reading   **1 John 2:18-21**

Children, it is the last hour; and just as you heard that the antichrist was coming, so now many antichrists have appeared. Thus we know this is the last hour. They went out from us, but they were not really of our number; if they had been, they would have remained with us. Their desertion shows that none of them was of our number. But you have the anointing that comes from the Holy One, and you all have knowledge. I write to you not because you do not know the truth but because you do, and because every lie is alien to the truth.

Responsorial Psalm   **Psalm 96:1-2, 11-12, 13**

R. (11a) Let the heavens be glad and the earth rejoice!

Sing to the LORD a new song; sing to the LORD, all you lands. Sing to the LORD; bless his name; announce his salvation, day after day. **R.**

Let the heavens be glad and the earth rejoice; let the sea and what fills it resound; let the plains be joyful and all that is in them! Then shall all the trees of the forest exult before the LORD. **R.**

The LORD comes, he comes to rule the earth. He shall rule the world with justice and the peoples with his constancy. **R.**

Alleluia   **John 1:14a, 12a**

R. Alleluia, alleluia.

The Word of God became flesh and dwelt among us. To those who accepted him he gave power to become the children of God. **R.**

In the beginning was the Word, and the Word was with God, and the Word was God. He was in the beginning with God. All things came to be through him, and without him nothing came to be. What came to be through him was life, and this life was the light of the human race; the light shines in the darkness, and the darkness has not overcome it.

A man named John was sent from God. He came for testimony, to testify to the light, so that all might believe through him. He was not the light, but came to testify to the light. The true light, which enlightens everyone, was coming into the world. He was in the world, and the world came to be through him, but the world did not know him. He came to what was his own, but his own people did not accept him. But to those who did accept him he gave power to become children of God, to those who believe in his name, who were born not by natural generation nor by human choice nor by a man's decision but of God. And the Word became flesh and made his dwelling among us, and we saw his glory, the glory as of the Father's only-begotten Son, full of grace and truth.

John testified to him and cried out, saying, "This was he of whom I said, 'The one who is coming after me ranks ahead of me because he existed before me.'" From his fullness we have all received, grace in place of grace, because while the law was given through Moses, grace and truth came through Jesus Christ. No one has ever seen God. The only-begotten Son, God, who is at the Father's side, has revealed him.

SOLEMNITY OF MARY, THE MOTHER OF GOD

First Reading   **Numbers 6:22-27**

The LORD said to Moses:

"Speak to Aaron and his sons and tell them: This is how you shall bless the Israelites. Say to them: The LORD bless you and keep you! The LORD let his face shine upon you, and be gracious to you! The LORD look upon you kindly and give you peace! So shall they invoke my name upon the Israelites, and I will bless them."

Responsorial Psalm   **Psalm 67:2-3, 5, 6, 8**

R. (2a) May God bless us in his mercy.

May God have pity on us and bless us; may he let his face shine upon us. So may your way be known upon earth; among all nations, your salvation. **R.**

May the nations be glad and exult because you rule the peoples in equity; the nations on the earth you guide. **R.**

May the peoples praise you, O God; may all the peoples praise you! May God bless us, and may all the ends of the earth fear him! **R.**

Second Reading   **Galatians 4:4-7**

Brothers and sisters:

When the fullness of time had come, God sent his Son, born of a woman, born under the law, to ransom those under the law, so that we might receive adoption as sons. As proof that you are sons, God sent the Spirit of his Son into our hearts, crying out, "Abba,

Father!" So you are no longer a slave but a son, and if a son then also an heir, through God.

Alleluia Hebrews 1:1-2

R. Alleluia, alleluia.

In the past God spoke to our ancestors through the prophets; in these last days, he has spoken to us through the Son. **R.**

Gospel Luke 2:16-21

The shepherds went in haste to Bethlehem and found Mary and Joseph, and the infant lying in the manger. When they saw this, they made known the message that had been told them about this child. All who heard it were amazed by what had been told them by the shepherds. And Mary kept all these things, reflecting on them in her heart. Then the shepherds returned, glorifying and praising God for all they had heard and seen, just as it had been told to them. When eight days were completed for his circumcision, he was named Jesus, the name given him by the angel before he was conceived in the womb.

SATURDAY, JANUARY 2, 2021

MEMORIAL OF SAINTS BASIL THE GREAT AND GREGORY NAZIANZEN, BISHOPS AND DOCTORS OF THE CHURCH

First Reading 1 John 2:22-28

Beloved:

Who is the liar? Whoever denies that Jesus is the Christ. Whoever denies the Father and the Son, this is the antichrist. Anyone who denies the Son does not have the Father, but whoever confesses the Son has the Father as well. Let what you heard from the beginning remain in you. If what you heard from the beginning remains in you, then you will remain in the Son and in the Father. And this is the promise that he made us: eternal life.

I write you these things about those who would deceive you. As for you, the anointing that you received from him remains in you, so that you do not need anyone to teach you. But his anointing teaches you about everything and is true and not false; just as it taught you, remain in him.

And now, children, remain in him, so that when he appears we may have confidence and not be put to shame by him at his coming.

Responsorial Psalm   Psalm 98:1, 2-3ab, 3cd-4

R. (3cd) All the ends of the earth have seen the saving power of God.

Sing to the LORD a new song, for he has done wondrous deeds;
His right hand has won victory for him, his holy arm. **R.**
The LORD has made his salvation known: in the sight of the
nations he has revealed his justice. He has remembered his
kindness and his faithfulness toward the house of Israel. **R.**
All the ends of the earth have seen the salvation by our God. Sing
joyfully to the LORD, all you lands; break into song; sing praise. **R.**

Alleluia   Hebrews 1:1-2

R. Alleluia, alleluia.

In times, past, God spoke to our ancestors through the prophets:
in these last days, he has spoken to us through his Son. **R.**

Gospel   John 1:19-28

This is the testimony of John. When the Jews from Jerusalem sent priests and Levites to him to ask him, "Who are you?" He admitted and did not deny it, but admitted, "I am not the Christ." So they asked him, "What are you then? Are you Elijah?" And he said, "I am not." "Are you the Prophet?" He answered, "No." So they said to him, "Who are you, so we can give an answer to those who sent us? What do you have to say for yourself?" He said: "I am *the voice of one crying out in the desert, 'Make straight the way of the Lord,'* as Isaiah the prophet said." Some Pharisees were also sent. They asked him, "Why then do you baptize if you are not the Christ or Elijah or the Prophet?" John answered them, "I baptize with water; but there is one among you whom you do not recognize, the one who is coming after me, whose sandal strap I am not worthy to untie." This happened in Bethany across the Jordan, where John was baptizing.

SUNDAY, JANUARY 3, 2021

THE EPIPHANY OF THE LORD

First Reading   Isaiah 60:1-6

Rise up in splendor, Jerusalem! Your light has come, the glory of the Lord shines upon you. See, darkness covers the earth, and thick clouds cover the peoples; but upon you the LORD shines, and over you appears his glory. Nations shall walk by your light, and kings by your shining radiance. Raise your eyes and look about; they all gather and come to you: your sons come from afar, and your daughters in the arms of their nurses. Then you shall be radiant at what you see, your heart shall throb and overflow, for the riches of the sea shall be emptied out before you, the wealth of nations shall be brought to you. Caravans of camels shall fill you, dromedaries from Midian and Ephah; all from Sheba shall come bearing gold and frankincense, and proclaiming the praises of the LORD.

Responsorial Psalm　　　　Psalm 72:1-2, 7-8, 10-11, 12-13
R. (11) Lord, every nation on earth will adore you.

O God, with your judgment endow the king, and with your justice, the king's son; He shall govern your people with justice and your afflicted ones with judgment. **R.**

Justice shall flower in his days, and profound peace, till the moon be no more. May he rule from sea to sea, and from the River to the ends of the earth. **R.**

The kings of Tarshish and the Isles shall offer gifts; the kings of Arabia and Seba shall bring tribute. All kings shall pay him homage, all nations shall serve him. **R.**

For he shall rescue the poor when he cries out, and the afflicted when he has no one to help him. He shall have pity for the lowly and the poor; the lives of the poor he shall save. **R.**

Second Reading　　　　　　Ephesians 3:2-3a, 5-6

Brothers and sisters:

You have heard of the stewardship of God's grace that was given to me for your benefit, namely, that the mystery was made known to me by revelation. It was not made known to people in other generations as it has now been revealed to his holy apostles and prophets by the Spirit: that the Gentiles are coheirs, members of the same body, and copartners in the promise in Christ Jesus through the gospel.

Alleluia

Matthew 2:2

R. Alleluia, alleluia.

We saw his star at its rising and have come to do him homage. **R.**

Gospel

Matthew 2:1-12

When Jesus was born in Bethlehem of Judea, in the days of King Herod, behold, magi from the east arrived in Jerusalem, saying, "Where is the newborn king of the Jews? We saw his star at its rising and have come to do him homage." When King Herod heard this, he was greatly troubled, and all Jerusalem with him. Assembling all the chief priests and the scribes of the people, He inquired of them where the Christ was to be born. They said to him, "In Bethlehem of Judea, for thus it has been written through the prophet: *And you, Bethlehem, land of Judah, are by no means least among the rulers of Judah; since from you shall come a ruler, who is to shepherd my people Israel.*" Then Herod called the magi secretly and ascertained from them the time of the star's appearance. He sent them to Bethlehem and said, "Go and search diligently for the child. When you have found him, bring me word, that I too may go and do him homage." After their audience with the king they set out. And behold, the star that they had seen at its rising preceded them, until it came and stopped over the place where the child was. They were overjoyed at seeing the star, and on entering the house they saw the child with Mary his mother. They prostrated themselves and did him homage. Then they opened their treasures and offered him gifts of gold, frankincense, and myrrh. And having been warned in a dream not to return to Herod, they departed for their country by another way.

MEMORIAL OF SAINT ELIZABETH ANN SETON, RELIGIOUS

First Reading   **1 John 3:22–4:6**

Beloved:

We receive from him whatever we ask, because we keep his commandments and do what pleases him. And his commandment is this: we should believe in the name of his Son, Jesus Christ, and love one another just as he commanded us. Those who keep his commandments remain in him, and he in them, and the way we know that he remains in us is from the Spirit whom he gave us.

Beloved, do not trust every spirit but test the spirits to see whether they belong to God, because many false prophets have gone out into the world. This is how you can know the Spirit of God: every spirit that acknowledges Jesus Christ come in the flesh belongs to God, and every spirit that does not acknowledge Jesus does not belong to God. This is the spirit of the antichrist who, as you heard, is to come, but in fact is already in the world. You belong to God, children, and you have conquered them, for the one who is in you is greater than the one who is in the world. They belong to the world; accordingly, their teaching belongs to the world, and the world listens to them. We belong to God, and anyone who knows God listens to us, while anyone who does not belong to God refuses to hear us. This is how we know the spirit of truth and the spirit of deceit.

Responsorial Psalm   Psalm 2:7bc-8, 10-12a

R. (8ab) I will give you all the nations for an inheritance.

The LORD said to me, "You are my Son; this day I have begotten you. Ask of me and I will give you the nations for an inheritance and the ends of the earth for your possession." **R.**
And now, O kings, give heed; take warning, you rulers of the earth. Serve the LORD with fear, and rejoice before him; with trembling rejoice. **R.**

Alleluia   Matthew 4:23

R. Alleluia, alleluia.
Jesus proclaimed the Gospel of the Kingdom and cured every disease among the people. **R.**

Gospel   Matthew 4:12-17, 23-25

When Jesus heard that John had been arrested, he withdrew to Galilee. He left Nazareth and went to live in Capernaum by the sea, in the region of Zebulun and Naphtali, that what had been said through Isaiah the prophet might be fulfilled: *Land of Zebulun and land of Naphtali, the way to the sea, beyond the Jordan, Galilee of the Gentiles, the people who sit in darkness have seen a great light, on those dwelling in a land overshadowed by death light has arisen.*

From that time on, Jesus began to preach and say, "Repent, for the Kingdom of heaven is at hand." He went around all of Galilee, teaching in their synagogues, proclaiming the Gospel of the Kingdom, and curing every disease and illness among the people.

His fame spread to all of Syria, and they brought to him all who were sick with various diseases and racked with pain, those who were possessed, lunatics, and paralytics, and he cured them. And great crowds from Galilee, the Decapolis, Jerusalem, and Judea, and from beyond the Jordan followed him.

TUESDAY, JANUARY 5, 2021

MEMORIAL OF SAINT JOHN NEUMANN, BISHOP

First Reading   **1 John 4:7-10**

Beloved, let us love one another, because love is of God; everyone who loves is begotten by God and knows God. Whoever is without love does not know God, for God is love. In this way the love of God was revealed to us: God sent his only-begotten Son into the world so that we might have life through him. In this is love: not that we have loved God, but that he loved us and sent his Son as expiation for our sins.

Responsorial Psalm   **Psalm 72:1-2, 3-4, 7-8**

R. (11) Lord, every nation on earth will adore you.

O God, with your judgment endow the king, and with your justice, the king's son; He shall govern your people with justice and your afflicted ones with judgment. **R.**

The mountains shall yield peace for the people, and the hills justice. He shall defend the afflicted among the people, save the children of the poor. **R.**

Justice shall flower in his days, and profound peace, till the moon be no more. May he rule from sea to sea, and from the River to the ends of the earth. **R.**

R. Alleluia, alleluia.

The Lord has sent me to bring glad tidings to the poor and to proclaim liberty to captives. **R.**

Gospel   Mark 6:34-44

When Jesus saw the vast crowd, his heart was moved with pity for them, for they were like sheep without a shepherd; and he began to teach them many things. By now it was already late and his disciples approached him and said, "This is a deserted place and it is already very late. Dismiss them so that they can go to the surrounding farms and villages and buy themselves something to eat." He said to them in reply, "Give them some food yourselves." But they said to him, "Are we to buy two hundred days' wages worth of food and give it to them to eat?" He asked them, "How many loaves do you have? Go and see." And when they had found out they said, "Five loaves and two fish." So he gave orders to have them sit down in groups on the green grass. The people took their places in rows by hundreds and by fifties. Then, taking the five loaves and the two fish and looking up to heaven, he said the blessing, broke the loaves, and gave them to his disciples to set before the people; he also divided the two fish among them all. They all ate and were satisfied. And they picked up twelve wicker baskets full of fragments and what was left of the fish. Those who ate of the loaves were five thousand men.

WEDNESDAY AFTER EPIPHANY

First Reading   1 John 4:11-18

Beloved, if God so loved us, we also must love one another. No one has ever seen God. Yet, if we love one another, God remains in us, and his love is brought to perfection in us. This is how we know that we remain in him and he in us, that he has given us of his Spirit. Moreover, we have seen and testify that the Father sent his Son as savior of the world. Whoever acknowledges that Jesus is the Son of God, God remains in him and he in God. We have come to know and to believe in the love God has for us. God is love, and whoever remains in love remains in God and God in him. In this is love brought to perfection among us, that we have confidence on the day of judgment because as he is, so are we in this world. There is no fear in love, but perfect love drives out fear because fear has to do with punishment, and so one who fears is not yet perfect in love.

Responsorial Psalm   Psalm 72:1-2, 10, 12-13

R. (11) Lord, every nation on earth will adore you.

O God, with your judgment endow the king, and with your justice, the king's son; He shall govern your people with justice and your afflicted ones with judgment. **R.**

The kings of Tarshish and the Isles shall offer gifts; the kings of Arabia and Seba shall bring tribute. **R.**

For he shall rescue the poor when he cries out, and the afflicted when he has no one to help him. He shall have pity for the lowly and the poor; the lives of the poor he shall save. **R.**

R. Alleluia, alleluia.

Glory to you, O Christ, proclaimed to the Gentiles. Glory to you, O Christ, believed in throughout the world. **R.**

Gospel Mark 6:45-52

After the five thousand had eaten and were satisfied, Jesus made his disciples get into the boat and precede him to the other side toward Bethsaida, while he dismissed the crowd. And when he had taken leave of them, he went off to the mountain to pray. When it was evening, the boat was far out on the sea and he was alone on shore. Then he saw that they were tossed about while rowing, for the wind was against them. About the fourth watch of the night, he came toward them walking on the sea. He meant to pass by them. But when they saw him walking on the sea, they thought it was a ghost and cried out. They had all seen him and were terrified. But at once he spoke with them, "Take courage, it is I, do not be afraid!" He got into the boat with them and the wind died down. They were completely astounded. They had not understood the incident of the loaves. On the contrary, their hearts were hardened.

THURSDAY, JANUARY 7, 2021
THURSDAY AFTER EPIPHANY

First Reading 1 John 4:19-5:4

Beloved, we love God because he first loved us. If anyone says, "I love God," but hates his brother, he is a liar; for whoever does not love a brother whom he has seen cannot love God whom he has not seen. This is the commandment we have from him: Whoever loves God must also love his brother. Everyone who believes that Jesus is the Christ is begotten by God, and everyone who loves the Father loves also the one begotten by him. In this way we know that we love the children of God when we love God and obey his commandments. For the love of God is this, that we keep his commandments. And his commandments are not burdensome, for whoever is begotten by God conquers the world. And the victory that conquers the world is our faith.

Responsorial Psalm   Psalm 72:1-2, 14 and 15bc, 17

R. (11) Lord, every nation on earth will adore you.

O God, with your judgment endow the king, and with your justice, the king's son;

He shall govern your people with justice and your afflicted ones with judgment. **R.**

From fraud and violence he shall redeem them, and precious shall their blood be in his sight. May they be prayed for continually; day by day shall they bless him. **R.**

May his name be blessed forever; as long as the sun his name shall remain. In him shall all the tribes of the earth be blessed; all the nations shall proclaim his happiness. **R.**

Alleluia   Luke 4:18

R. Alleluia, alleluia.

The Lord has sent me to bring glad tidings to the poor and to proclaim liberty to captives. **R.**

Gospel   Luke 4:14-22

Jesus returned to Galilee in the power of the Spirit, and news of him spread throughout the whole region. He taught in their synagogues and was praised by all. He came to Nazareth, where he had grown up, and went according to his custom into the synagogue on the Sabbath day. He stood up to read and was handed a scroll of the prophet Isaiah. He unrolled the scroll and found the passage where it was written: *The Spirit of the Lord is upon me, because he has anointed me to bring glad tidings to the poor. He has sent me to proclaim liberty to captives and recovery of sight to the blind, to let the oppressed go free, and to proclaim a year acceptable to the Lord.*

Rolling up the scroll, he handed it back to the attendant and sat down, and the eyes of all in the synagogue looked intently at him. He said to them, "Today this Scripture passage is fulfilled in your hearing." And all spoke highly of him and were amazed at the gracious words that came from his mouth.

FRIDAY, JANUARY 8, 2021
FRIDAY AFTER EPIPHANY

First Reading   **1 John 5:5-13**

Beloved:

Who indeed is the victor over the world but the one who believes that Jesus is the Son of God? This is the one who came through water and Blood, Jesus Christ, not by water alone, but by water and Blood. The Spirit is the one who testifies, and the Spirit is truth. So there are three who testify, the Spirit, the water, and the Blood, and the three are of one accord. If we accept human testimony, the testimony of God is surely greater. Now the testimony of God is this, that he has testified on behalf of his Son.

Whoever believes in the Son of God has this testimony within himself. Whoever does not believe God has made him a liar by not believing the testimony God has given about his Son. And this is the testimony: God gave us eternal life, and this life is in his Son. Whoever possesses the Son has life; whoever does not possess the Son of God does not have life. I write these things to you so that you may know that you have eternal life, you who believe in the name of the Son of God.

Responsorial Psalm — Psalm 147:12-13, 14-15, 19-20

R. (12a) Praise the Lord, Jerusalem.

Or:

R. Alleluia.

Glorify the LORD, O Jerusalem; praise your God, O Zion. For he has strengthened the bars of your gates; he has blessed your children within you. **R.**

He has granted peace in your borders; with the best of wheat he fills you. He sends forth his command to the earth; swiftly runs his word! **R.**

He has proclaimed his word to Jacob, his statutes and his ordinances to Israel. He has not done thus for any other nation; his ordinances he has not made known to them. Alleluia. **R.**

Alleluia — Matthew 4:23

R. Alleluia, alleluia.

Jesus proclaimed the Gospel of the Kingdom and cured every disease among the people. **R.**

Gospel — Luke 5:12-16

It happened that there was a man full of leprosy in one of the towns where Jesus was; and when he saw Jesus, he fell prostrate, pleaded with him, and said, "Lord, if you wish, you can make me clean." Jesus stretched out his hand, touched him, and said, "I do will it. Be made clean." And the leprosy left him immediately. Then he ordered him not to tell anyone, but "Go, show yourself to the priest and offer for your cleansing what Moses prescribed; that will be proof for them." The report about him spread all the more, and great crowds assembled to listen to him and to be cured of their ailments, but he would withdraw to deserted places to pray.

SATURDAY, JANUARY 9, 2021
SATURDAY AFTER EPIPHANY

First Reading   1 John 5:14-21

Beloved:

We have this confidence in him that if we ask anything according to his will, he hears us. And if we know that he hears us in regard to whatever we ask, we know that what we have asked him for is ours. If anyone sees his brother sinning, if the sin is not deadly, he should pray to God and he will give him life. This is only for those whose sin is not deadly. There is such a thing as deadly sin, about which I do not say that you should pray. All wrongdoing is sin, but there is sin that is not deadly. We know that anyone begotten by God does not sin; but the one begotten by God he protects, and the Evil One cannot touch him. We know that we belong to God, and the whole world is under the power of the Evil One. We also know that the Son of God has come and has given us discernment to know the one who is true. And we are in the one who is true, in his

Son Jesus Christ. He is the true God and eternal life. Children, be on your guard against idols.

Responsorial Psalm   Psalm 149:1-2, 3-4, 5-6a and 9b
R. (4a) The Lord takes delight in his people.
Or:
R. Alleluia.

Sing to the LORD a new song of praise in the assembly of the faithful. Let Israel be glad in their maker, let the children of Zion rejoice in their king. **R.**
Let them praise his name in the festive dance, let them sing praise to him with timbrel and harp. For the LORD loves his people, and he adorns the lowly with victory. **R.**
Let the faithful exult in glory; let them sing for joy upon their couches; Let the high praises of God be in their throats. This is the glory of all his faithful. Alleluia. **R.**

Alleluia   Matthew 4:16
R. Alleluia, alleluia.
The people who sit in darkness have seen a great light, on those dwelling in a land overshadowed by death light has arisen. **R.**

Gospel   John 3:22-30
Jesus and his disciples went into the region of Judea, where he spent some time with them baptizing. John was also baptizing in Aenon near Salim, because there was an abundance of water there, and people came to be baptized, for John had not yet been imprisoned. Now a dispute arose between the disciples of John

and a Jew about ceremonial washings. So they came to John and said to him, "Rabbi, the one who was with you across the Jordan, to whom you testified, here he is baptizing and everyone is coming to him." John answered and said, "No one can receive anything except what has been given from heaven. You yourselves can testify that I said that I am not the Christ, but that I was sent before him. The one who has the bride is the bridegroom; the best man, who stands and listens for him, rejoices greatly at the bridegroom's voice. So this joy of mine has been made complete. He must increase; I must decrease."

SUNDAY, JANUARY 10, 2021
THE BAPTISM OF THE LORD

First Reading　　　　**Isaiah 42:1-4, 6-7 or Isaiah 55:1-11**

Isaiah 42:1-4, 6-7

Thus says the LORD:

Here is my servant whom I uphold, my chosen one with whom I am pleased, upon whom I have put my spirit; he shall bring forth justice to the nations, not crying out, not shouting, not making his voice heard in the street. A bruised reed he shall not break, and a smoldering wick he shall not quench, until he establishes justice on the earth; the coastlands will wait for his teaching. I, the LORD, have called you for the victory of justice, I have grasped you by the hand; I formed you, and set you as a covenant of the people, a light for the nations, to open the eyes of the blind, to bring out prisoners from confinement, and from the dungeon, those who live in darkness.

Or:

Isaiah 55:1-11

Thus says the LORD:

All you who are thirsty, come to the water! You who have no money, come, receive grain and eat; come, without paying and without cost, drink wine and milk! Why spend your money for what is not bread, your wages for what fails to satisfy? Heed me, and you shall eat well, you shall delight in rich fare. Come to me heedfully, listen, that you may have life. I will renew with you the everlasting covenant, the benefits assured to David. As I made him a witness to the peoples, a leader and commander of nations, so shall you summon a nation you knew not, and nations that knew you not shall run to you, because of the LORD, your God, the Holy One of Israel, who has glorified you.

Seek the LORD while he may be found, call him while he is near. Let the scoundrel forsake his way, and the wicked man his thoughts; let him turn to the LORD for mercy; to our God, who is generous in forgiving. For my thoughts are not your thoughts, nor are your ways my ways, says the LORD. As high as the heavens are above the earth so high are my ways above your ways and my thoughts above your thoughts.

For just as from the heavens the rain and snow come down and do not return there till they have watered the earth, making it fertile and fruitful, giving seed to the one who sows and bread to the one who eats, so shall my word be that goes forth from my mouth; my word shall not return to me void, but shall do my will, achieving the end for which I sent it.

Responsorial Psalm	**Psalm 29:1-2, 3-4, 9-10 or Isaiah 12:2-3, 4bcd, 5-6**

Psalm 29:1-2, 3-4, 9-10

R (11b) The Lord will bless his people with peace.

Give to the LORD, you sons of God, give to the LORD glory and praise, Give to the LORD the glory due his name; adore the LORD in holy attire. **R.**

The voice of the LORD is over the waters, the LORD, over vast waters. The voice of the LORD is mighty; the voice of the LORD is majestic. **R.**

The God of glory thunders, and in his temple all say, "Glory!" The LORD is enthroned above the flood; the LORD is enthroned as king forever. **R.**

Or:

Isaiah 12:2-3, 4bcd, 5-6

R. (3) You will draw water joyfully from the springs of salvation.

God indeed is my savior; I am confident and unafraid. My strength and my courage is the LORD, and he has been my savior. With joy you will draw water at the fountain of salvation. **R.**

Give thanks to the LORD, acclaim his name; among the nations make known his deeds, proclaim how exalted is his name. **R.**

Sing praise to the LORD for his glorious achievement; let this be known throughout all the earth. Shout with exultation, O city of Zion, for great in your midst is the Holy One of Israel! **R.**

Second Reading   Acts 10:34-38 or 1 John 5:1-9

Acts 10:34-38

Peter proceeded to speak to those gathered in the house of Cornelius, saying: "In truth, I see that God shows no partiality.

Rather, in every nation whoever fears him and acts uprightly is acceptable to him. You know the word that he sent to the Israelites as he proclaimed peace through Jesus Christ, who is Lord of all, what has happened all over Judea, beginning in Galilee after the baptism that John preached, how God anointed Jesus of Nazareth with the Holy Spirit and power. He went about doing good and healing all those oppressed by the devil, for God was with him."

Or:

1 John 5:1-9

Beloved:

Everyone who believes that Jesus is the Christ is begotten by God, and everyone who loves the Father loves also the one begotten by him. In this way we know that we love the children of God when we love God and obey his commandments. For the love of God is this, that we keep his commandments. And his commandments are not burdensome, for whoever is begotten by God conquers the world. And the victory that conquers the world is our faith. Who indeed is the victor over the world but the one who believes that Jesus is the Son of God?

This is the one who came through water and blood, Jesus Christ, not by water alone, but by water and blood. The Spirit is the one who testifies, and the Spirit is truth. So there are three that testify, the Spirit, the water, and the blood, and the three are of one accord. If we accept human testimony, the testimony of God is surely greater. Now the testimony of God is this, that he has testified on behalf of his Son.

Alleluia   **John 1:29**

R. Alleluia, alleluia.

John saw Jesus approaching him, and said: Behold the Lamb of God who takes away the sin of the world. **R.**

Gospel   Mark 1:7-11

This is what John the Baptist proclaimed: "One mightier than I is coming after me. I am not worthy to stoop and loosen the thongs of his sandals. I have baptized you with water; he will baptize you with the Holy Spirit."

It happened in those days that Jesus came from Nazareth of Galilee and was baptized in the Jordan by John. On coming up out of the water he saw the heavens being torn open and the Spirit, like a dove, descending upon him. And a voice came from the heavens, "You are my beloved Son; with you I am well pleased."

MONDAY, JANUARY 11, 2021
MONDAY OF THE FIRST WEEK IN ORDINARY TIME

First Reading   Hebrew 1:1-6

Brothers and sisters:

In times past, God spoke in partial and various ways to our ancestors through the prophets; in these last days, he spoke to us through the Son, whom he made heir of all things and through whom he created the universe,

Who is the refulgence of his glory, the very imprint of his being, and who sustains all things by his mighty word. When he had accomplished purification from sins, he took his seat at the right hand of the Majesty on high, as far superior to the angels as the name he has inherited is more excellent than theirs.

For to which of the angels did God ever say:

You are my Son; this day I have begotten you?

Or again:

I will be a father to him, and he shall be a Son to me?

And again, when he leads the first born into the world, he says:

Let all the angels of God worship him.

Responsorial Psalm   Psalm 97:1 and 2b, 6 and 7c, 9

R. (7c) Let all his angels worship him.

The LORD is king; let the earth rejoice; let the many isles be glad.

Justice and judgment are the foundation of his throne. **R.**

The heavens proclaim his justice, and all peoples see his glory. Let

all his angels worship him. **R.**

Because you, O LORD, are the Most High over all the earth,

exalted far above all gods. **R.**

Alleluia   Mark 1:15

R. Alleluia, alleluia.

The Kingdom of God is at hand; repent and believe in the Gospel.

R.

Gospel   Mark 1:14-20

After John had been arrested, Jesus came to Galilee proclaiming
the Gospel of God:

"This is the time of fulfillment. The Kingdom of God is at hand.
Repent, and believe in the Gospel." As he passed by the Sea of
Galilee, he saw Simon and his brother Andrew casting their nets
into the sea; they were fishermen. Jesus said to them, "Come after
me, and I will make you fishers of men."

Then they left their nets and followed him. He walked along a little farther and saw James, the son of Zebedee, and his brother John. They too were in a boat mending their nets. Then he called them. So they left their father Zebedee in the boat along with the hired men and followed him.

TUESDAY, JANUARY 12, 2021
TUESDAY OF THE FIRST WEEK IN ORDINARY TIME
First Reading   **Hebrew 2:5-12**

It was not to angels that God subjected the world to come, of which we are speaking. Instead, someone has testified somewhere: *What is man that you are mindful of him, or the son of man that you care for him? You made him for a little while lower than the angels; you crowned him with glory and honor, subjecting all things under his feet.*

In "subjecting" all things to him, he left nothing not "subject to him." Yet at present we do not see "all things subject to him," but we do see Jesus "crowned with glory and honor" because he suffered death, he who "for a little while" was made "lower than the angels," that by the grace of God he might taste death for everyone.

For it was fitting that he, for whom and through whom all things exist, in bringing many children to glory, should make the leader to their salvation perfect through suffering. He who consecrates and those who are being consecrated all have one origin.

Therefore, he is not ashamed to call them "brothers" saying: *I will proclaim your name to my brethren, in the midst of the assembly I will praise you.*

Responsorial Psalm   Psalm 8:2ab and 5, 6-7, 8-9

R. (7) You have given your Son rule over the works of your hands.

O LORD, our Lord, how glorious is your name over all the earth! What is man that you should be mindful of him, or the son of man that you should care for him? **R.**

You have made him little less than the angels, and crowned him with glory and honor. You have given him rule over the works of your hands, putting all things under his feet. **R.**

All sheep and oxen, yes, and the beasts of the field, the birds of the air, the fishes of the sea, and whatever swims the paths of the seas. **R.**

Alleluia   1 Thessalonians 2:13

R. Alleluia, alleluia.

Receive the word of God, not as the word of men, but as it truly is, the word of God. **R.**

Gospel   Mark 1:21-28

Jesus came to Capernaum with his followers, and on the Sabbath he entered the synagogue and taught. The people were astonished at his teaching, for he taught them as one having authority and not as the scribes.

In their synagogue was a man with an unclean spirit; he cried out, "What have you to do with us, Jesus of Nazareth? Have you come to destroy us? I know who you are–the Holy One of God!" Jesus rebuked him and said, "Quiet! Come out of him!" The unclean spirit convulsed him and with a loud cry came out of him. All were amazed and asked one another, "What is this? A new teaching with authority. He commands even the unclean spirits and they obey him." His fame spread everywhere throughout the whole region of Galilee.

WEDNESDAY OF THE FIRST WEEK IN ORDINARY TIME

First Reading   **Hebrew 2:14-18**

Since the children share in blood and Flesh, Jesus likewise shared in them, that through death he might destroy the one who has the power of death, that is, the Devil, and free those who through fear of death had been subject to slavery all their life. Surely he did not help angels but rather the descendants of Abraham; therefore, he had to become like his brothers and sisters in every way, that he might be a merciful and faithful high priest before God to expiate the sins of the people. Because he himself was tested through what he suffered, he is able to help those who are being tested.

Responsorial Psalm   **Psalm 105:1-2, 3-4, 6-7, 8-9**

R. (8a) The Lord remembers his covenant for ever.
Or:
R. Alleluia.

Give thanks to the LORD, invoke his name; make known among the nations his deeds. Sing to him, sing his praise, proclaim all his wondrous deeds. **R.**

Glory in his holy name; rejoice, O hearts that seek the LORD! Look to the LORD in his strength; seek to serve him constantly. **R.**

You descendants of Abraham, his servants, sons of Jacob, his chosen ones! He, the LORD, is our God; throughout the earth his judgments prevail. **R.**

He remembers forever his covenant which he made binding for a thousand generations-- Which he entered into with Abraham and by his oath to Isaac. **R.**

Alleluia   John 10:27

R. Alleluia, alleluia.

My sheep hear my voice, says the Lord. I know them, and they follow me. **R.**

Gospel   Mark 1:29-39

On leaving the synagogue Jesus entered the house of Simon and Andrew with James and John. Simon's mother-in-law lay sick with a fever. They immediately told him about her. He approached, grasped her hand, and helped her up. Then the fever left her and she waited on them. When it was evening, after sunset, they brought to him all who were ill or possessed by demons. The whole town was gathered at the door. He cured many who were sick with various diseases, and he drove out many demons, not permitting them to speak because they knew him. Rising very early before dawn, he left and went off to a deserted place, where he prayed. Simon and those who were with him pursued him and on finding him said, "Everyone is looking for you." He told them, "Let us go on to the nearby villages that I may preach there also. For this purpose have I come." So he went into their synagogues, preaching and driving out demons throughout the whole of Galilee.

THURSDAY OF THE FIRST WEEK IN ORDINARY TIME

First Reading   **Hebrew 3:7-14**

The Holy Spirit says:

Oh, that today you would hear his voice, "Harden not your hearts as at the rebellion in the day of testing in the desert, where your ancestors tested and tried me and saw my works for forty years. Because of this I was provoked with that generation and I said, 'They have always been of erring heart, and they do not know my ways.' As I swore in my wrath, 'They shall not enter into my rest.'"

Take care, brothers and sisters, that none of you may have an evil and unfaithful heart, so as to forsake the living God. Encourage yourselves daily while it is still "today," so that none of you may grow hardened by the deceit of sin. We have become partners of Christ if only we hold the beginning of the reality firm until the end.

Responsorial Psalm   **Psalm 95:6-7c, 8-9, 10-11**

R. (8) If today you hear his voice, harden not your hearts.

Come, let us bow down in worship; let us kneel before the LORD who made us. For he is our God, and we are the people he shepherds, the flock he guides. **R.**

Oh, that today you would hear his voice: "Harden not your hearts as at Meribah, as in the day of Massah in the desert, where your fathers tempted me; they tested me though they had seen my works." **R.**

Forty years I was wearied of that generation; I said: "This people's heart goes astray, they do not know my ways." Therefore I swore in my anger: "They shall never enter my rest." **R.**

Alleluia   Matthew 4:23

R. Alleluia, alleluia.

Jesus preached the Gospel of the Kingdom and cured every disease among the people. **R.**

Gospel   Mark 1:40-45

A leper came to him and kneeling down begged him and said, "If you wish, you can make me clean." Moved with pity, he stretched out his hand, touched the leper, and said to him, "I do will it. Be made clean." The leprosy left him immediately, and he was made clean. Then, warning him sternly, he dismissed him at once. Then he said to him, "See that you tell no one anything, but go, show yourself to the priest and offer for your cleansing what Moses prescribed; that will be proof for them." The man went away and began to publicize the whole matter. He spread the report abroad so that it was impossible for Jesus to enter a town openly. He remained outside in deserted places, and people kept coming to him from everywhere.

FRIDAY, JANUARY 15, 2021

FRIDAY OF THE FIRST WEEK IN ORDINARY TIME

First Reading   Hebrew   4:1-5, 11

Let us be on our guard while the promise of entering into his rest remains, that none of you seem to have failed. For in fact we have received the Good News just as our ancestors did. But the word that they heard did not profit them, for they were not united in faith with those who listened. For we who believed enter into that rest, just as he has said:

As I swore in my wrath, "They shall not enter into my rest,"

and yet his works were accomplished at the foundation of the world. For he has spoken somewhere about the seventh day in this manner,

And God rested on the seventh day from all his works;

and again, in the previously mentioned place,

They shall not enter into my rest.

Therefore, let us strive to enter into that rest, so that no one may fall after the same example of disobedience.

Responsorial Psalm   Psalm 78:3 and 4bc, 6c-7, 8

R. (7b) Do not forget the works of the Lord!

What we have heard and know, and what our fathers have declared to us, we will declare to the generation to come the glorious deeds of the LORD and his strength. **R.**

That they too may rise and declare to their sons that they should put their hope in God, and not forget the deeds of God but keep his commands. **R.**

And not be like their fathers, a generation wayward and rebellious, A generation that kept not its heart steadfast nor its spirit faithful toward God. **R.**

Alleluia   Luke 7:16

R. Alleluia, alleluia.

A great prophet has arisen in our midst and God has visited his people. **R.**

Gospel   Mark 2:1-12

When Jesus returned to Capernaum after some days, it became known that he was at home. Many gathered together so that there was no longer room for them, not even around the door, and he preached the word to them. They came bringing to him a paralytic carried by four men. Unable to get near Jesus because of the crowd, they opened up the roof above him. After they had broken through, they let down the mat on which the paralytic was lying. When Jesus saw their faith, he said to him, "Child, your sins are forgiven." Now some of the scribes were sitting there asking themselves, "Why does this man speak that way? He is blaspheming. Who but God alone can forgive sins?" Jesus immediately knew in his mind what they were thinking to themselves, so he said, "Why are you thinking such things in your hearts? Which is easier, to say to the paralytic, 'Your sins are forgiven,' or to say, 'Rise, pick up your mat and walk'? But that you may know that the Son of Man has authority to forgive sins on earth" –he said to the paralytic, "I say to you, rise, pick up your mat, and go home." He rose, picked up his mat at once, and went away in the sight of everyone. They were all astounded and glorified God, saying, "We have never seen anything like this."

SATURDAY, JANUARY 16, 2021

SATURDAY OF THE FIRST WEEK IN ORDINARY TIME

First Reading   Hebrew 4:12-16

The word of God is living and effective, sharper than any two-edged sword, penetrating even between soul and spirit, joints and marrow, and able to discern reflections and thoughts of the heart. No creature is concealed from him, but everything is naked and exposed to the eyes of him to whom we must render an account.

Since we have a great high priest who has passed through the heavens, Jesus, the Son of God, let us hold fast to our confession. For we do not have a high priest who is unable to sympathize with our weaknesses, but one who has similarly been tested in every way, yet without sin. So let us confidently approach the throne of grace to receive mercy and to find grace for timely help.

Responsorial Psalm   Psalm 19:8, 9, 10, 15

R. (John 6:63c) Your words, Lord, are Spirit and life.

The law of the LORD is perfect, refreshing the soul; the decree of the LORD is trustworthy, giving wisdom to the simple. **R.**

The precepts of the LORD are right, rejoicing the heart; the command of the LORD is clear, enlightening the eye. **R.**

The fear of the LORD is pure, enduring forever; the ordinances of the LORD are true, all of them just. **R.**

Let the words of my mouth and the thought of my heart find favor before you, O LORD, my rock and my redeemer. **R.**

Alleluia   Luke 4:18

R. Alleluia, alleluia.

The Lord sent me to bring glad tidings to the poor and to proclaim liberty to captives. **R.**

Gospel   Mark 2:13-17

Jesus went out along the sea. All the crowd came to him and he taught them. As he passed by, he saw Levi, son of Alphaeus, sitting at the customs post. Jesus said to him, "Follow me." And he got up and followed Jesus. While he was at table in his house, many tax collectors and sinners sat with Jesus and his disciples; for there were many who followed him. Some scribes who were Pharisees saw that Jesus was eating with sinners and tax collectors and said to his disciples, "Why does he eat with tax collectors and sinners?" Jesus heard this and said to them, "Those who are well do not need a physician, but the sick do. I did not come to call the righteous but sinners."

SUNDAY, JANUARY 17, 2021
SECOND SUNDAY OF ORDINARY TIME

First Reading   **1 Samuel 3:3b-10, 19**

Samuel was sleeping in the temple of the LORD where the ark of God was. The LORD called to Samuel, who answered, "Here I am." Samuel ran to Eli and said, "Here I am. You called me." "I did not call you," Eli said. "Go back to sleep." So he went back to sleep. Again the LORD called Samuel, who rose and went to Eli. "Here I am," he said. "You called me." But Eli answered, "I did not call you, my son. Go back to sleep."

At that time Samuel was not familiar with the LORD, because the LORD had not revealed anything to him as yet. The LORD called Samuel again, for the third time. Getting up and going to Eli, he said, "Here I am. You called me." Then Eli understood that the LORD was calling the youth. So he said to Samuel, "Go to sleep, and if you are called, reply, Speak, LORD, for your servant is listening." When Samuel went to sleep in his place, the LORD came and revealed his presence, calling out as before, "Samuel, Samuel!" Samuel answered, "Speak, for your servant is listening." Samuel grew up, and the LORD was with him, not permitting any word of his to be without effect.

Responsorial Psalm   Psalm 40:2, 4, 7-8, 8-9, 10

R. (8a and 9a) Here am I, Lord; I come to do your will.

I have waited, waited for the LORD, and he stooped toward me and heard my cry. And he put a new song into my mouth, a hymn to our God. **R.**

Sacrifice or offering you wished not, but ears open to obedience you gave me. Holocausts or sin-offerings you sought not; then said I, "Behold I come." **R.**

"In the written scroll it is prescribed for me, to do your will, O my God, is my delight, and your law is within my heart!" **R.**

I announced your justice in the vast assembly; I did not restrain my lips, as you, O LORD, know. **R.**

Second Reading   1 Corinthians 6:13c-15a, 17-20

Brothers and sisters:

The body is not for immorality, but for the Lord, and the Lord is for the body; God raised the Lord and will also raise us by his power.

Do you not know that your bodies are members of Christ? But whoever is joined to the Lord becomes one Spirit with him. Avoid immorality. Every other sin a person commits is outside the body, but the immoral person sins against his own body. Do you not know that your body is a temple of the Holy Spirit within you, whom you have from God, and that you are not your own? For you have been purchased at a price. Therefore glorify God in your body.

Alleluia   John 1:41, 17b

R. Alleluia, alleluia.

We have found the Messiah: Jesus Christ, who brings us truth and grace. **R.**

Gospel   John 1:35-42

John was standing with two of his disciples, and as he watched Jesus walk by, he said, "Behold, the Lamb of God." The two disciples heard what he said and followed Jesus. Jesus turned and saw them following him and said to them, "What are you looking for?" They said to him, "Rabbi" — which translated means Teacher — "where are you staying?" He said to them, "Come, and you will see." So they went and saw where Jesus was staying, and they stayed with him that day. It was about four in the afternoon. Andrew, the brother of Simon Peter, was one of the two who heard John and followed Jesus. He first found his own brother Simon and told him, "We have found the Messiah" — which is translated Christ. Then he brought him to Jesus. Jesus looked at him and said, "You are Simon the son of John; you will be called Cephas" — which is translated Peter.

MONDAY OF THE SECOND WEEK IN ORDINARY TIME

First Reading   **Hebrew 5:1-10**

Brothers and sisters:

Every high priest is taken from among men and made their representative before God, to offer gifts and sacrifices for sins. He is able to deal patiently with the ignorant and erring, for he himself is beset by weakness and so, for this reason, must make sin offerings for himself as well as for the people. No one takes this honor upon himself but only when called by God, just as Aaron was. In the same way, it was not Christ who glorified himself in becoming high priest, but rather the one who said to him:

You are my Son: this day I have begotten you; just as he says in another place, *You are a priest forever according to the order of Melchizedek.*

In the days when he was in the Flesh, he offered prayers and supplications with loud cries and tears to the one who was able to save him from death, and he was heard because of his reverence. Son though he was, he learned obedience from what he suffered; and when he was made perfect, he became the source of eternal salvation for all who obey him.

Responsorial Psalm   Psalm 110:1, 2, 3, 4

R. (4b) You are a priest for ever, in the line of Melchizedek.

The LORD said to my Lord: "Sit at my right hand till I make your enemies your footstool." **R.**

The scepter of your power the LORD will stretch forth from Zion: "Rule in the midst of your enemies." **R.**

"Yours is princely power in the day of your birth, in holy splendor; before the daystar, like the dew, I have begotten you." **R.**

The LORD has sworn, and he will not repent: "You are a priest forever, according to the order of Melchizedek." **R.**

Alleluia   Hebrew 4:12

R. Alleluia, alleluia.

The word of God is living and effective, able to discern reflections and thoughts of the heart. **R.**

Gospel   Mark 2:18-22

The disciples of John and of the Pharisees were accustomed to fast. People came to Jesus and objected, "Why do the disciples of John and the disciples of the Pharisees fast, but your disciples do not fast?" Jesus answered them, "Can the wedding guests fast while the bridegroom is with them? As long as they have the bridegroom with them they cannot fast. But the days will come when the bridegroom is taken away from them, and then they will fast on that day. No one sews a piece of unshrunken cloth on an old cloak. If he does, its fullness pulls away, the new from the old, and the tear gets worse. Likewise, no one pours new wine into old wineskins. Otherwise, the wine will burst the skins, and both the wine and the skins are ruined. Rather, new wine is poured into fresh wineskins."

TUESDAY OF THE SECOND WEEK IN ORDINARY TIME

First Reading   **Hebrew 6:10-20**

Brothers and sisters:

God is not unjust so as to overlook your work and the love you have demonstrated for his name by having served and continuing to serve the holy ones. We earnestly desire each of you to demonstrate the same eagerness for the fulfillment of hope until the end, so that you may not become sluggish, but imitators of those who, through faith and patience, are inheriting the promises. When God made the promise to Abraham, since he had no one greater by whom to swear, *he swore by himself,* and said, *I will indeed bless you and multiply* you. And so, after patient waiting, Abraham obtained the promise. Now, men swear by someone greater than themselves; for them an oath serves as a guarantee and puts an end to all argument. So when God wanted to give the heirs of his promise an even clearer demonstration of the immutability of his purpose, he intervened with an oath, so that by two immutable things, in which it was impossible for God to lie, we who have taken refuge might be strongly encouraged to hold fast to the hope that lies before us. This we have as an anchor of the soul, sure and firm, which reaches into the interior behind the veil, where Jesus has

entered on our behalf as forerunner, becoming high priest forever according to the order of Melchizedek.

Responsorial Psalm   **Psalm 111:1-2, 4-5, 9 and 10c**

R. (5) The Lord will remember his covenant for ever.

Or:

R. Alleluia.

I will give thanks to the LORD with all my heart in the company and assembly of the just. Great are the works of the LORD, exquisite in all their delights. **R.**

He has won renown for his wondrous deeds; gracious and merciful is the LORD. He has given food to those who fear him; he will forever be mindful of his covenant. **R.**

He has sent deliverance to his people; he has ratified his covenant forever; holy and awesome is his name. His praise endures forever. **R.**

Alleluia   Ephesians 1:17-18

R. Alleluia, alleluia.

May the Father of our Lord Jesus Christ enlighten the eyes of our hearts, that we may know what is the hope that belongs to our call. **R.**

Gospel   Mark 2:23-28

As Jesus was passing through a field of grain on the Sabbath, his disciples began to make a path while picking the heads of grain. At this the Pharisees said to him, "Look, why are they doing what is unlawful on the Sabbath?" He said to them, "Have you never read what David did when he was in need and he and his companions were hungry? How he went into the house of God when Abiathar was high priest and ate the bread of offering that only the priests could lawfully eat, and shared it with his companions?" Then he said to them, "The Sabbath was made for man, not man for the Sabbath. That is why the Son of Man is lord even of the Sabbath."

WEDNESDAY OF THE SECOND WEEK IN ORDINARY TIME

First Reading   **Hebrew 7:1-3, 15-17**

Melchizedek, king of Salem and priest of God Most High, met Abraham as he returned from his defeat of the kings and *blessed him.* And Abraham apportioned to him *a tenth of everything.* His name first means righteous king, and he was also "king of Salem," that is, king of peace. Without father, mother, or ancestry, without beginning of days or end of life, thus made to resemble the Son of God, he remains a priest forever.

It is even more obvious if another priest is raised up after the likeness of Melchizedek, who has become so, not by a law expressed in a commandment concerning physical descent but by the power of a life that cannot be destroyed. For it is testified:

You are a priest forever according to the order of Melchizedek.

Responsorial Psalm   **Psalm 110:1, 2, 3, 4**

R. (4b) You are a priest for ever, in the line of Melchizedek.

The LORD said to my Lord: "Sit at my right hand till I make your enemies your footstool." **R.**

The scepter of your power the LORD will stretch forth from Zion: "Rule in the midst of your enemies." **R.**

"Yours is princely power in the day of your birth, in holy splendor; before the daystar, like the dew, I have begotten you." **R.**

The LORD has sworn, and he will not repent: "You are a priest forever, according to the order of Melchizedek." **R.**

<u>Alleluia</u>   **Matthew 4:23**

R. Alleluia, alleluia.

Jesus preached the Gospel of the Kingdom and cured every disease among the people. **R.**

<u>Gospel</u>   **Mark 3:1-6**

Jesus entered the synagogue. There was a man there who had a withered hand.

They watched Jesus closely to see if he would cure him on the Sabbath so that they might accuse him. He said to the man with the withered hand, "Come up here before us." Then he said to the Pharisees, "Is it lawful to do good on the Sabbath rather than to do evil, to save life rather than to destroy it?" But they remained silent. Looking around at them with anger and grieved at their hardness of heart, Jesus said to the man, "Stretch out your hand." He stretched it out and his hand was restored.

The Pharisees went out and immediately took counsel with the Herodians against him to put him to death.

THURSDAY, JANUARY 21, 2021

MEMORIAL OF SAINT AGNES, VIRGIN AND MARTYR

<u>First Reading</u>   **ebrew 7:25—8:6**

Jesus is always able to save those who approach God through him, since he lives forever to make intercession for them.

It was fitting that we should have such a high priest: holy, innocent, undefiled, separated from sinners, higher than the heavens. He has no need, as did the high priests, to offer sacrifice day after day, first for his own sins and then for those of the people; he did that once for all when he offered himself. For the law appoints men subject to weakness to be high priests, but the word of the oath, which was taken after the law, appoints a son, who has been made perfect forever.

The main point of what has been said is this: we have such a high priest, who has taken his seat at the right hand of the throne of the Majesty in heaven, a minister of the sanctuary and of the true tabernacle that the Lord, not man, set up. Now every high priest is appointed to offer gifts and sacrifices; thus the necessity for this one also to have something to offer. If then he were on earth, he would not be a priest, since there are those who offer gifts according to the law. They worship in a copy and shadow of the heavenly sanctuary, as Moses was warned when he was about to erect the tabernacle. For God says, "See that you make everything according to the pattern shown you on the mountain." Now he has obtained so much more excellent a ministry as he is mediator of a better covenant, enacted on better promises.

Responsorial   Psalm 40:7-8a, 8b-9, 10, 17
R. (8a and 9a) Here am I, Lord; I come to do your will.
Sacrifice or oblation you wished not, but ears open to obedience you gave me. Burnt offerings or sin-offerings you sought not; then said I, "Behold I come." **R.**
"In the written scroll it is prescribed for me, to do your will, O my God, is my delight, and your law is within my heart!" **R.**
I announced your justice in the vast assembly; I did not restrain my lips, as you, O LORD, know. **R.**

May all who seek you exult and be glad in you, and may those who love your salvation say ever, "The LORD be glorified." **R.**

Alleluia   2 Timothy 1:10

R. Alleluia, alleluia.

Our Savior Jesus Christ has destroyed death and brought life to light through the Gospel. **R.**

Gospel   Mark 3:7-12

Jesus withdrew toward the sea with his disciples.

A large number of people followed from Galilee and from Judea. Hearing what he was doing, a large number of people came to him also from Jerusalem, from Idumea, from beyond the Jordan, and from the neighborhood of Tyre and Sidon.

He told his disciples to have a boat ready for him because of the crowd, so that they would not crush him. He had cured many and, as a result, those who had diseases were pressing upon him to touch him. And whenever unclean spirits saw him they would fall down before him and shout, "You are the Son of God." He warned them sternly not to make him known.

FRIDAY, JANUARY 22, 2021

DAY OF PRAYER FOR THE LEGAL PROTECTION OF UNBORN CHILDREN

First Reading   Hebrew 8:6-13

Brothers and sisters:

Now our high priest has obtained so much more excellent a ministry as he is mediator of a better covenant, enacted on better promises. For if that first covenant had been faultless, no place would have been sought for a second one. But he finds fault with them and says:

Behold, the days are coming, says the Lord, when I will conclude a new covenant with the house of Israel and the house of Judah. It will not be like the covenant I made with their fathers the day I took them by the hand to lead them forth from the land of Egypt; for they did not stand by my covenant and I ignored them, says the Lord. But this is the covenant I will establish with the house of Israel after those days, says the Lord:

I will put my laws in their minds and I will write them upon their hearts. I will be their God, and they shall be my people. And they shall not teach, each one his fellow citizen and kin, saying, "Know the Lord," for all shall know me, from least to greatest. For I will forgive their evildoing and remember their sins no more.

When he speaks of a "new" covenant, he declares the first one obsolete. And what has become obsolete and has grown old is close to disappearing.

Responsorial Psalm   Psalm 85:8 and 10, 11-12, 13-14

R. (11a) Kindness and truth shall meet.

Show us, O LORD, your mercy, and grant us your salvation. Near indeed is his salvation to those who fear him, glory dwelling in our land. **R.**

Kindness and truth shall meet; justice and peace shall kiss. Truth shall spring out of the earth, and justice shall look down from heaven. **R.**

The LORD himself will give his benefits; our land shall yield its increase. Justice shall walk before him, and salvation, along the way of his steps. **R.**

Alleluia
2 Corinthians 5:19

R. Alleluia, alleluia.

God was reconciling the world to himself in Christ, and entrusting to us the message of reconciliation. **R.**

Gospel
Mark 3:13-19

Jesus went up the mountain and summoned those whom he wanted and they came to him. He appointed twelve, whom he also named Apostles, that they might be with him and he might send them forth to preach and to have authority to drive out demons:

He appointed the Twelve: Simon, whom he named Peter; James, son of Zebedee, and John the brother of James, whom he named Boanerges, that is, sons of thunder; Andrew, Philip, Bartholomew, Matthew, Thomas, James the son of Alphaeus; Thaddeus, Simon the Cananean, and Judas Iscariot who betrayed him.

SATURDAY, JANUARY 23, 2021

SATURDAY OF THE SECOND WEEK IN ORDINARY TIME

First Reading
Hebrew 9:2-3, 11-14

A tabernacle was constructed, the outer one, in which were the lampstand, the table, and the bread of offering; this is called the Holy Place. Behind the second veil was the tabernacle called the Holy of Holies.

But when Christ came as high priest of the good things that have come to be, passing through the greater and more perfect tabernacle not made by hands, that is, not belonging to this creation, he entered once for all into the sanctuary, not with the blood of goats and calves but with his own Blood, thus obtaining eternal redemption. For if the blood of goats and bulls and the sprinkling of a heifer's ashes can sanctify those who are defiled so that their flesh is cleansed, how much more will the Blood of Christ, who through the eternal spirit offered himself unblemished to God, cleanse our consciences from dead works to worship the living God.

Responsorial Psalm   Psalm 47:2-3, 6-7, 8-9

R. (6) God mounts his throne to shouts of joy: a blare of trumpets for the Lord.

All you peoples, clap your hands, shout to God with cries of gladness, For the LORD, the Most High, the awesome, is the great king over all the earth. **R.**

God mounts his throne amid shouts of joy; the LORD, amid trumpet blasts. Sing praise to God, sing praise; sing praise to our king, sing praise. **R.**

For king of all the earth is God: sing hymns of praise. God reigns over the nations, God sits upon his holy throne. **R.**

Alleluia   Acts 16:14b

R. Alleluia, alleluia.

Open our hearts, O Lord, to listen to the words of your Son. **R.**

Gospel   Mark 3:20-21

Jesus came with his disciples into the house. Again the crowd gathered, making it impossible for them even to eat. When his relatives heard of this they set out to seize him, for they said, "He is out of his mind."

THIRD SUNDAY IN ORDINARY TIME

First Reading   **Jonah 3:1-5, 10**

The word of the LORD came to Jonah, saying: "Set out for the great city of Nineveh, and announce to it the message that I will tell you." So Jonah made ready and went to Nineveh, according to the LORD'S bidding. Now Nineveh was an enormously large city; it took three days to go through it. Jonah began his journey through the city, and had gone but a single day's walk announcing, "Forty days more and Nineveh shall be destroyed, " when the people of Nineveh believed God; they proclaimed a fast and all of them, great and small, put on sackcloth.

When God saw by their actions how they turned from their evil way, he repented of the evil that he had threatened to do to them; he did not carry it out.

Responsorial Psalm   **Psalm 25:4-5, 6-7, 8-9**

R. (4a) Teach me your ways, O Lord.

Your ways, O LORD, make known to me; teach me your paths,
Guide me in your truth and teach me, for you are God my savior.
R.

Remember that your compassion, O LORD, and your love are from of old. In your kindness remember me, because of your goodness, O LORD. **R.**

Good and upright is the LORD; thus he shows sinners the way. He guides the humble to justice and teaches the humble his way. **R.**

Second Reading   **1 Corinthians 7:29-31**

I tell you, brothers and sisters, the time is running out. From now on, let those having wives act as not having them, those weeping as not weeping, those rejoicing as not rejoicing, those buying as not owning, those using the world as not using it fully. For the world in its present form is passing away.

Alleluia   Mark 1:15

R. Alleluia, alleluia.

The kingdom of God is at hand. Repent and believe in the Gospel.
R.

Gospel   Mark 1:14-20

After John had been arrested, Jesus came to Galilee proclaiming the gospel of God: "This is the time of fulfillment. The kingdom of God is at hand. Repent, and believe in the gospel."

As he passed by the Sea of Galilee, he saw Simon and his brother Andrew casting their nets into the sea; they were fishermen. Jesus said to them, "Come after me, and I will make you fishers of men." Then they abandoned their nets and followed him. He walked along a little farther and saw James, the son of Zebedee, and his brother John. They too were in a boat mending their nets. Then he called them. So they left their father Zebedee in the boat along with the hired men and followed him.

MONDAY, JANUARY 25, 2021
FEAST OF THE CONVERSION OF SAINT PAUL, APOSTLE

First Reading   Acts 22:3-16 or Acts 9:1-22

Acts 22:3-16

Paul addressed the people in these words:

"I am a Jew, born in Tarsus in Cilicia, but brought up in this city. At the feet of Gamaliel I was educated strictly in our ancestral law and was zealous for God, just as all of you are today. I persecuted this Way to death, binding both men and women and delivering them to prison. Even the high priest and the whole council of elders can testify on my behalf. For from them I even received letters to the brothers and set out for Damascus to bring back to Jerusalem in chains for punishment those there as well.

"On that journey as I drew near to Damascus, about noon a great light from the sky suddenly shone around me. I fell to the ground and heard a voice saying to me, 'Saul, Saul, why are you persecuting me?' I replied, 'Who are you, sir?' And he said to me, 'I am Jesus the Nazorean whom you are persecuting.' My companions saw the light but did not hear the voice of the one who spoke to me. I asked, 'What shall I do, sir?' The Lord answered me, 'Get up and go into Damascus, and there you will be told about everything appointed for you to do.' Since I could see nothing because of the brightness of that light, I was led by hand by my companions and entered Damascus.

"A certain Ananias, a devout observer of the law, and highly spoken of by all the Jews who lived there, came to me and stood there and said, 'Saul, my brother, regain your sight.' And at that very moment I regained my sight and saw him. Then he said, 'The God of our ancestors designated you to know his will, to see the Righteous One, and to hear the sound of his voice; for you will be his witness before all to what you have seen and heard. Now, why delay? Get up and have yourself baptized and your sins washed away, calling upon his name.'"

Or:

Acts 9:1-22

Saul, still breathing murderous threats against the disciples of the Lord, went to the high priest and asked him for letters to the synagogues in Damascus, that, if he should find any men or women who belonged to the Way, he might bring them back to Jerusalem in chains. On his journey, as he was nearing Damascus, a light from the sky suddenly flashed around him. He fell to the ground and heard a voice saying to him, "Saul, Saul, why are you persecuting me?" He said, "Who are you, sir?" The reply came, "I am Jesus, whom you are persecuting. Now get up and go into the city and you will be told what you must do." The men who were traveling with him stood speechless, for they heard the voice but could see no one. Saul got up from the ground, but when he opened his eyes he could see nothing; so they led him by the hand and brought him to

Damascus. For three days he was unable to see, and he neither ate nor drank.

There was a disciple in Damascus named Ananias, and the Lord said to him in a vision, Ananias." He answered, "Here I am, Lord." The Lord said to him, "Get up and go to the street called Straight and ask at the house of Judas for a man from Tarsus named Saul. He is there praying, and in a vision he has seen a man named Ananias come in and lay his hands on him, that he may regain his sight." But Ananias replied, "Lord, I have heard from many sources about this man, what evil things he has done to your holy ones in Jerusalem. And here he has authority from the chief priests to imprison all who call upon your name." But the Lord said to him, "Go, for this man is a chosen instrument of mine to carry my name before Gentiles, kings, and children of Israel, and I will show him what he will have to suffer for my name." So Ananias went and entered the house; laying his hands on him, he said, "Saul, my brother, the Lord has sent me, Jesus who appeared to you on the way by which you came, that you may regain your sight and be filled with the Holy Spirit." Immediately things like scales fell from his eyes and he regained his sight. He got up and was baptized, and when he had eaten, he recovered his strength.

He stayed some days with the disciples in Damascus, and he began at once to proclaim Jesus in the synagogues, that he is the Son of God. All who heard him were astounded and said, "Is not this the man who in Jerusalem ravaged those who call upon this name, and came here expressly to take them back in chains to the chief priests?" But Saul grew all the stronger and confounded the Jews who lived in Damascus, proving that this is the Christ.

Responsorial Psalm   **Psalm 117:1bc, 2**

R. (Mark 16:15) Go out to all the world, and tell the Good News.

Or:

R. Alleluia, alleluia.

Praise the LORD, all you nations; glorify him, all you peoples! **R.**
For steadfast is his kindness toward us, and the fidelity of the Lord endures forever. **R.**

Alleluia   **John 15:16**

R. Alleluia, alleluia.

I chose you from the world, to go and bear fruit that will last, says the Lord. **R.**

Gospel   Mark 16:15-18

Jesus appeared to the Eleven and said to them:

"Go into the whole world and proclaim the Gospel to every creature. Whoever believes and is baptized will be saved; whoever does not believe will be condemned. These signs will accompany those who believe: in my name they will drive out demons, they will speak new languages. They will pick up serpents with their hands, and if they drink any deadly thing, it will not harm them. They will lay hands on the sick, and they will recover."

TUESDAY, JANUARY 26, 2021
MEMORIAL OF SAINTS TIMOTHY AND TITUS, BISHOPS

First Reading   2 Timothy 1:1-8 or Titus 1:1-5

2Timothy 1:1-8

Paul, an Apostle of Christ Jesus by the will of God for the promise of life in Christ Jesus, to Timothy, my dear child: grace, mercy, and peace from God the Father and Christ Jesus our Lord.

I am grateful to God, whom I worship with a clear conscience as my ancestors did, as I remember you constantly in my prayers, night and day. I yearn to see you again, recalling your tears, so that I may be filled with joy, as I recall your sincere faith that first lived in your grandmother Lois and in your mother Eunice and that I am confident lives also in you.

For this reason, I remind you to stir into flame the gift of God that you have through the imposition of my hands. For God did not give us a spirit of cowardice but rather of power and love and self-control. So do not be ashamed of your testimony to our Lord, nor of me, a prisoner for his sake; but bear your share of hardship for the Gospel with the strength that comes from God.

Or:
Titus 1:1-5

Paul, a slave of God and Apostle of Jesus Christ for the sake of the faith of God's chosen ones and the recognition of religious truth, in the hope of eternal life that God, who does not lie, promised before time began, who indeed at the proper time revealed his word in the proclamation with which I was entrusted by the command of God our savior, to Titus, my true child in our common faith: grace and peace from God the Father and Christ Jesus our savior.

For this reason I left you in Crete so that you might set right what remains to be done and appoint presbyters in every town, as I directed you.

Responsorial Psalm　　　Psalm 96:1-2a, 2b-3, 7-8a, 10

R. (3) Proclaim God's marvelous deeds to all the nations.

Sing to the LORD a new song; sing to the LORD, all you lands.
Sing to the LORD; bless his name. **R.**

Announce his salvation, day after day. Tell his glory among the
nations; among all peoples, his wondrous deeds. **R.**

Give to the LORD, you families of nations, give to the LORD glory
and praise; give to the LORD the glory due his name! **R.**

Say among the nations: The LORD is king. He has made the world
firm, not to be moved; he governs the peoples with equity. **R.**

R. Alleluia, alleluia.

Blessed are you, Father, Lord of heaven and earth; you have revealed to little ones the mysteries of the Kingdom. **R.**

Gospel _____ Mark 3:31-35

The mother of Jesus and his brothers arrived at the house. Standing outside, they sent word to Jesus and called him. A crowd seated around him told him, "Your mother and your brothers and your sisters are outside asking for you." But he said to them in reply, "Who are my mother and my brothers?" And looking around at those seated in the circle he said, "Here are my mother and my brothers. For whoever does the will of God is my brother and sister and mother."

WEDNESDAY, JANUARY 27, 2021

WEDNESDAY OF THE THIRD WEEK IN ORDINARY TIME

First Reading _____ Hebrew 10:11-18

Every priest stands daily at his ministry, offering frequently those same sacrifices that can never take away sins. But this one offered one sacrifice for sins, and took his seat forever at the right hand of God; now he waits until his enemies are made his footstool. For by one offering he has made perfect forever those who are being consecrated. The Holy Spirit also testifies to us, for after saying:

This is the covenant I will establish with them after those days, says the Lord: "I will put my laws in their hearts, and I will write them upon their minds,"

He also says:

Their sins and their evildoing I will remember no more.

Where there is forgiveness of these, there is no longer offering for sin.

Responsorial Psalm   Psalm 110:1, 2, 3, 4

R. (4b) You are a priest for ever, in the line of Melchizedek.

The LORD said to my Lord: "Sit at my right hand till I make your enemies your footstool." **R.**

The scepter of your power the LORD will stretch forth from Zion: "Rule in the midst of your enemies." **R.**

"Yours is princely power in the day of your birth, in holy splendor; before the daystar, like the dew, I have begotten you." **R.**

The LORD has sworn, and he will not repent: "You are a priest forever, according to the order of Melchizedek." **R.**

Alleluia

R. Alleluia, alleluia.

The seed is the word of God, Christ is the sower; all who come to him will live forever. **R.**

Gospel   Mark 4:1-20

On another occasion, Jesus began to teach by the sea. A very large crowd gathered around him so that he got into a boat on the sea and sat down. And the whole crowd was beside the sea on land. And he taught them at length in parables, and in the course of his instruction he said to them, "Hear this! A sower went out to sow. And as he sowed, some seed fell on the path, and the birds came and ate it up. Other seed fell on rocky ground where it had little soil. It sprang up at once because the soil was not deep. And when the sun rose, it was scorched and it withered for lack of roots. Some seed fell among thorns, and the thorns grew up and choked it and it produced no grain. And some seed fell on rich soil and produced fruit. It came up and grew and yielded thirty, sixty, and a hundredfold." He added, "Whoever has ears to hear ought to hear."

And when he was alone, those present along with the Twelve questioned him about the parables. He answered them, "The mystery of the Kingdom of God has been granted to you. But to those outside everything comes in parables, so that

they may look and see but not perceive, and hear and listen but not understand, in order that they may not be converted and be forgiven."

Jesus said to them, "Do you not understand this parable? Then how will you understand any of the parables? The sower sows the word. These are the ones on the path where the word is sown. As soon as they hear, Satan comes at once and takes away the word sown in them. And these are the ones sown on rocky ground who, when they hear the word, receive it at once with joy. But they have no roots; they last only for a time. Then when tribulation or persecution comes because of the word, they quickly fall away. Those sown among thorns are another sort. They are the people who hear the word, but worldly anxiety, the lure of riches, and the craving for other things intrude and choke the word, and it bears no fruit. But those sown on rich soil are the ones who hear the word and accept it and bear fruit thirty and sixty and a hundredfold."

MEMORIAL OF SAINT THOMAS AQUINAS, PRIEST AND DOCTOR OF THE CHURCH

First Reading   **Hebrew 10:19-25**

Brothers and sisters:

Since through the Blood of Jesus we have confidence of entrance into the sanctuary by the new and living way he opened for us through the veil, that is, his flesh, and since we have "a great priest over the house of God," let us approach with a sincere heart and in absolute trust, with our hearts sprinkled clean from an evil conscience and our bodies washed in pure water. Let us hold unwaveringly to our confession that gives us hope, for he who made the promise is trustworthy. We must consider how to rouse one another to love and good works. We should not stay away from our assembly, as is the custom of some, but encourage one another, and this all the more as you see the day drawing near.

Responsorial Psalm   **Psalm 24:1-2, 3-4ab, 5-6**

R. (6) Lord, this is the people that longs to see your face.

The LORD's are the earth and its fullness; the world and those who dwell in it. For he founded it upon the seas and established it upon the rivers. **R.**

Who can ascend the mountain of the LORD? Or who may stand in his holy place? He whose hands are sinless, whose heart is clean, who desires not what is vain. **R.**

He shall receive a blessing from the LORD, a reward from God his savior. Such is the race that seeks for him, that seeks the face of the God of Jacob. **R.**

Alleluia
Psalm 119:105

R. Alleluia, alleluia.

A lamp to my feet is your word, a light to my path. **R.**

Gospel
Mark 4:21-25

Jesus said to his disciples, "Is a lamp brought in to be placed under a bushel basket or under a bed, and not to be placed on a lampstand? For there is nothing hidden except to be made visible; nothing is secret except to come to light. Anyone who has ears to hear ought to hear." He also told them, "Take care what you hear. The measure with which you measure will be measured out to you, and still more will be given to you. To the one who has, more will be given; from the one who has not, even what he has will be taken away."

FRIDAY, JANUARY 29, 2021

FRIDAY OF THE THIRD WEEK IN ORDINARY TIME

First Reading
Hebrew 10:32-39

Remember the days past when, after you had been enlightened, you endured a great contest of suffering. At times you were publicly exposed to abuse and affliction; at other times you associated yourselves with those so treated. You even joined in the sufferings of those in prison and joyfully accepted the confiscation of your property, knowing that you had a better and lasting possession. Therefore, do not throw away your confidence; it will have great recompense. You need endurance to do the will of God and receive what he has promised.

For, after just a brief moment, he who is to come shall come; he shall not delay. But my just one shall live by faith, and if he draws back I take no pleasure in him.

We are not among those who draw back and perish, but among those who have faith and will possess life.

Responsorial Psalm   Psalm 37:3-4, 5-6, 23-24, 39-40

R. (39a) The salvation of the just comes from the Lord.

Trust in the LORD and do good, that you may dwell in the land and be fed in security. Take delight in the LORD, and he will grant you your heart's requests. **R.**

Commit to the LORD your way; trust in him, and he will act. He will make justice dawn for you like the light; bright as the noonday shall be your vindication. **R.**

By the LORD are the steps of a man made firm, and he approves his way. Though he fall, he does not lie prostrate, for the hand of the LORD sustains him. **R.**

The salvation of the just is from the LORD; he is their refuge in time of distress. And the LORD helps them and delivers them; he delivers them from the wicked and saves them, because they take refuge in him. **R.**

Alleluia   Matthew 11:25

R. Alleluia, alleluia.

Blessed are you, Father, Lord of heaven and earth; you have revealed to little ones the mysteries of the Kingdom. **R.**

Gospel   Mark 4:26-34

Jesus said to the crowds:

"This is how it is with the Kingdom of God; it is as if a man were to scatter seed on the land and would sleep and rise night and day and the seed would sprout and grow, he knows not how. Of its own accord the land yields fruit, first the blade, then the ear, then the full grain in the ear. And when the grain is ripe, he wields the sickle at once, for the harvest has come." He said, "To what shall we compare the Kingdom of God, or what parable can we use for it? It is like a mustard seed that, when it is sown in the ground, is the smallest of all the seeds on the earth. But once it is sown, it springs up and becomes the largest of plants and puts forth large branches, so that the birds of the sky can dwell in its shade." With many such parables he spoke the word to them as they were able to understand it. Without parables he did not speak to them, but to his own disciples he explained everything in private.

SATURDAY OF THE THIRD WEEK IN ORDINARY TIME

First Reading   **Hebrew 11:1-2, 8-19**

Brothers and sisters:

Faith is the realization of what is hoped for and evidence of things not seen. Because of it the ancients were well attested. By faith Abraham obeyed when he was called to go out to a place that he was to receive as an inheritance; he went out, not knowing where he was to go. By faith he sojourned in the promised land as in a foreign country, dwelling in tents with Isaac and Jacob, heirs of the same promise; for he was looking forward to the city with foundations, whose architect and maker is God. By faith he received power to generate, even though he was past the normal age and Sarah herself was sterile for he thought that the one who had made the promise was trustworthy. So it was that there came forth from one man, himself as good as dead, descendants as numerous as the stars in the sky and as countless as the sands on the seashore.

All these died in faith. They did not receive what had been promised but saw it and greeted it from afar and acknowledged themselves to be strangers and aliens on earth, for those who speak thus show that they are seeking a homeland. If they had been thinking of the land from which they had come, they would have had opportunity to return. But now they desire a better homeland, a heavenly one. Therefore, God is not ashamed to be called their God, for he has prepared a city for them.

By faith Abraham, when put to the test, offered up Isaac, and he who had received the promises was ready to offer his only son, of whom it was said, *Through Isaac descendants shall bear your name.* He reasoned that God was able to raise even from the dead, and he received Isaac back as a symbol.

Responsorial Psalm   **Luke 1:69-70, 71-72, 73-75**

R. (68) Blessed be the Lord the God of Israel; he has come to his people.

He has raised up for us a mighty savior, born of the house of his servant David. **R.**

Through his holy prophets he promised of old. That he would save us from our sins from the hands of all who hate us. He promised to show mercy to our fathers and to remember his holy covenant. **R.**

This was the oath he swore to our father Abraham: to set us free from the bonds of our enemies, free to worship him without fear, holy and righteous in his sight all the days of our life. **R.**

Alleluia   John 3:16

R. Alleluia, alleluia.

God so loved the world that he gave his only-begotten Son, so that everyone who believes in him might have eternal life. **R.**

Gospel   Mark 4:35-41

On that day, as evening drew on, Jesus said to his disciples: "Let us cross to the other side." Leaving the crowd, they took Jesus with them in the boat just as he was. And other boats were with him. A violent squall came up and waves were breaking over the boat, so that it was already filling up. Jesus was in the stern, asleep on a cushion. They woke him and said to him, "Teacher, do you not care that we are perishing?" He woke up, rebuked the wind, and said to the sea, "Quiet! Be still!" The wind ceased and there was great calm. Then he asked them, "Why are you terrified? Do you not yet have faith?" They were filled with great awe and said to one another, "Who then is this whom even wind and sea obey?"

SUNDAY, JANUARY 31, 2021

FOURTH SUNDAY IN ORDINARY TIME

First Reading   Deuteronomy 18:15-20

Moses spoke to all the people, saying:

"A prophet like me will the LORD, your God, raise up for you from among your own kin; to him you shall listen. This is exactly what you requested of the LORD, your God, at Horeb on the day of the assembly, when you said, 'Let us not again hear the voice of the LORD, our God, nor see this great fire any more, lest we die.' And the LORD said to me, 'This was well said. I will raise up for them a prophet like you from among their kin, and will put my words into his mouth; he shall tell them all that I command him. Whoever will not listen to my words which he speaks in my name, I myself will make him answer for it. But if a prophet presumes to speak in my name an oracle that I have not commanded him to speak, or speaks in the name of other gods, he shall die.'"

Responsorial Psalm   Psalm 95:1-2, 6-7, 7-9

R. (8) If today you hear his voice, harden not your hearts.
Come, let us sing joyfully to the LORD; let us acclaim the rock of our salvation. Let us come into his presence with thanksgiving; let us joyfully sing psalms to him. **R.**
Come, let us bow down in worship; let us kneel before the LORD who made us. For he is our God, and we are the people he shepherds, the flock he guides. **R.**
Oh, that today you would hear his voice: "Harden not your hearts as at Meribah, as in the day of Massah in the desert, where your fathers tempted me; they tested me though they had seen my works." **R.**

Second Reading   1 Corinthians 7:32-35

Brothers and sisters:
I should like you to be free of anxieties. An unmarried man is anxious about the things of the Lord, how he may please the Lord. But a married man is anxious about the things of the world, how he may please his wife, and he is divided. An unmarried woman or a virgin is anxious about the things of the Lord, so that she may be holy in both body and spirit. A married woman, on the other hand, is anxious about the things of the world, how she may please her

husband. I am telling you this for your own benefit, not to impose a restraint upon you, but for the sake of propriety and adherence to the Lord without distraction.

Alleluia — Matthew 4:16

R. Alleluia, alleluia.

The people who sit in darkness have seen a great light; on those dwelling in a land overshadowed by death, light has arisen. **R.**

Gospel — Mark 1:21-28

Then they came to Capernaum, and on the Sabbath Jesus entered the synagogue and taught. The people were astonished at his teaching, for he taught them as one having authority and not as the scribes. In their synagogue was a man with an unclean spirit; he cried out, "What have you to do with us, Jesus of Nazareth? Have you come to destroy us? I know who you are—the Holy One of God!" Jesus rebuked him and said, "Quiet! Come out of him!" The unclean spirit convulsed him and with a loud cry came out of him. All were amazed and asked one another, "What is this? A new teaching with authority. He commands even the unclean spirits and they obey him." His fame spread everywhere throughout the whole region of Galilee.

MONDAY OF THE FOURTH WEEK IN ORDINARY TIME

First Reading **Hebrew 11:32-40**

Brothers and sisters:

What more shall I say? I have not time to tell of Gideon, Barak, Samson, Jephthah, of David and Samuel and the prophets, who by faith conquered kingdoms, did what was righteous, obtained the promises; they closed the mouths of lions, put out raging fires, escaped the devouring sword; out of weakness they were made powerful, became strong in battle, and turned back foreign invaders. Women received back their dead through resurrection. Some were tortured and would not accept deliverance, in order to obtain a better resurrection. Others endured mockery, scourging, even chains and imprisonment. They were stoned, sawed in two, put to death at sword's point; they went about in skins of sheep or goats, needy, afflicted, tormented. The world was not worthy of them. They wandered about in deserts and on mountains, in caves and in crevices in the earth.

Yet all these, though approved because of their faith, did not receive what had been promised. God had foreseen something better for us, so that without us they should not be made perfect.

Responsorial Psalm **Psalm 31:20, 21, 22, 23, 24**

R. (25) Let your hearts take comfort, all who hope in the Lord.

How great is the goodness, O LORD, which you have in store for those who fear you, and which, toward those who take refuge in you, you show in the sight of the children of men. **R.**

You hide them in the shelter of your presence from the plottings of men; you screen them within your abode from the strife of tongues. **R.**

Blessed be the LORD whose wondrous mercy he has shown me in a fortified city. **R.**

Once I said in my anguish, "I am cut off from your sight"; yet you heard the sound of my pleading when I cried out to you. **R.**

Love the LORD, all you his faithful ones! The LORD keeps those who are constant, but more than requites those who act proudly. **R.**

Alleluia   Luke 7:16

R. Alleluia, alleluia.

A great prophet has arisen in our midst and God has visited his people. **R.**

Gospel   Mark 5:1-20

Jesus and his disciples came to the other side of the sea, to the territory of the Gerasenes. When he got out of the boat, at once a man from the tombs who had an unclean spirit met him. The man had been dwelling among the tombs, and no one could restrain him any longer, even with a chain. In fact, he had frequently been bound with shackles and chains, but the chains had been pulled apart by him and the shackles smashed, and no one was strong enough to subdue him. Night and day among the tombs and on the hillsides he was always crying out and bruising himself with stones.

Catching sight of Jesus from a distance, he ran up and prostrated himself before him, crying out in a loud voice, "What have you to do with me, Jesus, Son of the Most High God? I adjure you by God, do not torment me!" (He had been saying to him, "Unclean spirit, come out of the man!") He asked him, "What is your name?" He replied, "Legion is my name. There are many of us." And he pleaded earnestly with him not to drive them away from that territory. Now a large herd of swine was feeding there on the hillside. And they pleaded with him, "Send us into the swine. Let us enter them." And he let them, and the unclean spirits came out and entered the swine. The herd of about two thousand rushed down a steep bank into the sea, where they were drowned. The swineherds ran away and reported the incident in the town and throughout the countryside. And people came out to see what had happened. As they approached Jesus, they caught sight of the man who had been possessed by Legion, sitting there clothed and in his right mind. And they were seized with fear. Those who witnessed the incident explained to them what had happened to the possessed man and to the swine. Then they began to beg him to leave their district.

As he was getting into the boat, the man who had been possessed pleaded to remain with him. But Jesus would not permit him but told him instead, "Go home to your family and announce to them all that the Lord in his pity has done for you." Then the man went off and began to proclaim in the Decapolis what Jesus had done for him; and all were amazed.

FEAST OF THE PRESENTATION OF THE LORD

First Reading   **Malachi 3:1-4**

Thus says the Lord God:

Lo, I am sending my messenger to prepare the way before me; And suddenly there will come to the temple the LORD whom you seek, And the messenger of the covenant whom you desire. Yes, he is coming, says the LORD of hosts. But who will endure the day of his coming? And who can stand when he appears? For he is like the refiner's fire, or like the fuller's lye. He will sit refining and purifying silver, and he will purify the sons of Levi, Refining them like gold or like silver that they may offer due sacrifice to the LORD. Then the sacrifice of Judah and Jerusalem will please the LORD, as in the days of old, as in years gone by.

Responsorial Psalm   **Psalm 24:7, 8, 9, 10**

R. (8) Who is this king of glory? It is the Lord!

Lift up, O gates, your lintels; reach up, you ancient portals, that the king of glory may come in! **R.**

Who is this king of glory? The LORD, strong and mighty, the LORD, mighty in battle. **R.**

Lift up, O gates, your lintels; reach up, you ancient portals, that the king of glory may come in! **R.**

Who is this king of glory? The LORD of hosts; he is the king of glory. **R.**

Second Reading   **Hebrew 2:14-18**

Since the children share in blood and flesh, Jesus likewise shared in them, that through death he might destroy the one who has the power of death, that is, the Devil, and free those who through fear of death had been subject to slavery all their life. Surely he did not help angels but rather the descendants of Abraham; therefore, he had to become like his brothers and sisters in every way, that he might be a merciful and faithful high priest before God to expiate the sins of the people. Because he himself was tested through what he suffered, he is able to help those who are being tested.

Alleluia   Luke 2:32
R. Alleluia, alleluia.

A light of revelation to the Gentiles, and glory for your people Israel. **R.**

Gospel   Luke 2:22-40 or Luke 2:22-32
Luke 2:22-40

When the days were completed for their purification according to the law of Moses, Mary and Joseph took Jesus up to Jerusalem to present him to the Lord, just as it is written in the law of the Lord, *Every male that opens the womb shall be consecrated to the Lord,* and to offer the sacrifice of *a pair of turtledoves or two young pigeons,* in accordance with the dictate in the law of the Lord.

Now there was a man in Jerusalem whose name was Simeon. This man was righteous and devout, awaiting the consolation of Israel, and the Holy Spirit was upon him. It had been revealed to him by the Holy Spirit that he should not see death before he had seen the Christ of the Lord. He came in the Spirit into the temple; and when the parents brought in the child Jesus to perform the custom of the law in regard to him, he took him into his arms and blessed God, saying:

"Now, Master, you may let your servant go in peace, according to your word, for my eyes have seen your salvation, which you prepared in the sight of all the peoples: a light for revelation to the Gentiles, and glory for your people Israel."

The child's father and mother were amazed at what was said about him; and Simeon blessed them and said to Mary his mother, "Behold, this child is destined for the fall and rise of many in Israel, and to be a sign that will be contradicted -and you yourself a sword will pierce- so that the thoughts of many hearts may be revealed."

There was also a prophetess, Anna, the daughter of Phanuel, of the tribe of Asher. She was advanced in years, having lived seven years with her husband after her marriage, and then as a widow until she was eighty-four. She never left the temple, but worshiped night and day with fasting and prayer. And coming forward at that very time, she gave thanks to God and spoke about the child to all who were awaiting the redemption of Jerusalem.

When they had fulfilled all the prescriptions of the law of the Lord, they returned to Galilee, to their own town of Nazareth. The child grew and became strong, filled with wisdom; and the favor of God was upon him.

Or:

Luke 2:22-32

When the days were completed for their purification according to the law of Moses, Mary and Joseph took Jesus up to Jerusalem to present him to the Lord, just as it is written in the law of the Lord, *Every male that opens the womb shall be consecrated to the Lord,* and to offer the sacrifice of *a pair of turtledoves or two young pigeons,* in accordance with the dictate in the law of the Lord.

Now there was a man in Jerusalem whose name was Simeon. This man was righteous and devout, awaiting the consolation of Israel, and the Holy Spirit was upon him. It had been revealed to him by the Holy Spirit that he should not see death before he had seen the Christ of the Lord. He came in the Spirit into the temple; and when the parents brought in the child Jesus to perform the custom of the law in regard to him, he took him into his arms and blessed God, saying:

"Now, Master, you may let your servant go in peace, according to your word, for my eyes have seen your salvation, which you prepared in the sight of all the peoples: a light for revelation to the Gentiles, and glory for your people Israel."

WEDNESDAY OF THE FOURTH WEEK IN ORDINARY TIME

First Reading   **Hebrew 12:4-7, 11-15**

Brothers and sisters:

In your struggle against sin you have not yet resisted to the point of shedding blood. You have also forgotten the exhortation addressed to you as children:

My son, do not disdain the discipline of the Lord or lose heart when reproved by him; for whom the Lord loves, he disciplines; he scourges every son he acknowledges.

Endure your trials as "discipline"; God treats you as his sons. For what "son" is there whom his father does not discipline? At the time, all discipline seems a cause not for joy but for pain, yet later it brings the peaceful fruit of righteousness to those who are trained by it.

So strengthen your drooping hands and your weak knees. Make straight paths for your feet, that what is lame may not be dislocated but healed.

Strive for peace with everyone, and for that holiness without which no one will see the Lord. See to it that no one be deprived of the grace of God, that no bitter root spring up and cause trouble, through which many may become defiled.

Responsorial Psalm   Psalm 103:1-2, 13-14, 17-18a

R. (see 17) The Lord's kindness is everlasting to those who fear him.

Bless the LORD, O my soul; and all my being, bless his holy name.
Bless the LORD, O my soul, and forget not all his benefits. **R.**

As a father has compassion on his children, so the LORD has compassion on those who fear him, for he knows how we are formed; he remembers that we are dust. **R.**

But the kindness of the LORD is from eternity to eternity toward those who fear him, and his justice toward children's children among those who keep his covenant. **R.**

Alleluia   John 10:27

R. Alleluia, alleluia.

My sheep hear my voice, says the Lord; I know them, and they follow me. **R.**

Gospel   Mark 6:1-6

Jesus departed from there and came to his native place, accompanied by his disciples. When the Sabbath came he began to teach in the synagogue, and many who heard him were astonished. They said, "Where did this man get all this? What kind of wisdom has been given him? What mighty deeds are wrought by his hands! Is he not the carpenter, the son of Mary, and the brother of James and Joseph and Judas and Simon? And are not his sisters here with us?" And they took offense at him. Jesus said to them, "A prophet is not without honor except in his native place and among his own kin and in his own house." So he was not able to perform any mighty deed there, apart from curing a few sick people by laying his hands on them. He was amazed at their lack of faith.

THURSDAY OF THE FOURTH WEEK IN ORDINARY TIME

First Reading   **Hebrew 12:18-19, 21-24**

Brothers and sisters:

You have not approached that which could be touched and a blazing fire and gloomy darkness and storm and a trumpet blast and a voice speaking words such that those who heard begged that no message be further addressed to them. Indeed, so fearful was the spectacle that Moses said, "I am terrified and trembling." No, you have approached Mount Zion and the city of the living God, the heavenly Jerusalem, and countless angels in festal gathering, and the assembly of the firstborn enrolled in heaven, and God the judge of all, and the spirits of the just made perfect, and Jesus, the mediator of a new covenant, and the sprinkled Blood that speaks more eloquently than that of Abel.

Responsorial Psalm   Psalm 48:2-3ab, 3cd-4, 9, 10-11

R. (10) O God, we ponder your mercy within your temple.

Great is the LORD and wholly to be praised in the city of our God.
His holy mountain, fairest of heights, is the joy of all the earth. **R.**

Mount Zion, "the recesses of the North," the city of the great King.
God is with her castles; renowned is he as a stronghold. **R.**

As we had heard, so have we seen in the city of the LORD of hosts,
in the city of our God; God makes it firm forever. **R.**

O God, we ponder your mercy within your temple. As your name,
O God, so also your praise reaches to the ends of the earth. Of
justice your right hand is full. **R.**

Alleluia   Mark 1:15

R. Alleluia, alleluia.

The Kingdom of God is at hand; repent and believe in the Gospel.
R.

Gospel   Mark 6:7-13

Jesus summoned the Twelve and began to send them out two by
two and gave them authority over unclean spirits. He instructed
them to take nothing for the journey but a walking stick –no food,
no sack, no money in their belts. They were, however, to wear
sandals but not a second tunic. He said to them, "Wherever you
enter a house, stay there until you leave from there. Whatever
place does not welcome you or listen to you, leave there and shake
the dust off your feet in testimony against them." So they went off
and preached repentance. The Twelve drove out many demons,
and they anointed with oil many who were sick and cured them.

MEMORIAL OF SAINT AGATHA, VIRGIN AND MARTYR

First Reading   **Hebrew 13:1-8**

Let brotherly love continue. Do not neglect hospitality, for through it some have unknowingly entertained angels. Be mindful of prisoners as if sharing their imprisonment, and of the ill-treated as of yourselves, for you also are in the body. Let marriage be honored among all and the marriage bed be kept undefiled, for God will judge the immoral and adulterers. Let your life be free from love of money but be content with what you have, for he has said, *I will never forsake you or abandon you.* Thus we may say with confidence: *The Lord is my helper, and I will not be afraid. What can anyone do to me?*

Remember your leaders who spoke the word of God to you. Consider the outcome of their way of life and imitate their faith. Jesus Christ is the same yesterday, today, and forever.

Responsorial Psalm   **Psalm 27:1, 3, 5, 8b-9abc**

R. (1a) The Lord is my light and my salvation.

The LORD is my light and my salvation; whom should I fear? The LORD is my life's refuge; of whom should I be afraid? **R.**

Though an army encamp against me, my heart will not fear; though war be waged upon me, even then will I trust. **R.**

For he will hide me in his abode in the day of trouble; He will conceal me in the shelter of his tent, he will set me high upon a rock. **R.**

Your presence, O LORD, I seek. Hide not your face from me; do not in anger repel your servant. You are my helper: cast me not off. **R.**

Alleluia   Luke 8:15

R. Alleluia, alleluia.

Blessed are they who have kept the word with a generous heart, and yield a harvest through perseverance. **R.**

Gospel   Mark 6:14-29

King Herod heard about Jesus, for his fame had become widespread, and people were saying, "John the Baptist has been raised from the dead; that is why mighty powers are at work in him." Others were saying, "He is Elijah"; still others, "He is a prophet like any of the prophets." But when Herod learned of it, he said, "It is John whom I beheaded. He has been raised up." Herod was the one who had John arrested and bound in prison on account of Herodias, the wife of his brother Philip, whom he had married. John had said to Herod, "It is not lawful for you to have your brother's wife." Herodias harbored a grudge against him and wanted to kill him but was unable to do so. Herod feared John, knowing him to be a righteous and holy man, and kept him in custody. When he heard him speak he was very much perplexed, yet he liked to listen to him. Herodias had an opportunity one day when Herod, on his birthday, gave a banquet for his courtiers, his military officers, and the leading men of Galilee. His own daughter came in and performed a dance that delighted Herod and his guests. The king said to the girl, "Ask of me whatever you wish and I will grant it to you." He even swore many things to her, "I will grant you whatever you ask of me, even to half of my kingdom."

She went out and said to her mother, "What shall I ask for?" Her mother replied, "The head of John the Baptist." The girl hurried back to the king's presence and made her request, "I want you to give me at once on a platter the head of John the Baptist." The king was deeply distressed, but because of his oaths and the guests he did not wish to break his word to her. So he promptly dispatched an executioner with orders to bring back his head. He went off and beheaded him in the prison. He brought in the head on a platter and gave it to the girl. The girl in turn gave it to her mother. When his disciples heard about it, they came and took his body and laid it in a tomb.

SATURDAY, FEBRUARY 6, 2021

MEMORIAL OF SAINT PAUL MIKI AND COMPANIONS, MARTYRS

First Reading   **Hebrew 13:15-17, 20-21**

Brothers and sisters:

Through Jesus, let us continually offer God a sacrifice of praise, that is, the fruit of lips that confess his name. Do not neglect to do good and to share what you have; God is pleased by sacrifices of that kind.

Obey your leaders and defer to them, for they keep watch over you and will have to give an account, that they may fulfill their task with joy and not with sorrow, for that would be of no advantage to you.

May the God of peace, who brought up from the dead the great shepherd of the sheep by the Blood of the eternal covenant, furnish you with all that is good, that you may do his will. May he carry out in you what is pleasing to him through Jesus Christ, to whom be glory forever and ever. Amen.

Responsorial Psalm   Psalm 23:1-3a, 3b-4, 5, 6

R. (1) The Lord is my shepherd; there is nothing I shall want.

The LORD is my shepherd; I shall not want. In verdant pastures he gives me repose. Beside restful waters he leads me; he refreshes my soul. **R.**

He guides me in right paths for his name's sake. Even though I walk in the dark valley I fear no evil; for you are at my side with your rod and your staff that give me courage. **R.**

You spread the table before me in the sight of my foes; you anoint my head with oil; my cup overflows. **R.**

Only goodness and kindness follow me all the days of my life; and I shall dwell in the house of the LORD for years to come. **R.**

Alleluia   John 10:27

R. Alleluia, alleluia.

My sheep hear my voice, says the Lord; I know them, and they follow me. **R.**

Gospel   Mark 6:30-34

The Apostles gathered together with Jesus and reported all they had done and taught. He said to them, "Come away by yourselves to a deserted place and rest a while." People were coming and going in great numbers, and they had no opportunity even to eat. So they went off in the boat by themselves to a deserted place.

People saw them leaving and many came to know about it. They hastened there on foot from all the towns and arrived at the place before them. When Jesus disembarked and saw the vast crowd, his heart was moved with pity for them, for they were like sheep without a shepherd; and he began to teach them many things.

SUNDAY, FEBRUARY 7, 2021

FIFTH SUNDAY IN ORDINARY TIME

First Reading   Job 7:1-4, 6-7

Job spoke, saying:

Is not man's life on earth a drudgery? Are not his days those of hirelings? He is a slave who longs for the shade, a hireling who waits for his wages. So I have been assigned months of misery, and troubled nights have been allotted to me. If in bed I say, "When shall I arise?" then the night drags on; I am filled with restlessness until the dawn. My days are swifter than a weaver's shuttle; they come to an end without hope. Remember that my life is like the wind; I shall not see happiness again.

Responsorial Psalm   Psalm 147:1-2, 3-4, 5-6

R. (3a) Praise the Lord, who heals the brokenhearted.

Or:

R. Alleluia.

Praise the LORD, for he is good; sing praise to our God, for he is gracious; it is fitting to praise him. The LORD rebuilds Jerusalem; the dispersed of Israel he gathers. **R.**

He heals the brokenhearted and binds up their wounds. He tells the number of the stars; he calls each by name. **R.**

Great is our Lord and mighty in power; to his wisdom there is no limit. The LORD sustains the lowly; the wicked he casts to the ground. **R.**

Second Reading   1 Corinthians 9:16-19, 22-23

Brothers and sisters:

If I preach the gospel, this is no reason for me to boast, for an obligation has been imposed on me, and woe to me if I do not preach it! If I do so willingly, I have a recompense, but if unwillingly, then I have been entrusted with a stewardship. What then is my recompense? That, when I preach, I offer the gospel free of charge so as not to make full use of my right in the gospel. Although I am free in regard to all, I have made myself a slave to all so as to win over as many as possible. To the weak I became weak, to win over the weak. I have become all things to all, to save at least some. All this I do for the sake of the gospel, so that I too may have a share in it.

Alleluia   Matthew 8:17

R. Alleluia, alleluia.

Christ took away our infirmities and bore our diseases. **R.**

Gospel   Mark 1:29-39

On leaving the synagogue Jesus entered the house of Simon and Andrew with James and John. Simon's mother-in-law lay sick with a fever. They immediately told him about her. He approached, grasped her hand, and helped her up. Then the fever left her and she waited on them.

When it was evening, after sunset, they brought to him all who were ill or possessed by demons. The whole town was gathered at the door. He cured many who were sick with various diseases, and he drove out many demons, not permitting them to speak because they knew him.

Rising very early before dawn, he left and went off to a deserted place, where he prayed. Simon and those who were with him pursued him and on finding him said, "Everyone is looking for you." He told them, "Let us go on to the nearby villages that I may preach there also. For this purpose have I come." So he went into their synagogues, preaching and driving out demons throughout the whole of Galilee.

MONDAY OF THE FIFTH WEEK IN ORDINARY TIME

First Reading   **Genesis 1:1-19**

In the beginning, when God created the heavens and the earth, the earth was a formless wasteland, and darkness covered the abyss, while a mighty wind swept over the waters.

Then God said, "Let there be light," and there was light. God saw how good the light was. God then separated the light from the darkness. God called the light "day," and the darkness he called "night." Thus evening came, and morning followed–the first day.

Then God said, "Let there be a dome in the middle of the waters, to separate one body of water from the other." And so it happened: God made the dome, and it separated the water above the dome from the water below it. God called the dome "the sky." Evening came, and morning followed–the second day.

Then God said, "Let the water under the sky be gathered into a single basin, so that the dry land may appear." And so it happened: the water under the sky was gathered into its basin, and the dry land appeared. God called the dry land "the earth," and the basin of the water he called "the sea." God saw how good it was.

Then God said, "Let the earth bring forth vegetation: every kind of plant that bears seed and every kind of fruit tree on earth that bears fruit with its seed in it." And so it happened: the earth brought forth every kind of plant that bears seed and every kind of fruit tree on earth that bears fruit with its seed in it. God saw how good it was. Evening came, and morning followed–the third day.

Then God said: "Let there be lights in the dome of the sky, to separate day from night. Let them mark the fixed times, the days and the years, and serve as luminaries in the dome of the sky, to shed light upon the earth."

And so it happened: God made the two great lights, the greater one to govern the day, and the lesser one to govern the night; and he made the stars. God set them in the dome of the sky, to shed light upon the earth, to govern the day and the night, and to separate the light from the darkness. God saw how good it was. Evening came, and morning followed–the fourth day.

Responsorial Psalm   Psalm 104:1-2a, 5-6, 10 and 12, 24 and 35c

R. (31b) May the Lord be glad in his works.
Bless the LORD, O my soul! O LORD, my God, you are great indeed! You are clothed with majesty and glory, robed in light as with a cloak. **R.**

You fixed the earth upon its foundation, not to be moved forever; with the ocean, as with a garment, you covered it; above the mountains the waters stood. **R.**

You send forth springs into the watercourses that wind among the mountains. Beside them the birds of heaven dwell; from among the branches they send forth their song. **R.**

How manifold are your works, O LORD! In wisdom you have wrought them all— the earth is full of your creatures; bless the LORD, O my soul! Alleluia. **R.**

Alleluia   Matthew 4:23

R. Alleluia, alleluia.

Jesus preached the Gospel of the Kingdom and cured every disease among the people. **R.**

Gospel   Mark 6:53-56

After making the crossing to the other side of the sea, Jesus and his disciples came to land at Gennesaret and tied up there. As they were leaving the boat, people immediately recognized him. They scurried about the surrounding country and began to bring in the sick on mats to wherever they heard he was. Whatever villages or towns or countryside he entered, they laid the sick in the marketplaces and begged him that they might touch only the tassel on his cloak; and as many as touched it were healed.

TUESDAY OF THE FIFTH WEEK IN ORDINARY TIME

First Reading   **Genesis 1:20—2:4a**

God said,

"Let the water teem with an abundance of living creatures, and on the earth let birds fly beneath the dome of the sky." And so it happened: God created the great sea monsters and all kinds of swimming creatures with which the water teems, and all kinds of winged birds. God saw how good it was, and God blessed them, saying, "Be fertile, multiply, and fill the water of the seas; and let the birds multiply on the earth." Evening came, and morning followed–the fifth day.

Then God said, "Let the earth bring forth all kinds of living creatures: cattle, creeping things, and wild animals of all kinds." And so it happened: God made all kinds of wild animals, all kinds of cattle, and all kinds of creeping things of the earth. God saw how good it was. Then God said: "Let us make man in our image, after our likeness. Let them have dominion over the fish of the sea, the birds of the air, and the cattle, and over all the wild animals and all the creatures that crawl on the ground."

God created man in his image; in the divine image he created him; male and female he created them. God blessed them, saying: "Be fertile and multiply; fill the earth and subdue it. Have dominion over the fish of the sea, the birds of the air, and all the living things that move on the earth."

God also said: "See, I give you every seed-bearing plant all over the earth and every tree that has seed-bearing fruit on it to be your food; and to all the animals of the land, all the birds of the air, and all the living creatures that crawl on the ground, I give all the green plants for food." And so it happened. God looked at everything he had made, and he found it very good. Evening came, and morning followed–the sixth day.

Thus the heavens and the earth and all their array were completed. Since on the seventh day God was finished with the work he had been doing, he rested on the seventh day from all the work he had undertaken. So God blessed the seventh day and made it holy, because on it he rested from all the work he had done in creation. Such is the story of the heavens and the earth at their creation.

Responsorial Psalm　　　　　　　　**Psalm 8:4-5, 6-7, 8-9**

R. (2ab) O Lord, our God, how wonderful your name in all the earth!

When I behold your heavens, the work of your fingers, the moon and the stars which you set in place— what is man that you should be mindful of him, or the son of man that you should care for him? **R.**

You have made him little less than the angels, and crowned him with glory and honor. You have given him rule over the works of your hands, putting all things under his feet. **R.**

All sheep and oxen, yes, and the beasts of the field, the birds of the air, the fishes of the sea, and whatever swims the paths of the seas. **R.**

Alleluia　　　　　　　　　　　　**Psalm 119:36, 29b**

R. Alleluia, alleluia.

Incline my heart, O God, to your decrees; and favor me with your law. **R.**

When the Pharisees with some scribes who had come from Jerusalem gathered around Jesus, they observed that some of his disciples ate their meals with unclean, that is, unwashed, hands. (For the Pharisees and, in fact, all Jews, do not eat without carefully washing their hands, keeping the tradition of the elders. And on coming from the marketplace they do not eat without purifying themselves. And there are many other things that they have traditionally observed, the purification of cups and jugs and kettles and beds.) So the Pharisees and scribes questioned him, "Why do your disciples not follow the tradition of the elders but instead eat a meal with unclean hands?" He responded, "Well did Isaiah prophesy about you hypocrites, as it is written:

This people honors me with their lips, but their hearts are far from me; in vain do they worship me, teaching as doctrines human precepts.

You disregard God's commandment but cling to human tradition." He went on to say, "How well you have set aside the commandment of God in order to uphold your tradition! For Moses said,

Honor your father and your mother, and *whoever curses father or mother shall die.* Yet you say, 'If someone says to father or mother, "Any support you might have had from me is qorban"' (meaning, dedicated to God), you allow him to do nothing more for his father or mother. You nullify the word of God in favor of your tradition that you have handed on. And you do many such things."

MEMORIAL OF SAINT SCHOLASTICA, VIRGIN

First Reading   **Genesis 2:4b-9, 15-17**

At the time when the LORD God made the earth and the heavens while as yet there was no field shrub on earth and no grass of the field had sprouted, for the LORD God had sent no rain upon the earth and there was no man to till the soil, but a stream was welling up out of the earth and was watering all the surface of the ground the LORD God formed man out of the clay of the ground and blew into his nostrils the breath of life, and so man became a living being.

Then the LORD God planted a garden in Eden, in the east, and he placed there the man whom he had formed. Out of the ground the LORD God made various trees grow that were delightful to look at and good for food, with the tree of life in the middle of the garden and the tree of the knowledge of good and evil.

The LORD God then took the man and settled him in the garden of Eden, to cultivate and care for it. The LORD God gave man this order: "You are free to eat from any of the trees of the garden except the tree of knowledge of good and evil. From that tree you shall not eat; the moment you eat from it you are surely doomed to die."

Responsorial Psalm   **Psalm 104:1-2a, 27-28, 29bc-30**

R. (1a) O bless the Lord, my soul!

Bless the LORD, O my soul! O LORD, my God, you are great indeed! You are clothed with majesty and glory, robed in light as with a cloak. **R.**

All creatures look to you to give them food in due time. When you give it to them, they gather it; when you open your hand, they are filled with good things. **R.**

If you take away their breath, they perish and return to their dust. When you send forth your spirit, they are created, and you renew the face of the earth. **R.**

Alleluia   John 17:17b, 17a
R. Alleluia, alleluia.

Your word, O Lord, is truth: consecrate us in the truth. **R.**

Gospel   Mark 7:14-23

Jesus summoned the crowd again and said to them, "Hear me, all of you, and understand. Nothing that enters one from outside can defile that person; but the things that come out from within are what defile." When he got home away from the crowd his disciples questioned him about the parable. He said to them, "Are even you likewise without understanding? Do you not realize that everything that goes into a person from outside cannot defile, since it enters not the heart but the stomach and passes out into the latrine?" (Thus he declared all foods clean.) "But what comes out of the man, that is what defiles him. From within the man, from his heart, come evil thoughts, unchastity, theft, murder, adultery, greed, malice, deceit, licentiousness, envy, blasphemy, arrogance, folly. All these evils come from within and they defile."

THURSDAY, FEBRUARY 11, 2021

THURSDAY OF THE FIFTH WEEK IN ORDINARY TIME
First Reading   Genesis 2:18-25

The LORD God said:

"It is not good for the man to be alone. I will make a suitable partner for him." So the LORD God formed out of the ground various wild animals and various birds of the air, and he brought them to the man to see what he would call them; whatever the man called each of them would be its name. The man gave names to all the cattle, all the birds of the air, and all the wild animals; but none proved to be the suitable partner for the man.

So the LORD God cast a deep sleep on the man, and while he was asleep, he took out one of his ribs and closed up its place with flesh. The LORD God then built up into a woman the rib that he had taken from the man. When he brought her to the man, the man said: "This one, at last, is bone of my bones and flesh of my flesh; this one shall be called 'woman,' for out of 'her man' this one has been taken." That is why a man leaves his father and mother and clings to his wife, and the two of them become one flesh.

The man and his wife were both naked, yet they felt no shame.

Responsorial Psalm   Psalm 128:1-2, 3, 4-5

R. (1a) Blessed are those who fear the Lord.

Blessed are you who fear the LORD, who walk in his ways! For you shall eat the fruit of your handiwork; blessed shall you be, and favored. **R.**

Your wife shall be like a fruitful vine in the recesses of your home; your children like olive plants around your table. **R.**

Behold, thus is the man blessed who fears the LORD. The LORD bless you from Zion: may you see the prosperity of Jerusalem all the days of your life. **R.**

Alleluia   James 1:21bc

R. Alleluia, alleluia.

Humbly welcome the word that has been planted in you and is
able to save your souls. **R.**

Gospel   Mark 7:24-30

Jesus went to the district of Tyre. He entered a house and wanted
no one to know about it, but he could not escape notice. Soon a
woman whose daughter had an unclean spirit heard about him.
She came and fell at his feet. The woman was a Greek, a
Syrophoenician by birth, and she begged him to drive the demon
out of her daughter. He said to her, "Let the children be fed first.
For it is not right to take the food of the children and throw it to
the dogs." She replied and said to him, "Lord, even the dogs under
the table eat the children's scraps." Then he said to her, "For
saying this, you may go. The demon has gone out of your
daughter." When the woman went home, she found the child lying
in bed and the demon gone.

FRIDAY, FEBRUARY 12, 2021

FRIDAY OF THE FIFTH WEEK IN ORDINARY TIME

First Reading   Genesis 3:1-8

Now the serpent was the most cunning of all the animals that the
LORD God had made. The serpent asked the woman, "Did God
really tell you not to eat from any of the trees in the garden?" The
woman answered the serpent: "We may eat of the fruit of the trees
in the garden; it is only about the fruit of the tree in the middle of
the garden that God said, 'You shall not eat it or even touch it, lest
you die.'" But the serpent said to the woman: "You certainly will

not die! No, God knows well that the moment you eat of it your eyes will be opened and you will be like gods who know what is good and what is evil."

The woman saw that the tree was good for food, pleasing to the eyes, and desirable for gaining wisdom. So she took some of its fruit and ate it; and she also gave some to her husband, who was with her, and he ate it. Then the eyes of both of them were opened, and they realized that they were naked; so they sewed fig leaves together and made loincloths for themselves.

When they heard the sound of the LORD God moving about in the garden at the breezy time of the day, the man and his wife hid themselves from the LORD God among the trees of the garden.

Responsorial Psalm   Psalm 32:1-2, 5, 6, 7

R. (1a) Blessed are those whose sins are forgiven.

Blessed is he whose fault is taken away, whose sin is covered. Blessed the man to whom the LORD imputes not guilt, in whose spirit there is no guile. **R.**

Then I acknowledged my sin to you, my guilt I covered not. I said, "I confess my faults to the LORD," and you took away the guilt of my sin. **R.**

For this shall every faithful man pray to you in time of stress. Though deep waters overflow, they shall not reach him. **R.**

You are my shelter; from distress you will preserve me; with glad cries of freedom you will ring me round. **R.**

Alleluia   Acts 16:14b

R. Alleluia, alleluia.

Open our hearts, O Lord, to listen to the words of your Son. **R.**

Gospel   Mark 7:31-37

Jesus left the district of Tyre and went by way of Sidon to the Sea of Galilee, into the district of the Decapolis. And people brought to him a deaf man who had a speech impediment and begged him to lay his hand on him. He took him off by himself away from the crowd. He put his finger into the man's ears and, spitting, touched his tongue; then he looked up to heaven and groaned, and said to him, *"Ephphatha!"* (that is, "Be opened!") And immediately the man's ears were opened, his speech impediment was removed, and he spoke plainly. He ordered them not to tell anyone. But the more he ordered them not to, the more they proclaimed it. They were exceedingly astonished and they said, "He has done all things well. He makes the deaf hear and the mute speak."

SATURDAY, FEBRUARY 13, 2021

SATURDAY OF THE FIFTH WEEK IN ORDINARY TIME

First Reading   Genesis 3:9-24

The LORD God called to Adam and asked him, "Where are you?" He answered, "I heard you in the garden; but I was afraid, because I was naked, so I hid myself." Then he asked, "Who told you that you were naked? You have eaten, then, from the tree of which I had forbidden you to eat!" The man replied, "The woman whom you put here with me she gave me fruit from the tree, and so I ate it." The LORD God then asked the woman, "Why did you do such a thing?" The woman answered, "The serpent tricked me into it, so I ate it."

Then the LORD God said to the serpent: "Because you have done this, you shall be banned from all the animals and from all the wild creatures; on your belly shall you crawl, and dirt shall you eat all the days of your life. I will put enmity between you and the woman, and between your offspring and hers; He will strike at your head, while you strike at his heel."

To the woman he said: "I will intensify the pangs of your childbearing; in pain shall you bring forth children. Yet your urge shall be for your husband, and he shall be your master."

To the man he said: "Because you listened to your wife and ate from the tree of which I had forbidden you to eat, "Cursed be the ground because of you! In toil shall you eat its yield all the days of your life. Thorns and thistles shall it bring forth to you, as you eat of the plants of the field. By the sweat of your face shall you get bread to eat, until you return to the ground, from which you were taken; for you are dirt, and to dirt you shall return."

The man called his wife Eve, because she became the mother of all the living.

For the man and his wife the LORD God made leather garments, with which he clothed them. Then the LORD God said: "See! The man has become like one of us, knowing what is good and what is evil! Therefore, he must not be allowed to put out his hand to take fruit from the tree of life also, and thus eat of it and live forever." The LORD God therefore banished him from the Garden of Eden, to till the ground from which he had been taken. When he expelled the man, he settled him east of the Garden of Eden; and he stationed the cherubim and the fiery revolving sword, to guard the way to the tree of life.

Responsorial Psalm   **Psalm 90:2, 3-4abc, 5-6, 12-13**

R. (1) In every age, O Lord, you have been our refuge.

Before the mountains were begotten and the earth and the world were brought forth, from everlasting to everlasting you are God. **R.**

You turn man back to dust, saying, "Return, O children of men." For a thousand years in your sight are as yesterday, now that it is past, or as a watch of the night. **R.**

You make an end of them in their sleep; the next morning they are like the changing grass, which at dawn springs up anew, but by evening wilts and fades. **R.**

Teach us to number our days aright, that we may gain wisdom of heart. Return, O LORD! How long? Have pity on your servants! **R.**

Alleluia   **Matthew 4:4b**

R. Alleluia, alleluia.

One does not live on bread alone, but on every word that comes forth from the mouth of God. **R.**

Gospel   **Mark 8:1-10**

In those days when there again was a great crowd without anything to eat, Jesus summoned the disciples and said, "My heart is moved with pity for the crowd, because they have been with me now for three days and have nothing to eat. If I send them away hungry to their homes, they will collapse on the way, and some of them have come a great distance." His disciples answered him, "Where can anyone get enough bread to satisfy them here in this deserted place?" Still he asked them, "How many loaves do you have?" They replied, "Seven." He ordered the crowd to sit down on the ground. Then, taking the seven loaves he gave thanks, broke them, and gave them to his disciples to distribute, and they distributed them to the crowd. They also had a few fish. He said the blessing over them and ordered them distributed also. They ate and were satisfied. They picked up the fragments left over– seven baskets. There were about four thousand people. He dismissed the crowd and got into the boat with his disciples and came to the region of Dalmanutha.

SUNDAY, FEBRUARY 14, 2021

SIXTH SUNDAY IN ORDINARY TIME

First Reading   **Leviticus 13:1-2, 44-46**

The Lord said to Moses and Aaron, "If someone has on his skin a scab or pustule or blotch which appears to be the sore of leprosy, he shall be brought to Aaron, the priest, or to one of the priests among his descendants. If the man is leprous and unclean, the priest shall declare him unclean by reason of the sore on his head.

"The one who bears the sore of leprosy shall keep his garments rent and his head bare, and shall muffle his beard; he shall cry out, 'Unclean, unclean!' As long as the sore is on him he shall declare himself unclean, since he is in fact unclean. He shall dwell apart, making his abode outside the camp."

Responsorial Psalm   **Psalm 32:1-2, 5, 11**

R. (7) I turn to you, Lord, in time of trouble, and you fill me with the joy of salvation.

Blessed is he whose fault is taken away, whose sin is covered. Blessed the man to whom the LORD imputes not guilt, in whose spirit there is no guile. **R.**

Then I acknowledged my sin to you, my guilt I covered not. I said, "I confess my faults to the LORD," and you took away the guilt of my sin. **R.**

Be glad in the LORD and rejoice, you just; exult, all you upright of heart. **R.**

Second Reading   1 Corinthians 10:31—11:1

Brothers and sisters,

Whether you eat or drink, or whatever you do, do everything for the glory of God. Avoid giving offense, whether to the Jews or Greeks or the church of God, just as I try to please everyone in every way, not seeking my own benefit but that of the many, that they may be saved. Be imitators of me, as I am of Christ.

Alleluia   Luke 7:16

R. Alleluia, alleluia.

A great prophet has arisen in our midst, God has visited his people. **R.**

Gospel   Mark 1:40-45

A leper came to Jesus and kneeling down begged him and said, "If you wish, you can make me clean." Moved with pity, he stretched out his hand, touched him, and said to him, "I do will it. Be made clean." The leprosy left him immediately, and he was made clean. Then, warning him sternly, he dismissed him at once.

He said to him, "See that you tell no one anything, but go, show yourself to the priest and offer for your cleansing what Moses prescribed; that will be proof for them."

The man went away and began to publicize the whole matter. He spread the report abroad so that it was impossible for Jesus to enter a town openly. He remained outside in deserted places, and people kept coming to him from everywhere.

MONDAY OF THE SIXTH WEEK IN ORDINARY TIME

First Reading   **Genesis 4:1-15, 25**

The man had relations with his wife Eve, and she conceived and bore Cain, saying, "I have produced a man with the help of the LORD." Next she bore his brother Abel. Abel became a keeper of flocks, and Cain a tiller of the soil. In the course of time Cain brought an offering to the LORD from the fruit of the soil, while Abel, for his part, brought one of the best firstlings of his flock. The LORD looked with favor on Abel and his offering, but on Cain and his offering he did not. Cain greatly resented this and was crestfallen. So the LORD said to Cain: "Why are you so resentful and crestfallen. If you do well, you can hold up your head; but if not, sin is a demon lurking at the door: his urge is toward you, yet you can be his master."

Cain said to his brother Abel, "Let us go out in the field." When they were in the field, Cain attacked his brother Abel and killed him. Then the LORD asked Cain, "Where is your brother Abel?" He answered, "I do not know. Am I my brother's keeper?" The LORD then said: "What have you done! Listen: your brother's blood cries out to me from the soil! Therefore you shall be banned from the soil that opened its mouth to receive your brother's blood from your hand. If you till the soil, it shall no longer give you its produce. You shall become a restless wanderer on the earth." Cain said to the LORD: "My punishment is too great to bear. Since you have now banished me from the soil, and I must avoid your presence and become a restless wanderer on the earth, anyone may kill me at sight." "Not so!" the LORD said to him. "If anyone kills Cain, Cain shall be avenged sevenfold." So the LORD put a mark on Cain, lest anyone should kill him at sight.

Adam again had relations with his wife, and she gave birth to a son whom she called Seth. "God has granted me more offspring in place of Abel," she said, "because Cain slew him."

Responsorial Psalm   **Psalm 50:1 and 8, 16bc-17, 20-21**

R. (14a) Offer to God a sacrifice of praise.

God the LORD has spoken and summoned the earth, from the rising of the sun to its setting. "Not for your sacrifices do I rebuke you, for your burnt offerings are before me always." **R.**

"Why do you recite my statutes, and profess my covenant with your mouth though you hate discipline and cast my words behind you?" **R.**

"You sit speaking against your brother; against your mother's son you spread rumors. When you do these things, shall I be deaf to it? Or do you think that I am like yourself? I will correct you by drawing them up before your eyes." **R.**

Alleluia   **John 14:6**

R. Alleluia, alleluia.

I am the way and the truth and the life, says the Lord; no one comes to the Father except through me. **R.**

Gospel   Mark 8:11-13

The Pharisees came forward and began to argue with Jesus, seeking from him a sign from heaven to test him. He sighed from the depth of his spirit and said, "Why does this generation seek a sign? Amen, I say to you, no sign will be given to this generation." Then he left them, got into the boat again, and went off to the other shore.

TUESDAY OF THE SIXTH WEEK IN ORDINARY TIME

First Reading   Genesis 6:5-8; 7:1-5, 10

When the LORD saw how great was man's wickedness on earth, and how no desire that his heart conceived was ever anything but evil, he regretted that he had made man on the earth, and his heart was grieved. So the LORD said: "I will wipe out from the earth the men whom I have created, and not only the men, but also the beasts and the creeping things and the birds of the air, for I am sorry that I made them." But Noah found favor with the LORD.

Then the LORD said to Noah: "Go into the ark, you and all your household, for you alone in this age have I found to be truly just. Of every clean animal, take with you seven pairs, a male and its mate; and of the unclean animals, one pair, a male and its mate; likewise, of every clean bird of the air, seven pairs, a male and a female, and of all the unclean birds, one pair, a male and a female. Thus you will keep their issue alive over all the earth. Seven days from now I will bring rain down on the earth for forty days and forty nights, and so I will wipe out from the surface of the earth every moving creature that I have made." Noah did just as the LORD had commanded him.

As soon as the seven days were over, the waters of the flood came upon the earth.

Responsorial Psalm   Psalm 29:1a and 2, 3ac-4, 3b and 9c-10

R. (11b) The Lord will bless his people with peace.

Give to the LORD, you sons of God, give to the LORD glory and praise, Give to the LORD the glory due his name; adore the LORD in holy attire. **R.**

The voice of the LORD is over the waters, the LORD, over vast waters. The voice of the LORD is mighty; the voice of the LORD is majestic. **R.**

The God of glory thunders, and in his temple all say, "Glory!" The LORD is enthroned above the flood; the LORD is enthroned as king forever. **R.**

Alleluia   John 14:23

R. Alleluia, alleluia.

Whoever loves me will keep my word, says the Lord; and my Father will love him and we will come to him. **R.**

Gospel   Mark 8:14-21

The disciples had forgotten to bring bread, and they had only one loaf with them in the boat. Jesus enjoined them, "Watch out, guard against the leaven of the Pharisees and the leaven of Herod." They concluded among themselves that it was because they had no bread. When he became aware of this he said to them, "Why do you conclude that it is because you have no bread? Do you not yet understand or comprehend? Are your hearts hardened? Do you have eyes and not see, ears and not hear? And do you not remember, when I broke the five loaves for the five thousand, how many wicker baskets full of fragments you picked up?" They answered him, "Twelve." "When I broke the seven loaves for the four thousand, how many full baskets of fragments did you pick up?" They answered him, "Seven." He said to them, "Do you still not understand?"

WEDNESDAY, FEBRUARY 17, 2021
ASH WEDNESDAY

First Reading   **Joel 2:12-18**

Even now, says the LORD, return to me with your whole heart, with fasting, and weeping, and mourning; Rend your hearts, not your garments, and return to the LORD, your God. For gracious and merciful is he, slow to anger, rich in kindness, and relenting in punishment. Perhaps he will again relent and leave behind him a blessing, Offerings and libations for the LORD, your God.

Blow the trumpet in Zion! Proclaim a fast, call an assembly; Gather the people, notify the congregation; assemble the elders, gather the children and the infants at the breast; Let the bridegroom quit his room and the bride her chamber. Between the porch and the altar let the priests, the ministers of the LORD, weep, and say, "Spare, O LORD, your people, and make not your heritage a reproach, with the nations ruling over them! Why should they say among the peoples, 'Where is their God?'"

Then the LORD was stirred to concern for his land and took pity on his people.

Responsorial Psalm   Psalm 51:3-4, 5-6ab, 12-13, 14 and 17

R. (3a) Be merciful, O Lord, for we have sinned.

Have mercy on me, O God, in your goodness; in the greatness of your compassion wipe out my offense. Thoroughly wash me from my guilt and of my sin cleanse me. **R.**

For I acknowledge my offense, and my sin is before me always: "Against you only have I sinned, and done what is evil in your sight." **R.**

A clean heart create for me, O God, and a steadfast spirit renew within me. Cast me not out from your presence, and your Holy Spirit take not from me. **R.**

Give me back the joy of your salvation, and a willing spirit sustain in me. O Lord, open my lips, and my mouth shall proclaim your praise. **R.**

Second Reading   2 Corinthians 5:20—6:2

Brothers and sisters:

We are ambassadors for Christ, as if God were appealing through us. We implore you on behalf of Christ, be reconciled to God. For our sake he made him to be sin who did not know sin, so that we might become the righteousness of God in him.

Working together, then, we appeal to you not to receive the grace of God in vain. For he says: *In an acceptable time I heard you, and on the day of salvation I helped you.*

Behold, now is a very acceptable time; behold, now is the day of salvation.

If today you hear his voice, harden not your hearts.

<u>**Gospel**</u>   **Matthew 6:1-6, 16-18**

Jesus said to his disciples:

"Take care not to perform righteous deeds in order that people may see them; otherwise, you will have no recompense from your heavenly Father. When you give alms, do not blow a trumpet before you, as the hypocrites do in the synagogues and in the streets to win the praise of others. Amen, I say to you, they have received their reward. But when you give alms, do not let your left hand know what your right is doing, so that your almsgiving may be secret. And your Father who sees in secret will repay you.

"When you pray, do not be like the hypocrites, who love to stand and pray in the synagogues and on street corners so that others may see them. Amen, I say to you, they have received their reward. But when you pray, go to your inner room, close the door, and pray to your Father in secret. And your Father who sees in secret will repay you.

"When you fast, do not look gloomy like the hypocrites. They neglect their appearance, so that they may appear to others to be fasting. Amen, I say to you, they have received their reward. But when you fast, anoint your head and wash your face, so that you may not appear to be fasting, except to your Father who is hidden. And your Father who sees what is hidden will repay you."

THURSDAY AFTER ASH WEDNESDAY

First Reading   **Deuteronomy 30:15-20**

Moses said to the people:

"Today I have set before you life and prosperity, death and doom. If you obey the commandments of the LORD, your God, which I enjoin on you today, loving him, and walking in his ways, and keeping his commandments, statutes and decrees, you will live and grow numerous, and the LORD, your God, will bless you in the land you are entering to occupy. If, however, you turn away your hearts and will not listen, but are led astray and adore and serve other gods, I tell you now that you will certainly perish; you will not have a long life on the land that you are crossing the Jordan to enter and occupy. I call heaven and earth today to witness against you: I have set before you life and death, the blessing and the curse. Choose life, then, that you and your descendants may live, by loving the LORD, your God, heeding his voice, and holding fast to him. For that will mean life for you, a long life for you to live on the land that the LORD swore he would give to your fathers Abraham, Isaac and Jacob."

Responsorial Psalm   **Psalm 1:1-2, 3, 4 and 6**

R. (40:5a) Blessed are they who hope in the Lord.

Blessed the man who follows not the counsel of the wicked nor walks in the way of sinners, nor sits in the company of the

insolent, but delights in the law of the LORD and meditates on his law day and night. **R.**

He is like a tree planted near running water, that yields its fruit in due season, and whose leaves never fade. Whatever he does, prospers. **R.**

Not so the wicked, not so; they are like chaff which the wind drives away. For the LORD watches over the way of the just, but the way of the wicked vanishes. **R.**

Verse before the Gospel   Matthew 4:17

Repent, says the Lord; the Kingdom of heaven is at hand.

Gospel   Luke 9:22-25

Jesus said to his disciples:

"The Son of Man must suffer greatly and be rejected by the elders, the chief priests, and the scribes, and be killed and on the third day be raised." Then he said to all, "If anyone wishes to come after me, he must deny himself and take up his cross daily and follow me. For whoever wishes to save his life will lose it, but whoever loses his life for my sake will save it. What profit is there for one to gain the whole world yet lose or forfeit himself?"

FRIDAY, FEBRUARY 19, 2021
FRIDAY AFTER ASH WEDNESDAY

First Reading   Isaiah 58:1-9a

Thus says the Lord GOD:

Cry out full-throated and unsparingly, lift up your voice like a trumpet blast; Tell my people their wickedness, and the house of Jacob their sins. They seek me day after day, and desire to know my ways, like a nation that has done what is just and not abandoned the law of their God; they ask me to declare what is due them, pleased to gain access to God. "Why do we fast, and you do not see it? Afflict ourselves, and you take no note of it?"

Lo, on your fast day you carry out your own pursuits, and drive all your laborers. Yes, your fast ends in quarreling and fighting, striking with wicked claw. Would that today you might fast so as to make your voice heard on high! Is this the manner of fasting I wish, of keeping a day of penance: That a man bow his head like a reed and lie in sackcloth and ashes? Do you call this a fast, a day acceptable to the LORD? This, rather, is the fasting that I wish: releasing those bound unjustly, untying the thongs of the yoke; Setting free the oppressed, breaking every yoke; Sharing your bread with the hungry, sheltering the oppressed and the homeless; Clothing the naked when you see them, and not turning your back on your own. Then your light shall break forth like the dawn, and your wound shall quickly be healed; your vindication shall go before you, and the glory of the LORD shall be your rear guard. Then you shall call, and the LORD will answer, you shall cry for help, and he will say: Here I am!

Responsorial Psalm   Psalm 51:3-4, 5-6ab, 18-19

R. (19b) A heart contrite and humbled, O God, you will not spurn.

Have mercy on me, O God, in your goodness; in the greatness of your compassion wipe out my offense. Thoroughly wash me from my guilt and of my sin cleanse me. **R.**

For I acknowledge my offense, and my sin is before me always: "Against you only have I sinned, and done what is evil in your sight." **R.**

For you are not pleased with sacrifices; should I offer a burnt offering, you would not accept it. My sacrifice, O God, is a contrite spirit; a heart contrite and humbled, O God, you will not spurn. **R.**

Verse before the Gospel   Amos 5:14

Seek good and not evil so that you may live, and the Lord will be with you.

Gospel   Matthew 9:14-15

The disciples of John approached Jesus and said, "Why do we and the Pharisees fast much, but your disciples do not fast?" Jesus answered them, "Can the wedding guests mourn as long as the bridegroom is with them? The days will come when the bridegroom is taken away from them, and then they will fast."

SATURDAY, FEBRUARY 20, 2021
SATURDAY AFTER ASH WEDNESDAY

First Reading   Isaiah 58:9b-14

Thus says the LORD:

If you remove from your midst oppression, false accusation and malicious speech; If you bestow your bread on the hungry and satisfy the afflicted; Then light shall rise for you in the darkness, and the gloom shall become for you like midday; Then the LORD will guide you always and give you plenty even on the parched land. He will renew your strength, and you shall be like a watered garden, like a spring whose water never fails. The ancient ruins shall be rebuilt for your sake, and the foundations from ages past you shall raise up; "Repairer of the breach," they shall call you, "Restorer of ruined homesteads." If you hold back your foot on the

Sabbath from following your own pursuits on my holy day; If you call the Sabbath a delight, and the LORD's holy day honorable; If you honor it by not following your ways, seeking your own interests, or speaking with malice Then you shall delight in the LORD, and I will make you ride on the heights of the earth; I will nourish you with the heritage of Jacob, your father, for the mouth of the LORD has spoken.

Responsorial Psalm   Psalm 86:1-2, 3-4, 5-6

R. (11ab) Teach me your way, O Lord, that I may walk in your truth.

Incline your ear, O LORD; answer me, for I am afflicted and poor. Keep my life, for I am devoted to you; save your servant who trusts in you. You are my God. **R.**

Have mercy on me, O Lord, for to you I call all the day. Gladden the soul of your servant, for to you, O Lord, I lift up my soul. **R.**

For you, O Lord, are good and forgiving, abounding in kindness to all who call upon you. Hearken, O LORD, to my prayer and attend to the sound of my pleading. **R.**

Verse before the Gospel   Ezekiel 33:11

I take no pleasure in the death of the wicked man, says the Lord, but rather in his conversion, that he may live.

Gospel   Luke 5:27-32

Jesus saw a tax collector named Levi sitting at the customs post. He said to him, "Follow me." And leaving everything behind, he got up and followed him. Then Levi gave a great banquet for him in his house, and a large crowd of tax collectors and others were at table with them. The Pharisees and their scribes complained to his disciples, saying, "Why do you eat and drink with tax collectors and sinners?" Jesus said to them in reply, "Those who are healthy do not need a physician, but the sick do. I have not come to call the righteous to repentance but sinners."

FIRST SUNDAY OF LENT

First Reading   **Genesis 9:8-15**

God said to Noah and to his sons with him:

"See, I am now establishing my covenant with you and your descendants after you and with every living creature that was with you: all the birds, and the various tame and wild animals that were with you and came out of the ark. I will establish my covenant with you, that never again shall all bodily creatures be destroyed by the waters of a flood; there shall not be another flood to devastate the earth."

God added: "This is the sign that I am giving for all ages to come, of the covenant between me and you and every living creature with you: I set my bow in the clouds to serve as a sign of the covenant between me and the earth. When I bring clouds over the earth, and the bow appears in the clouds, I will recall the covenant I have made between me and you and all living beings, so that the waters shall never again become a flood to destroy all mortal beings."

Responsorial Psalm   **Psalm 25:4-5, 6-7, 8-9**

R. (10) Your ways, O Lord, are love and truth to those who keep your covenant.

Your ways, O LORD, make known to me; teach me your paths, Guide me in your truth and teach me, for you are God my savior. **R.**

Remember that your compassion, O LORD, and your love are from of old. In your kindness remember me, because of your goodness, O LORD. **R.**

Good and upright is the LORD, thus he shows sinners the way. He guides the humble to justice, and he teaches the humble his way. **R.**

Second Reading   1 Peter 3:18-22

Beloved:

Christ suffered for sins once, the righteous for the sake of the unrighteous, that he might lead you to God. Put to death in the flesh, he was brought to life in the Spirit. In it he also went to preach to the spirits in prison, who had once been disobedient while God patiently waited in the days of Noah during the building of the ark, in which a few persons, eight in all, were saved through water. This prefigured baptism, which saves you now. It is not a removal of dirt from the body but an appeal to God for a clear conscience, through the resurrection of Jesus Christ, who has gone into heaven and is at the right hand of God, with angels, authorities, and powers subject to him.

Verse before the Gospel   Matthew 4:4b

One does not live on bread alone, but on every word that comes forth from the mouth of God.

Gospel   Mark 1:12-15

The Spirit drove Jesus out into the desert, and he remained in the desert for forty days, tempted by Satan. He was among wild beasts, and the angels ministered to him.

After John had been arrested, Jesus came to Galilee proclaiming the gospel of God: "This is the time of fulfillment. The kingdom of God is at hand. Repent, and believe in the gospel."

FEAST OF THE CHAIR OF SAINT PETER, APOSTLE

First Reading   **1 Peter 5:1-4**

Beloved:

I exhort the presbyters among you, as a fellow presbyter and witness to the sufferings of Christ and one who has a share in the glory to be revealed. Tend the flock of God in your midst, overseeing not by constraint but willingly, as God would have it, not for shameful profit but eagerly. Do not lord it over those assigned to you, but be examples to the flock. And when the chief Shepherd is revealed, you will receive the unfading crown of glory.

Responsorial Psalm   **Psalm 23:1-3a, 4, 5, 6**

R. (1) The Lord is my shepherd; there is nothing I shall want.

The Lord is my shepherd; I shall not want. In verdant pastures he gives me repose; beside restful waters he leads me; he refreshes my soul. **R.**

Even though I walk in the dark valley I fear no evil; for you are at my side with your rod and your staff that give me courage. **R.**

You spread the table before me in the sight of my foes; you anoint my head with oil; my cup overflows. **R.**

Only goodness and kindness follow me all the days of my life; and I shall dwell in the house of the Lord for years to come. **R.**

Alleluia   Matthew 16:18
R. Alleluia, alleluia.
You are Peter, and upon this rock I will build my Church; the gates of the netherworld shall not prevail against it. **R.**

Gospel   Matthew 16:13-19
When Jesus went into the region of Caesarea Philippi he asked his disciples, "Who do people say that the Son of Man is?" They replied, "Some say John the Baptist, others Elijah, still others Jeremiah or one of the prophets." He said to them, "But who do you say that I am?" Simon Peter said in reply, "You are the Christ, the Son of the living God." Jesus said to him in reply, "Blessed are you, Simon son of Jonah. For flesh and blood has not revealed this to you, but my heavenly Father. And so I say to you, you are Peter, and upon this rock I will build my Church, and the gates of the netherworld shall not prevail against it. I will give you the keys to the Kingdom of heaven. Whatever you bind on earth shall be bound in heaven; and whatever you loose on earth shall be loosed in heaven."

TUESDAY, FEBRUARY 23, 2021
TUESDAY OF THE FIRST WEEK OF LENT
First Reading   Isaiah 55:10-11
Thus says the LORD:
Just as from the heavens the rain and snow come down And do not return there till they have watered the earth, making it fertile

and fruitful, Giving seed to the one who sows and bread to the one who eats, So shall my word be that goes forth from my mouth; It shall not return to me void, but shall do my will, achieving the end for which I sent it.

Responsorial Psalm   Psalm 34:4-5, 6-7, 16-17, 18-19
R. (18b) From all their distress God rescues the just.
Glorify the LORD with me, let us together extol his name. I sought the LORD, and he answered me and delivered me from all my fears. **R.**

Look to him that you may be radiant with joy, and your faces may not blush with shame. When the poor one called out, the LORD heard, and from all his distress he saved him. **R.**

The LORD has eyes for the just, and ears for their cry. The LORD confronts the evildoers, to destroy remembrance of them from the earth. **R.**

When the just cry out, the LORD hears them, and from all their distress he rescues them. The LORD is close to the brokenhearted; and those who are crushed in spirit he saves. **R.**

Verse before the Gospel   Matthew 4:4b
One does not live on bread alone, but on every word that comes forth from the mouth of God.

Gospel   Matthew 6:7-15
Jesus said to his disciples:

"In praying, do not babble like the pagans, who think that they will be heard because of their many words. Do not be like them. Your Father knows what you need before you ask him.

"This is how you are to pray:

Our Father who art in heaven, hallowed be thy name, thy Kingdom come, thy will be done, on earth as it is in heaven. Give us this day our daily bread; and forgive us our trespasses, as we forgive those who trespass against us; and lead us not into temptation, but deliver us from evil.

"If you forgive men their transgressions, your heavenly Father will forgive you. But if you do not forgive men, neither will your Father forgive your transgressions."

WEDNESDAY OF THE FIRST WEEK IN LENT

First Reading   **Jonah 3:1-10**

The word of the LORD came to Jonah a second time: "Set out for the great city of Nineveh, and announce to it the message that I will tell you." So Jonah made ready and went to Nineveh, according to the LORD's bidding. Now Nineveh was an enormously large city; it took three days to go through it. Jonah began his journey through the city, and had gone but a single day's walk announcing, "Forty days more and Nineveh shall be destroyed," when the people of Nineveh believed God; they proclaimed a fast and all of them, great and small, put on sackcloth.

When the news reached the king of Nineveh, he rose from his throne, laid aside his robe, covered himself with sackcloth, and sat in the ashes. Then he had this proclaimed throughout Nineveh, by decree of the king and his nobles: "Neither man nor beast, neither cattle nor sheep, shall taste anything; they shall not eat, nor shall they drink water. Man and beast shall be covered with sackcloth and call loudly to God; every man shall turn from his evil way and from the violence he has in hand. Who knows, God may relent and forgive, and withhold his blazing wrath, so that we shall not perish." When God saw by their actions how they turned from their evil way, he repented of the evil that he had threatened to do to them; he did not carry it out.

Responsorial Psalm   Psalm 51:3-4, 12-13, 18-19

R. (19b) A heart contrite and humbled, O God, you will not spurn.

Have mercy on me, O God, in your goodness; in the greatness of your compassion wipe out my offense. Thoroughly wash me from my guilt and of my sin cleanse me. **R.**

A clean heart create for me, O God, and a steadfast spirit renew within me. Cast me not out from your presence, and your Holy Spirit take not from me. **R.**

For you are not pleased with sacrifices; should I offer a burnt offering, you would not accept it. My sacrifice, O God, is a contrite spirit; a heart contrite and humbled, O God, you will not spurn. **R.**

Verse Before The Gospel   Joel 2:12-13

Even now, says the LORD, return to me with your whole heart for I am gracious and merciful.

Gospel   Luke 11:29-32

While still more people gathered in the crowd, Jesus said to them, "This generation is an evil generation; it seeks a sign, but no sign will be given it, except the sign of Jonah. Just as Jonah became a sign to the Ninevites, so will the Son of Man be to this generation. At the judgment the queen of the south will rise with the men of this generation and she will condemn them, because she came from the ends of the earth to hear the wisdom of Solomon, and there is something greater than Solomon here. At the judgment the men of Nineveh will arise with this generation and condemn it, because at the preaching of Jonah they repented, and there is something greater than Jonah here."

THURSDAY OF THE FIRST WEEK IN LENT

First Reading   **Esther C:12, 14-16, 23-25**

Queen Esther, seized with mortal anguish, had recourse to the LORD. She lay prostrate upon the ground, together with her handmaids, from morning until evening, and said:

"God of Abraham, God of Isaac, and God of Jacob, blessed are you. Help me, who am alone and have no help but you, for I am taking my life in my hand. As a child I used to hear from the books of my forefathers that you, O LORD, always free those who are pleasing to you. Now help me, who am alone and have no one but you, O LORD, my God.

"And now, come to help me, an orphan. Put in my mouth persuasive words in the presence of the lion and turn his heart to hatred for our enemy, so that he and those who are in league with him may perish. Save us from the hand of our enemies; turn our mourning into gladness and our sorrows into wholeness."

Responsorial Psalm   **Psalm 138:1-2ab, 2cde-3, 7c-8**

R. (3a) Lord, on the day I called for help, you answered me.

I will give thanks to you, O LORD, with all my heart, for you have heard the words of my mouth; in the presence of the angels I will sing your praise; I will worship at your holy temple and give thanks to your name. **R.**

Because of your kindness and your truth; for you have made great above all things your name and your promise. When I called, you answered me; you built up strength within me. **R.**

Your right hand saves me. The LORD will complete what he has done for me; your kindness, O LORD, endures forever; forsake not the work of your hands. **R.**

Verse before the Gospel　　　　　Psalm 51:12a, 14a

A clean heart create for me, O God; give me back the joy of your salvation.

Gospel　　　　　　　　　　　Matthew 7:7-12

Jesus said to his disciples:

"Ask and it will be given to you; seek and you will find; knock and the door will be opened to you. For everyone who asks, receives; and the one who seeks, finds; and to the one who knocks, the door will be opened. Which one of you would hand his son a stone when he asked for a loaf of bread, or a snake when he asked for a fish? If you then, who are wicked, know how to give good gifts to your children, how much more will your heavenly Father give good things to those who ask him.

"Do to others whatever you would have them do to you. This is the law and the prophets."

FRIDAY OF THE FIRST WEEK OF LENT

First Reading   **Ezekiel 18:21-28**

Thus says the Lord GOD:

If the wicked man turns away from all the sins he committed, if he keeps all my statutes and does what is right and just, he shall surely live, he shall not die. None of the crimes he committed shall be remembered against him; he shall live because of the virtue he has practiced. Do I indeed derive any pleasure from the death of the wicked? says the Lord GOD. Do I not rather rejoice when he turns from his evil way that he may live?

And if the virtuous man turns from the path of virtue to do evil, the same kind of abominable things that the wicked man does, can he do this and still live? None of his virtuous deeds shall be remembered, because he has broken faith and committed sin; because of this, he shall die. You say, "The LORD's way is not fair!" Hear now, house of Israel: Is it my way that is unfair, or rather, are not your ways unfair? When someone virtuous turns away from virtue to commit iniquity, and dies, it is because of the iniquity he committed that he must die. But if the wicked, turning from the wickedness he has committed, does what is right and just, he shall preserve his life; since he has turned away from all the sins that he committed, he shall surely live, he shall not die.

Responsorial Psalm   **Psalm 130:1-2, 3-4, 5-7a, 7bc-8**

R. (3) If you, O Lord, mark iniquities, who can stand?

Out of the depths I cry to you, O LORD; LORD, hear my voice! Let your ears be attentive to my voice in supplication. **R.**

If you, O LORD, mark iniquities, LORD, who can stand? But with you is forgiveness, that you may be revered. **R.**

I trust in the LORD; my soul trusts in his word. My soul waits for the LORD more than sentinels wait for the dawn. Let Israel wait for the LORD. **R.**

For with the LORD is kindness and with him is plenteous redemption; and he will redeem Israel from all their iniquities. **R.**

Verse Before The Gospel   Ezekiel 18:31

Cast away from you all the crimes you have committed, says the LORD, and make for yourselves a new heart and a new spirit.

Gospel   Matthew 5:20-26

Jesus said to his disciples:

"I tell you, unless your righteousness surpasses that of the scribes and Pharisees, you will not enter into the Kingdom of heaven.

"You have heard that it was said to your ancestors, *you shall not kill; and whoever kills will be liable to judgment.* But I say to you, whoever is angry with his brother will be liable to judgment, and whoever says to his brother, *Raqa*, will be answerable to the Sanhedrin, and whoever says, 'You fool,' will be liable to fiery Gehenna. Therefore, if you bring your gift to the altar, and there recall that your brother has anything against you, leave your gift there at the altar, go first and be reconciled with your brother, and then come and offer your gift. Settle with your opponent quickly while on the way to court. Otherwise your opponent will hand you over to the judge, and the judge will hand you over to the guard, and you will be thrown into prison. Amen, I say to you, you will not be released until you have paid the last penny."

SATURDAY OF THE FIRST WEEK OF LENT

First Reading   **Deuteronomy 26:16-19**

Moses spoke to the people, saying:

"This day the LORD, your God, commands you to observe these statutes and decrees. Be careful, then, to observe them with all your heart and with all your soul. Today you are making this agreement with the LORD: he is to be your God and you are to walk in his ways and observe his statutes, commandments and decrees, and to hearken to his voice. And today the LORD is making this agreement with you: you are to be a people peculiarly his own, as he promised you; and provided you keep all his commandments, he will then raise you high in praise and renown and glory above all other nations he has made, and you will be a people sacred to the LORD, your God, as he promised."

Responsorial Psalm   **Psalm 119:1-2, 4-5, 7-8**

R. (1b) Blessed are they who follow the law of the Lord!

Blessed are they whose way is blameless, who walk in the law of the LORD. Blessed are they who observe his decrees, who seek him with all their heart. **R.**

You have commanded that your precepts be diligently kept. Oh, that I might be firm in the ways of keeping your statutes! **R.**

I will give you thanks with an upright heart, when I have learned your just ordinances. I will keep your statutes; do not utterly forsake me. **R.**

Verse before the Gospel 2 Corinthians 6:2b

Behold, now is a very acceptable time; behold, now is the day of salvation.

Gospel Matthew 5:43-48

Jesus said to his disciples:

"You have heard that it was said, *you shall love your neighbor and hate your enemy.* But I say to you, love your enemies, and pray for those who persecute you, that you may be children of your heavenly Father, for he makes his sun rise on the bad and the good, and causes rain to fall on the just and the unjust. For if you love those who love you, what recompense will you have? Do not the tax collectors do the same? And if you greet your brothers and sisters only, what is unusual about that? Do not the pagans do the same? So be perfect, just as your heavenly Father is perfect."

SUNDAY, FEBRUARY 28, 2021
SECOND SUNDAY OF LENT

First Reading Genesis 22:1-2, 9a, 10-13, 15-18

God put Abraham to the test.

He called to him, "Abraham!" "Here I am!" he replied. Then God said: "Take your son Isaac, your only one, whom you love, and go to the land of Moriah. There you shall offer him up as a holocaust on a height that I will point out to you."

When they came to the place of which God had told him, Abraham built an altar there and arranged the wood on it. Then he reached out and took the knife to slaughter his son. But the LORD's messenger called to him from heaven, "Abraham, Abraham!"

"Here I am!" he answered. "Do not lay your hand on the boy," said the messenger. "Do not do the least thing to him. I know now how devoted you are to God, since you did not withhold from me your own beloved son." As Abraham looked about, he spied a ram caught by its horns in the thicket. So he went and took the ram and offered it up as a holocaust in place of his son.

Again the LORD's messenger called to Abraham from heaven and said: "I swear by myself, declares the LORD, that because you acted as you did in not withholding from me your beloved son, I will bless you abundantly and make your descendants as countless as the stars of the sky and the sands of the seashore; your descendants shall take possession of the gates of their enemies, and in your descendants all the nations of the earth shall find blessing— all this because you obeyed my command."

Responsorial Psalm   Psalm 116:10, 15, 16-17, 18-19

R. (116:9) I will walk before the Lord, in the land of the living.

I believed, even when I said, "I am greatly afflicted." Precious in the eyes of the LORD is the death of his faithful ones. **R.**

O LORD, I am your servant; I am your servant, the son of your handmaid; you have loosed my bonds. To you will I offer sacrifice of thanksgiving, and I will call upon the name of the LORD. **R.**

My vows to the LORD I will pay in the presence of all his people, in the courts of the house of the LORD, in your midst, O Jerusalem. **R.**

Second Reading   Romans 8:31b-34

Brothers and sisters:

If God is for us, who can be against us? He who did not spare his own Son but handed him over for us all, how will he not also give us everything else along with him?

Who will bring a charge against God's chosen ones? It is God who acquits us, who will condemn? Christ Jesus it is who died—or, rather, was raised— who also is at the right hand of God, who indeed intercedes for us.

Verse before the Gospel   Matthew 17:5

From the shining cloud the Father's voice is heard: This is my beloved Son, listen to him.

Gospel   Mark 9:2-10

Jesus took Peter, James, and John and led them up a high mountain apart by themselves. And he was transfigured before them, and his clothes became dazzling white, such as no fuller on earth could bleach them. Then Elijah appeared to them along with Moses, and they were conversing with Jesus. Then Peter said to Jesus in reply, "Rabbi, it is good that we are here! Let us make three tents: one for you, one for Moses, and one for Elijah." He hardly knew what to say, they were so terrified. Then a cloud came, casting a shadow over them; from the cloud came a voice, "This is my beloved Son. Listen to him." Suddenly, looking around, they no longer saw anyone but Jesus alone with them.

As they were coming down from the mountain, he charged them not to relate what they had seen to anyone, except when the Son of Man had risen from the dead. So they kept the matter to themselves, questioning what rising from the dead meant.

MONDAY OF THE SECOND WEEK IN LENT

First Reading   **Daniel 9:4b-10**

"Lord, great and awesome God, you who keep your merciful covenant toward those who love you and observe your commandments! We have sinned, been wicked and done evil; we have rebelled and departed from your commandments and your laws. We have not obeyed your servants the prophets, who spoke in your name to our kings, our princes, our fathers, and all the people of the land. Justice, O Lord, is on your side; we are shamefaced even to this day: we, the men of Judah, the residents of Jerusalem, and all Israel, near and far, in all the countries to which you have scattered them because of their treachery toward you. O LORD, we are shamefaced, like our kings, our princes, and our fathers, for having sinned against you. But yours, O Lord, our God, are compassion and forgiveness! Yet we rebelled against you and paid no heed to your command, O LORD, our God, to live by the law you gave us through your servants the prophets."

Responsorial Psalm   **Psalm 79:8, 9, 11 and 13**

R. (103:10a) Lord, do not deal with us according to our sins.

Remember not against us the iniquities of the past; may your compassion quickly come to us, for we are brought very low. **R.**
Help us, O God our savior, because of the glory of your name;
Deliver us and pardon our sins for your name's sake. **R.**

Let the prisoners' sighing come before you; with your great power free those doomed to death. Then we, your people and the sheep of your pasture, will give thanks to you forever; through all generations we will declare your praise. **R.**

Verse before the Gospel 2 Corinthians 6:2b

Your words, Lord, are Spirit and life; you have the words of everlasting life.

Gospel John 6:63c, 68c

Jesus said to his disciples:

"Be merciful, just as your Father is merciful. "Stop judging and you will not be judged. Stop condemning and you will not be condemned. Forgive and you will be forgiven. Give and gifts will be given to you; a good measure, packed together, shaken down, and overflowing, will be poured into your lap. For the measure with which you measure will in return be measured out to you."

TUESDAY, MARCH 2, 2021
TUESDAY OF THE SECOND WEEK OF LENT

First Reading Isaiah 1:10, 16-20

Hear the word of the LORD, princes of Sodom! Listen to the instruction of our God, people of Gomorrah!

Wash yourselves clean! Put away your misdeeds from before my eyes; cease doing evil; learn to do good. Make justice your aim: redress the wronged, hear the orphan's plea, defend the widow. Come now, let us set things right, says the LORD: Though your sins be like scarlet, they may become white as snow; though they be crimson red, they may become white as wool. If you are willing, and obey, you shall eat the good things of the land; but if you refuse and resist, the sword shall consume you: for the mouth of the LORD has spoken!

Responsorial Psalm   Psalm 50:8-9, 16bc-17, 21 and 23
R. (23b) To the upright I will show the saving power of God.

"Not for your sacrifices do I rebuke you, for your burnt offerings are before me always. I take from your house no bullock, no goats out of your fold." **R.**

"Why do you recite my statutes, and profess my covenant with your mouth, though you hate discipline and cast my words behind you?" **R.**

"When you do these things, shall I be deaf to it? Or do you think that I am like yourself? I will correct you by drawing them up before your eyes. He that offers praise as a sacrifice glorifies me; and to him that goes the right way I will show the salvation of God." **R.**

Verse Before The Gospel   Ezekiel 18:31
Cast away from you all the crimes you have committed, says the LORD, and make for yourselves a new heart and a new spirit.

Gospel   Matthew 23:1-12
Jesus spoke to the crowds and to his disciples, saying,

"The scribes and the Pharisees have taken their seat on the chair of Moses. Therefore, do and observe all things whatsoever they tell you, but do not follow their example. For they preach but they do not practice. They tie up heavy burdens hard to carry and lay them on people's shoulders, but they will not lift a finger to move them. All their works are performed to be seen. They widen their phylacteries and lengthen their tassels. They love places of honor at banquets, seats of honor in synagogues, greetings in marketplaces, and the salutation 'Rabbi.' As for you, do not be called 'Rabbi.' You have but one teacher, and you are all brothers. Call no one on earth your father; you have but one Father in heaven. Do not be called 'Master'; you have but one master, the Christ. The greatest among you must be your servant. Whoever exalts himself will be humbled; but whoever humbles himself will be exalted."

WEDNESDAY OF THE SECOND WEEK OF LENT

First Reading   **Jeremiah 18:18-20**

The people of Judah and the citizens of Jerusalem said,

"Come, let us contrive a plot against Jeremiah. It will not mean the loss of instruction from the priests, nor of counsel from the wise, nor of messages from the prophets. And so, let us destroy him by his own tongue; let us carefully note his every word."

Heed me, O LORD, and listen to what my adversaries say. Must good be repaid with evil that they should dig a pit to take my life? Remember that I stood before you to speak in their behalf, to turn away your wrath from them.

Responsorial Psalm   **Psalm 31:5-6, 14, 15-16**

R. (17b) Save me, O Lord, in your kindness.

You will free me from the snare they set for me, for you are my refuge. Into your hands I commend my spirit; you will redeem me, O LORD, O faithful God. **R.**

I hear the whispers of the crowd, that frighten me from every side, as they consult together against me, plotting to take my life. **R.**

But my trust is in you, O LORD; I say, "You are my God." In your hands is my destiny; rescue me from the clutches of my enemies and my persecutors. **R.**

Verse before the Gospel   John 8:12

I am the light of the world, says the Lord; whoever follows me will have the light of life.

Gospel   Matthew 20:17-28

As Jesus was going up to Jerusalem, he took the Twelve disciples aside by themselves, and said to them on the way, "Behold, we are going up to Jerusalem, and the Son of Man will be handed over to the chief priests and the scribes, and they will condemn him to death, and hand him over to the Gentiles to be mocked and scourged and crucified, and he will be raised on the third day."

Then the mother of the sons of Zebedee approached Jesus with her sons and did him homage, wishing to ask him for something. He said to her, "What do you wish?" She answered him, "Command that these two sons of mine sit, one at your right and the other at your left, in your kingdom." Jesus said in reply, "You do not know what you are asking. Can you drink the chalice that I am going to drink?" They said to him, "We can." He replied, "My chalice you will indeed drink, but to sit at my right and at my left, this is not mine to give but is for those for whom it has been prepared by my

Father." When the ten heard this, they became indignant at the two brothers. But Jesus summoned them and said, "You know that the rulers of the Gentiles lord it over them, and the great ones make their authority over them felt. But it shall not be so among you. Rather, whoever wishes to be great among you shall be your servant; whoever wishes to be first among you shall be your slave. Just so, the Son of Man did not come to be served but to serve and to give his life as a ransom for many."

THURSDAY OF THE SECOND WEEK OF LENT

First Reading   **Jeremiah 17:5-10**

Thus says the LORD: Cursed is the man who trusts in human beings, who seeks his strength in flesh, whose heart turns away from the LORD. He is like a barren bush in the desert that enjoys no change of season, but stands in a lava waste, a salt and empty earth. Blessed is the man who trusts in the LORD, whose hope is the LORD. He is like a tree planted beside the waters that stretches out its roots to the stream: It fears not the heat when it comes, its leaves stay green; in the year of drought it shows no distress, but still bears fruit. More tortuous than all else is the human heart, beyond remedy; who can understand it? I, the LORD, alone probe the mind and test the heart, to reward everyone according to his ways, according to the merit of his deeds.

Responsorial Psalm   **Psalm 1:1-2, 3, 4 and 6**

R. (40:5a) Blessed are they who hope in the Lord.

Blessed the man who follows not the counsel of the wicked nor walks in the way of sinners, nor sits in the company of the insolent, but delights in the law of the LORD and meditates on his law day and night. **R.**

He is like a tree planted near running water, that yields its fruit in due season, and whose leaves never fade. Whatever he does, prospers. **R.**

Not so, the wicked, not so; they are like chaff which the wind drives away. For the LORD watches over the way of the just, but the way of the wicked vanishes. **R.**

Verse before the Gospel   Luke 8:15

Blessed are they who have kept the word with a generous heart and yield a harvest through perseverance.

Gospel   Luke 16:19-31

Jesus said to the Pharisees:

"There was a rich man who dressed in purple garments and fine linen and dined sumptuously each day. And lying at his door was a poor man named Lazarus, covered with sores, who would gladly have eaten his fill of the scraps that fell from the rich man's table. Dogs even used to come and lick his sores. When the poor man died, he was carried away by angels to the bosom of Abraham. The rich man also died and was buried, and from the netherworld, where he was in torment, he raised his eyes and saw Abraham far off and Lazarus at his side. And he cried out, 'Father Abraham, have pity on me. Send Lazarus to dip the tip of his finger in water and cool my tongue, for I am suffering torment in these flames.'

Abraham replied, 'My child, remember that you received what was good during your lifetime while Lazarus likewise received what was bad; but now he is comforted here, whereas you are tormented. Moreover, between us and you a great chasm is established to prevent anyone from crossing who might wish to go from our side to yours or from your side to ours.' He said, 'Then I beg you, father, send him to my father's house, for I have five brothers, so that he may warn them, lest they too come to this place of torment.' But Abraham replied, 'They have Moses and the prophets. Let them listen to them.' He said, 'Oh no, father Abraham, but if someone from the dead goes to them, they will repent.' Then Abraham said, 'If they will not listen to Moses and the prophets, neither will they be persuaded if someone should rise from the dead.'"

FRIDAY OF THE SECOND WEEK IN LENT

First Reading   **Genesis 37:3-4, 12-13a, 17b-28a**

Israel loved Joseph best of all his sons, for he was the child of his old age; and he had made him a long tunic. When his brothers saw that their father loved him best of all his sons, they hated him so much that they would not even greet him. One day, when his brothers had gone to pasture their father's flocks at Shechem, Israel said to Joseph, "Your brothers, you know, are tending our flocks at Shechem. Get ready; I will send you to them." So Joseph went after his brothers and caught up with them in Dothan. They noticed him from a distance, and before he came up to them, they plotted to kill him. They said to one another: "Here comes that master dreamer! Come on, let us kill him and throw him into one of the cisterns here; we could say that a wild beast devoured him. We shall then see what comes of his dreams." When Reuben heard this, he tried to save him from their hands, saying, "We must not take his life. Instead of shedding blood," he continued, "just throw him into that cistern there in the desert; but do not kill him outright." His purpose was to rescue him from their hands and return him to his father. So when Joseph came up to them, they stripped him of the long tunic he had on; then they took him and threw him into the cistern, which was empty and dry. They then sat down to their meal. Looking up, they saw a caravan of Ishmaelites coming from Gilead, their camels laden with gum, balm and resin to be taken down to Egypt. Judah said to his brothers: "What is to be gained by killing our brother and concealing his blood? Rather, let us sell him to these Ishmaelites, instead of doing away with him ourselves. After all, he is our brother, our own flesh." His brothers agreed. They sold Joseph to the Ishmaelites for twenty pieces of silver.

Responsorial Psalm　　　**Psalm 105:16-17, 18-19, 20-21**

R. (5a) Remember the marvels the Lord has done.

When the LORD called down a famine on the land and ruined the crop that sustained them, He sent a man before them, Joseph, sold as a slave. **R.**

They had weighed him down with fetters, and he was bound with chains, till his prediction came to pass and the word of the LORD proved him true. **R.**

The king sent and released him, the ruler of the peoples set him free. He made him lord of his house and ruler of all his possessions. **R.**

God so loved the world that he gave his only-begotten Son; so that everyone who believes in him might have eternal life.

Gospel   **Matthew 21:33-43, 45-46**

Jesus said to the chief priests and the elders of the people:

"Hear another parable. There was a landowner who planted a vineyard, put a hedge around it, dug a wine press in it, and built a tower. Then he leased it to tenants and went on a journey. When vintage time drew near, he sent his servants to the tenants to obtain his produce. But the tenants seized the servants and one they beat, another they killed, and a third they stoned. Again he sent other servants, more numerous than the first ones, but they treated them in the same way. Finally, he sent his son to them, thinking, 'They will respect my son.' But when the tenants saw the son, they said to one another, 'This is the heir. Come, let us kill him and acquire his inheritance.' They seized him, threw him out of the vineyard, and killed him. What will the owner of the vineyard do to those tenants when he comes?" They answered him, He will put those wretched men to a wretched death and lease his vineyard to other tenants who will give him the produce at the proper times." Jesus said to them, did you never read in the Scriptures:

The stone that the builders rejected has become the cornerstone; by the Lord has this been done, and it is wonderful in our eyes?

Therefore, I say to you, the Kingdom of God will be taken away from you and given to a people that will produce its fruit." When the chief priests and the Pharisees heard his parables, they knew that he was speaking about them. And although they were attempting to arrest him, they feared the crowds, for they regarded him as a prophet.

SATURDAY, MARCH 6, 2021

SATURDAY OF THE SECOND WEEK IN LENT

First Reading   **Micah 7:14-15, 18-20**

Shepherd your people with your staff, the flock of your inheritance, that dwells apart in a woodland, in the midst of Carmel. Let them feed in Bashan and Gilead, as in the days of old; As in the days when you came from the land of Egypt, show us wonderful signs. Who is there like you, the God who removes guilt and pardons sin for the remnant of his inheritance; Who does not persist in anger forever, but delights rather in clemency, And will again have compassion on us, treading underfoot our guilt? You will cast into the depths of the sea all our sins; you will show faithfulness to Jacob, and grace to Abraham, as you have sworn to our fathers from days of old.

Responsorial Psalm   **Psalm 103:1-2, 3-4, 9-10, 11-12**

R. (8a) The Lord is kind and merciful.

Bless the LORD, O my soul; and all my being, bless his holy name. Bless the LORD, O my soul, and forget not all his benefits. **R.**

He pardons all your iniquities, he heals all your ills. He redeems your life from destruction, he crowns you with kindness and compassion. **R.**

He will not always chide, nor does he keep his wrath forever. Not according to our sins does he deal with us, nor does he requite us according to our crimes. **R.**

For as the heavens are high above the earth, so surpassing is his kindness toward those who fear him. As far as the east is from the west, so far has he put our transgressions from us. **R.**

Verse before the Gospel   Luke 15:18

I will get up and go to my father and shall say to him, Father, I have sinned against heaven and against you.

Gospel   Luke 15:1-3, 11-32

Tax collectors and sinners were all drawing near to listen to Jesus, but the Pharisees and scribes began to complain, saying, "This man welcomes sinners and eats with them." So to them Jesus addressed this parable. "A man had two sons, and the younger son said to his father, 'Father, give me the share of your estate that should come to me.' So the father divided the property between them. After a few days, the younger son collected all his belongings and set off to a distant country where he squandered his inheritance on a life of dissipation. When he had freely spent everything, a severe famine struck that country, and he found himself in dire need. So he hired himself out to one of the local citizens who sent him to his farm to tend the swine. And he longed to eat his fill of the pods on which the swine fed, but nobody gave him any. Coming to his senses he thought, 'How many of my father's hired workers have more than enough food to eat, but here am I, dying from hunger. I shall get up and go to my father and I shall say to him, "Father, I have sinned against heaven and against you. I no longer deserve to be called your son; treat me as you would treat one of your hired workers."' So he got up and went back to his father. While he was still a long way off, his father caught sight of him, and was filled with compassion. He ran to his son, embraced him and kissed him. His son said to him, 'Father, I have sinned against heaven and against you; I no longer deserve to be called your son.' But his father ordered his servants, 'Quickly, bring the finest robe and put it on him; put a ring on his finger and sandals on his feet. Take the fattened calf and slaughter it. Then let us celebrate with a feast, because this son of mine was dead, and has come to life again; he was lost, and has been found.' Then the celebration began.

Now the older son had been out in the field and, on his way back, as he neared the house, he heard the sound of music and dancing. He called one of the servants and asked what this might mean. The servant said to him, 'Your brother has returned and your father has slaughtered the fattened calf because he has him back safe and sound.' He became angry, and when he refused to enter the house, his father came out and pleaded with him. He said to his father in reply, 'Look, all these years I served you and not once did I disobey your orders; yet you never gave me even a young goat to feast on with my friends. But when your son returns who swallowed up your property with prostitutes, for him you slaughter the fattened calf.' He said to him, 'My son, you are here with me always; everything I have is yours. But now we must celebrate and rejoice, because your brother was dead and has come to life again; he was lost and has been found.'"

THIRD SUNDAY OF LENT

First Reading   **Exodus 20:1-17 or Exodus 20:1-3, 7-8, 12-17**

Exodus 20:1-17

In those days, God delivered all these commandments:

"I, the LORD, am your God, who brought you out of the land of Egypt, that place of slavery. You shall not have other gods besides me. You shall not carve idols for yourselves in the shape of anything in the sky above or on the earth below or in the waters beneath the earth; you shall not bow down before them or worship them. For I, the LORD, your God, am a jealous God, inflicting punishment for their fathers' wickedness on the children of those who hate me, down to the third and fourth generation; but bestowing mercy down to the thousandth generation on the children of those who love me and keep my commandments.

"You shall not take the name of the LORD, your God, in vain. For the LORD will not leave unpunished the one who takes his name in vain.

"Remember to keep holy the Sabbath day. Six days you may labor and do all your work, but the seventh day is the Sabbath of the LORD, your God. No work may be done then either by you, or your son or daughter, or your male or female slave, or your beast, or by the alien who lives with you. In six days the Lord made the heavens and the earth, the sea and all that is in them; but on the seventh day he rested. That is why the LORD has blessed the Sabbath day and made it holy.

"Honor your father and your mother, that you may have a long life in the land which the LORD, your God, is giving you.

You shall not kill.

You shall not commit adultery.

You shall not steal.

You shall not bear false witness against your neighbor.

You shall not covet your neighbor's house.

You shall not covet your neighbor's wife, nor his male or female slave, nor his ox or ass, nor anything else that belongs to him."

Or:

Exodus 20:1-3, 7-8, 12-17

In those days, God delivered all these commandments:

"I, the LORD am your God, who brought you out of the land of Egypt, that place of slavery. You shall not have other gods besides me.

"You shall not take the name of the LORD, your God, in vain. For the LORD will not leave unpunished the one who takes his name in vain.

"Remember to keep holy the sabbath day.

Honor your father and your mother, that you may have a long life in the land which the Lord, your God, is giving you.

You shall not kill.

You shall not commit adultery.

You shall not steal.

You shall not bear false witness against your neighbor.

You shall not covet your neighbor's house.

You shall not covet your neighbor's wife, nor his male or female slave, nor his ox or ass, nor anything else that belongs to him."

Responsorial Psalm   **Psalm 19:8, 9, 10, 11**

R. (John 6:68c) Lord, you have the words of everlasting life.

The law of the LORD is perfect, refreshing the soul; the decree of the LORD is trustworthy, giving wisdom to the simple. **R.**

The precepts of the LORD are right, rejoicing the heart; the command of the LORD is clear, enlightening the eye. **R.**

The fear of the LORD is pure, enduring forever; the ordinances of the LORD are true, all of them just. **R.**

They are more precious than gold, than a heap of purest gold; sweeter also than syrup or honey from the comb. **R.**

Second Reading   1 Corinthians 1:22-25

Brothers and sisters:

Jews demand signs and Greeks look for wisdom, but we proclaim Christ crucified, a stumbling block to Jews and foolishness to Gentiles, but to those who are called, Jews and Greeks alike, Christ the power of God and the wisdom of God. For the foolishness of God is wiser than human wisdom, and the weakness of God is stronger than human strength.

Verse before the Gospel   John 3:16

God so loved the world that he gave his only Son, so that everyone who believes in him might have eternal life.

Gospel   John 2:13-25

Since the Passover of the Jews was near, Jesus went up to Jerusalem. He found in the temple area those who sold oxen, sheep, and doves, as well as the money changers seated there. He made a whip out of cords and drove them all out of the temple area, with the sheep and oxen, and spilled the coins of the money changers and overturned their tables, and to those who sold doves he said, "Take these out of here, and stop making my Father's house a marketplace." His disciples recalled the words of Scripture, *Zeal for your house will consume me.*

At this the Jews answered and said to him, "What sign can you show us for doing this?" Jesus answered and said to them, "Destroy this temple and in three days I will raise it up." The Jews said, "This temple has been under construction for forty-six years, and you will raise it up in three days?" But he was speaking about the temple of his body. Therefore, when he was raised from the dead, his disciples remembered that he had said this, and they came to believe the Scripture and the word Jesus had spoken.

While he was in Jerusalem for the feast of Passover, many began to believe in his name when they saw the signs he was doing. But Jesus would not trust himself to them because he knew them all, and did not need anyone to testify about human nature. He himself understood it well.

MONDAY, MARCH 8, 2021
MONDAY OF THE THIRD WEEK OF LENT

First Reading   **2 Kings 5:1-15ab**

Naaman, the army commander of the king of Aram, was highly esteemed and respected by his master, for through him the LORD had brought victory to Aram. But valiant as he was, the man was a leper. Now the Arameans had captured in a raid on the land of Israel a little girl, who became the servant of Naaman's wife. "If only my master would present himself to the prophet in Samaria," she said to her mistress, "he would cure him of his leprosy."

Naaman went and told his lord just what the slave girl from the land of Israel had said. "Go," said the king of Aram. "I will send along a letter to the king of Israel."

So Naaman set out, taking along ten silver talents, six thousand gold pieces, and ten festal garments. To the king of Israel he brought the letter, which read: "With this letter I am sending my servant Naaman to you, that you may cure him of his leprosy."

When he read the letter, the king of Israel tore his garments and exclaimed: "Am I a god with power over life and death, that this man should send someone to me to be cured of leprosy? Take note! You can see he is only looking for a quarrel with me!" When Elisha, the man of God, heard that the king of Israel had torn his garments, he sent word to the king: "Why have you torn your garments? Let him come to me and find out that there is a prophet in Israel." Naaman came with his horses and chariots and stopped at the door of Elisha's house. The prophet sent him the message: "Go and wash seven times in the Jordan, and your flesh will heal, and you will be clean." But Naaman went away angry, saying, "I thought that he would surely come out and stand there to invoke the LORD his God, and would move his hand over the spot, and thus cure the leprosy. Are not the rivers of Damascus, the Abana and the Pharpar, better than all the waters of Israel? Could I not wash in them and be cleansed?" With this, he turned about in anger and left. But his servants came up and reasoned with him. "My father," they said, "if the prophet had told you to do something extraordinary, would you not have done it? All the more now, since he said to you, 'Wash and be clean,' should you do as he said." So Naaman went down and plunged into the Jordan seven times at the word of the man of God. His flesh became again like the flesh of a little child, and he was clean. He returned with his whole retinue to the man of God. On his arrival he stood before him and said, "Now I know that there is no God in all the earth, except in Israel."

Responsorial Psalm   Psalm 42:2, 3; 43:3, 4

R. (42:3) Athirst is my soul for the living God. When shall I go and behold the face of God?

As the hind longs for the running waters, so my soul longs for you, O God. **R.**

Athirst is my soul for God, the living God. When shall I go and behold the face of God? **R.**

Send forth your light and your fidelity; they shall lead me on and bring me to your holy mountain, to your dwelling-place. **R.**

Then will I go in to the altar of God, the God of my gladness and joy; then will I give you thanks upon the harp, O God, my God! **R.**

Verse before the Gospel   Psalm 130:5, 7

I hope in the LORD, I trust in his word; with him there is kindness and plenteous redemption.

Gospel   Luke 4:24-30

Jesus said to the people in the synagogue at Nazareth: "Amen, I say to you, no prophet is accepted in his own native place. Indeed, I tell you, there were many widows in Israel in the days of Elijah when the sky was closed for three and a half years and a severe famine spread over the entire land. It was to none of these that Elijah was sent, but only to a widow in Zarephath in the land of Sidon. Again, there were many lepers in Israel during the time of

Elisha the prophet; yet not one of them was cleansed, but only Naaman the Syrian." When the people in the synagogue heard this, they were all filled with fury. They rose up, drove him out of the town, and led him to the brow of the hill on which their town had been built, to hurl him down headlong. But he passed through the midst of them and went away.

TUESDAY OF THE THIRD WEEK OF LENT

First Reading   **Daniel 3:25, 34-43**

Azariah stood up in the fire and prayed aloud:

"For your name's sake, O Lord, do not deliver us up forever, or make void your covenant. Do not take away your mercy from us, for the sake of Abraham, your beloved, Isaac your servant, and Israel your holy one, to whom you promised to multiply their offspring like the stars of heaven, or the sand on the shore of the sea. For we are reduced, O Lord, beyond any other nation, brought low everywhere in the world this day because of our sins. We have in our day no prince, prophet, or leader, no burnt offering, sacrifice, oblation, or incense, no place to offer first fruits, to find favor with you. But with contrite heart and humble spirit let us be received; As though it were burnt offerings of rams and bullocks, or thousands of fat lambs, so let our sacrifice be in your presence today as we follow you unreservedly; for those who trust in you cannot be put to shame. And now we follow you with our whole heart, we fear you and we pray to you. Do not let us be put to shame, but deal with us in your kindness and great mercy. Deliver us by your wonders, and bring glory to your name, O Lord."

R. (6a) Remember your mercies, O Lord.

Your ways, O LORD, make known to me; teach me your paths,

Guide me in your truth and teach me, for you are God my savior.

R.

Remember that your compassion, O LORD, and your kindness are

from of old. In your kindness remember me, because of your

goodness, O LORD. **R.**

Good and upright is the LORD; thus he shows sinners the way. He

guides the humble to justice, he teaches the humble his way. **R.**

Verse before the Gospel   Joel 2:12-13

Even now, says the LORD, return to me with your whole heart; for

I am gracious and merciful.

Gospel   Matthew 18:21-35

Peter approached Jesus and asked him, "Lord, if my brother sins

against me, how often must I forgive him? As many as seven

times?" Jesus answered, "I say to you, not seven times but

seventy-seven times. That is why the Kingdom of heaven may be

likened to a king who decided to settle accounts with his servants.

When he began the accounting, a debtor was brought before him

who owed him a huge amount. Since he had no way of paying it

back, his master ordered him to be sold, along with his wife, his

children, and all his property, in payment of the debt. At that, the

servant fell down, did him homage, and said, 'Be patient with me,

and I will pay you back in full.' Moved with compassion the master

of that servant let him go and forgave him the loan. When that

servant had left, he found one of his fellow servants who owed him a much smaller amount. He seized him and started to choke him, demanding, 'pay back what you owe.' Falling to his knees, his fellow servant begged him, 'Be patient with me, and I will pay you back.' But he refused. Instead, he had him put in prison until he paid back the debt.

Now when his fellow servants saw what had happened, they were deeply disturbed, and went to their master and reported the whole affair. His master summoned him and said to him, 'You wicked servant! I forgave you your entire debt because you begged me to. Should you not have had pity on your fellow servant, as I had pity on you?' Then in anger his master handed him over to the torturers until he should pay back the whole debt. So will my heavenly Father do to you, unless each of you forgives your brother from your heart."

WEDNESDAY OF THE THIRD WEEK OF LENT

First Reading   **Deuteronomy 4:1, 5-9**

Moses spoke to the people and said: "Now, Israel, hear the statutes and decrees which I am teaching you to observe, that you may live, and may enter in and take possession of the land which the LORD, the God of your fathers, is giving you. Therefore, I teach you the statutes and decrees as the LORD, my God, has commanded me, that you may observe them in the land you are entering to occupy. Observe them carefully, for thus will you give evidence of your wisdom and intelligence to the nations, who will hear of all these statutes and say, 'This great nation is truly a wise and intelligent people.' For what great nation is there that has gods so close to it as the LORD, our God, is to us whenever we call upon him? Or what great nation has statutes and decrees that are as just as this whole law which I am setting before you today? "However, take care and be earnestly on your guard not to forget the things which your own eyes have seen, nor let them slip from your memory as long as you live, but teach them to your children and to your children's children."

Responsorial Psalm   Psalm 147:12-13, 15-16, 19-20
R. (12a) Praise the Lord, Jerusalem.
Glorify the LORD, O Jerusalem; praise your God, O Zion. For he has strengthened the bars of your gates; he has blessed your children within you. **R.**
He sends forth his command to the earth; swiftly runs his word! He spreads snow like wool; frost he strews like ashes. **R.**
He has proclaimed his word to Jacob, his statutes and his ordinances to Israel. He has not done thus for any other nation; his ordinances he has not made known to them. **R.**

Verse before the Gospel   John 6:63c, 68c
Your words, Lord, are Spirit and life; you have the words of everlasting life.

Gospel   Matthew 5:17-19
Jesus said to his disciples:
"Do not think that I have come to abolish the law or the prophets. I have come not to abolish but to fulfill. Amen, I say to you, until heaven and earth pass away, not the smallest letter or the smallest part of a letter will pass from the law, until all things have taken place. Therefore, whoever breaks one of the least of these

commandments and teaches others to do so will be called least in the Kingdom of heaven. But whoever obeys and teaches these commandments will be called greatest in the Kingdom of heaven."

THURSDAY OF THE THIRD WEEK OF LENT

First Reading   **Jeremiah 7:23-28**

Thus says the LORD:

This is what I commanded my people: Listen to my voice; then I will be your God and you shall be my people. Walk in all the ways that I command you, so that you may prosper. But they obeyed not, nor did they pay heed. They walked in the hardness of their evil hearts and turned their backs, not their faces, to me. From the day that your fathers left the land of Egypt even to this day, I have sent you untiringly all my servants the prophets. Yet they have not obeyed me nor paid heed; they have stiffened their necks and done worse than their fathers. When you speak all these words to them, they will not listen to you either; when you call to them, they will not answer you. Say to them: This is the nation that does not listen to the voice of the LORD, its God, or take correction. Faithfulness has disappeared; the word itself is banished from their speech.

Responsorial Psalm   **Psalm 95:1-2, 6-7, 8-9**

R. (8) If today you hear his voice, harden not your hearts.

Come, let us sing joyfully to the LORD; let us acclaim the Rock of our salvation. Let us come into his presence with thanksgiving; let us joyfully sing psalms to him. **R.**

Come, let us bow down in worship; let us kneel before the LORD who made us. For he is our God, and we are the people he shepherds, the flock he guides. **R.**

Oh, that today you would hear his voice: "Harden not your hearts as at Meribah, as in the day of Massah in the desert, Where your fathers tempted me; they tested me though they had seen my works." **R.**

Verse before the Gospel   Joel 2:12-13

Even now, says the LORD, return to me with your whole heart, for I am gracious and merciful.

Gospel   Luke 11:14-23

Jesus was driving out a demon that was mute, and when the demon had gone out, the mute man spoke and the crowds were amazed. Some of them said, "By the power of Beelzebul, the prince of demons, he drives out demons." Others, to test him, asked him for a sign from heaven. But he knew their thoughts and said to them, "Every kingdom divided against itself will be laid waste and house will fall against house. And if Satan is divided against himself, how will his kingdom stand? For you say that it is by Beelzebul that I drive out demons. If I, then, drive out demons by Beelzebul, by whom do your own people drive them out? Therefore they will be your judges. But if it is by the finger of God that I drive out demons, then the Kingdom of God has come upon you. When a strong man fully armed guards his palace, his possessions are safe. But when one stronger than he attacks and overcomes him, he takes away the armor on which he relied and distributes the spoils. Whoever is not with me is against me, and whoever does not gather with me scatters."

FRIDAY OF THE THIRD WEEK OF LENT

First Reading   Hosea 14:2-10

Thus says the LORD: Return, O Israel, to the LORD, your God; you have collapsed through your guilt. Take with you words, and return to the LORD; Say to him, "Forgive all iniquity, and receive what is good, that we may render as offerings the bullocks from our stalls. Assyria will not save us, nor shall we have horses to mount; we shall say no more, 'Our god,' to the work of our hands; for in you the orphan finds compassion." I will heal their defection, says the LORD, I will love them freely; for my wrath is turned away from them. I will be like the dew for Israel: he shall blossom like the lily; He shall strike root like the Lebanon cedar, and put forth his shoots. His splendor shall be like the olive tree and his fragrance like the Lebanon cedar. Again they shall dwell in his shade and raise grain; they shall blossom like the vine, and his fame shall be like the wine of Lebanon. Ephraim! What more has he to do with idols? I have humbled him, but I will prosper him. "I am like a verdant cypress tree"– Because of me you bear fruit! Let him who is wise understand these things; let him who is prudent know them. Straight are the paths of the LORD, in them the just walk, but sinners stumble in them.

Responsorial Psalm   Psalm 81:6c-8a, 8bc-9, 10-11ab, 14 and 17

R. (11 and 9a) I am the Lord your God: hear my voice.

An unfamiliar speech I hear: "I relieved his shoulder of the burden; his hands were freed from the basket. In distress you called, and I rescued you." **R.**

"Unseen, I answered you in thunder; I tested you at the waters of Meribah. Hear, my people, and I will admonish you; O Israel, will you not hear me?" **R.**

"There shall be no strange god among you nor shall you worship any alien god. I, the LORD, am your God who led you forth from the land of Egypt." **R.**

"If only my people would hear me, and Israel walk in my ways, I would feed them with the best of wheat, and with honey from the rock I would fill them." **R.**

Verse before the Gospel   Matthew 4:17

Repent, says the Lord; the Kingdom of heaven is at hand.

Gospel   Mark 12:28-34

One of the scribes came to Jesus and asked him, "Which is the first of all the commandments?" Jesus replied, "The first is this: *Hear, O Israel! The Lord our God is Lord alone! You shall love the Lord your God with all your heart, with all your soul, with all your mind, and with all your strength.*

The second is this: *You shall love your neighbor as yourself.* There is no other commandment greater than these."

The scribe said to him, "Well said, teacher. You are right in saying, *He is One and there is no other than he.* And *to love him with all your heart, with all your understanding, with all your strength, and to love your neighbor as yourself* is worth more than all burnt offerings and sacrifices." And when Jesus saw that he answered with understanding, he said to him, "You are not far from the Kingdom of God." And no one dared to ask him any more questions.

SATURDAY OF THE THIRD WEEK OF LENT

First Reading   **Hosea 6:1-6**

"Come, let us return to the LORD, it is he who has rent, but he will heal us; he has struck us, but he will bind our wounds. He will revive us after two days; on the third day he will raise us up, to live in his presence. Let us know, let us strive to know the LORD; as certain as the dawn is his coming, and his judgment shines forth like the light of day! He will come to us like the rain, like spring rain that waters the earth." What can I do with you, Ephraim? What can I do with you, Judah? Your piety is like a morning cloud, like the dew that early passes away. For this reason I smote them through the prophets, I slew them by the words of my mouth; for it is love that I desire, not sacrifice, and knowledge of God rather than burnt offerings.

Responsorial Psalm   **Psalm 51:3-4, 18-19, 20-21ab**

R. (Hosea 6:6) It is mercy I desire, and not sacrifice.

Have mercy on me, O God, in your goodness; in the greatness of your compassion wipe out my offense. Thoroughly wash me from my guilt and of my sin cleanse me. **R.**

For you are not pleased with sacrifices; should I offer a burnt offering, you would not accept it. My sacrifice, O God, is a contrite spirit; a heart contrite and humbled, O God, you will not spurn. **R.**

Be bountiful, O LORD, to Zion in your kindness by rebuilding the walls of Jerusalem; Then shall you be pleased with due sacrifices, burnt offerings and holocausts. **R.**

Verse before the Gospel Psalm 95:8

If today you hear his voice, harden not your hearts.

Gospel Luke 18:9-14

Jesus addressed this parable to those who were convinced of their own righteousness and despised everyone else. "Two people went up to the temple area to pray; one was a Pharisee and the other was a tax collector. The Pharisee took up his position and spoke this prayer to himself, 'O God, I thank you that I am not like the rest of humanity —greedy, dishonest, adulterous — or even like this tax collector. I fast twice a week, and I pay tithes on my whole income.' But the tax collector stood off at a distance and would not even raise his eyes to heaven but beat his breast and prayed, 'O God, be merciful to me a sinner.' I tell you, the latter went home justified, not the former; for everyone who exalts himself will be humbled, and the one who humbles himself will be exalted."

SUNDAY, MARCH 14, 2021
FOURTH SUNDAY OF LENT

First Reading 1 Samuel 16:1b, 6-7, 10-13a

The LORD said to Samuel:

"Fill your horn with oil, and be on your way. I am sending you to Jesse of Bethlehem, for I have chosen my king from among his sons."

As Jesse and his sons came to the sacrifice, Samuel looked at Eliab and thought, "Surely the LORD's anointed is here before him." But the LORD said to Samuel: "Do not judge from his appearance or from his lofty stature, because I have rejected him. Not as man sees does God see, because man sees the appearance but the LORD looks into the heart."

In the same way Jesse presented seven sons before Samuel, but Samuel said to Jesse, "The LORD has not chosen any one of these." Then Samuel asked Jesse, "Are these all the sons you have?" Jesse replied, "There is still the youngest, who is tending the sheep." Samuel said to Jesse, "Send for him; we will not begin the sacrificial banquet until he arrives here." Jesse sent and had the young man brought to them. He was ruddy, a youth handsome to behold and making a splendid appearance. The LORD said, "There—anoint him, for this is the one!" Then Samuel, with the horn of oil in hand, anointed David in the presence of his brothers; and from that day on, the spirit of the LORD rushed upon David.

Responsorial Psalm   Psalm 23: 1-3a, 3b-4, 5, 6.

R. (1) The Lord is my shepherd; there is nothing I shall want.

The LORD is my shepherd; I shall not want. In verdant pastures he gives me repose; beside restful waters he leads me; he refreshes my soul. **R.**

He guides me in right paths for his name's sake. Even though I walk in the dark valley I fear no evil; for you are at my side with your rod and your staff that give me courage. **R.**

You spread the table before me in the sight of my foes; you anoint my head with oil; my cup overflows. **R.**

Only goodness and kindness follow me all the days of my life; and I shall dwell in the house of the LORD for years to come. **R.**

Second Reading   Ephesians 5:8-14

Brothers and sisters:

You were once darkness, but now you are light in the Lord. Live as children of light, for light produces every kind of goodness and righteousness and truth. Try to learn what is pleasing to the Lord. Take no part in the fruitless works of darkness; rather expose them, for it is shameful even to mention the things done by them in secret; but everything exposed by the light becomes visible, for everything that becomes visible is light.

Therefore, it says: "Awake, O sleeper, and arise from the dead, and Christ will give you light."

Verse before the Gospel   John 8:12

I am the light of the world, says the Lord; whoever follows me will have the light of life.

Gospel   John 9:1-41 or John 9:1, 6-9, 13-17, 34-38

John 9:1-41

As Jesus passed by he saw a man blind from birth. His disciples asked him, "Rabbi, who sinned, this man or his parents, that he was born blind?"

Jesus answered, "Neither he nor his parents sinned; it is so that the works of God might be made visible through him. We have to do the works of the one who sent me while it is day. Night is coming when no one can work. While I am in the world, I am the light of the world." When he had said this, he spat on the ground and made clay with the saliva, and smeared the clay on his eyes, and said to him, "Go wash in the Pool of Siloam" —which means Sent—. So he went and washed, and came back able to see.

His neighbors and those who had seen him earlier as a beggar said, "Isn't this the one who used to sit and beg?" Some said, "It is, "but others said, "No, he just looks like him." He said, "I am." So they said to him, "How were your eyes opened?" He replied, "The man called Jesus made clay and anointed my eyes and told me, 'Go to Siloam and wash.' So I went there and washed and was able to see." And they said to him, "Where is he?" He said, "I don't know."

They brought the one who was once blind to the Pharisees. Now Jesus had made clay and opened his eyes on a Sabbath. So then the Pharisees also asked him how he was able to see. He said to them, "He put clay on my eyes, and I washed, and now I can see." So some of the Pharisees said, "This man is not from God, because he does not keep the Sabbath." But others said, "How can a sinful man do such signs?" And there was a division among them. So they said to the blind man again, "What do you have to say about him, since he opened your eyes?" He said, "He is a prophet."

Now the Jews did not believe that he had been blind and gained his sight until they summoned the parents of the one who had gained his sight. They asked them, "Is this your son, who you say was born blind? How does he now see?" His parents answered and said, "We know that this is our son and that he was born blind. We do not know how he sees now, nor do we know who opened his eyes. Ask him, he is of age; he can speak for himself." His parents said this because they were afraid of the Jews, for the Jews had already agreed that if anyone acknowledged him as the Christ, he would be expelled from the synagogue. For this reason his parents said, "He is of age; question him."

So a second time they called the man who had been blind and said to him, "Give God the praise! We know that this man is a sinner." He replied, "If he is a sinner, I do not know. One thing I do know is that I was blind and now I see." So they said to him, "What did he do to you? How did he open your eyes?" He answered them, "I told you already and you did not listen. Why do you want to hear it again? Do you want to become his disciples, too?" They ridiculed him and said, "You are that man's disciple; we are disciples of Moses! We know that God spoke to Moses, but we do not know where this one is from." The man answered and said to them, "This is what is so amazing, that you do not know where he is from, yet he opened my eyes. We know that God does not listen to sinners, but if one is devout and does his will, he listens to him. It is unheard of that anyone ever opened the eyes of a person born blind. If this man were not from God, he would not be able to do anything." They answered and said to him, "You were born totally in sin, and are you trying to teach us?" Then they threw him out.

When Jesus heard that they had thrown him out, he found him and said, do you believe in the Son of Man?" He answered and said, "Who is he, sir, that I may believe in him?" Jesus said to him, "You have seen him, the one speaking with you is he." He said, "I do believe, Lord," and he worshiped him. Then Jesus said, "I came into this world for judgment, so that those who do not see might see, and those who do see might become blind."

Some of the Pharisees who were with him heard this and said to him, "Surely we are not also blind, are we?" Jesus said to them, "If you were blind, you would have no sin; but now you are saying, 'We see,' so your sin remains.

Or:

John 9:1, 6-9, 13-17, 34-38

As Jesus passed by he saw a man blind from birth. He spat on the ground and made clay with the saliva, and smeared the clay on his eyes, and said to him, "Go wash in the Pool of Siloam" — which means Sent —. So he went and washed, and came back able to see. His neighbors and those who had seen him earlier as a beggar said, "Isn't this the one who used to sit and beg?" Some said, "It is, "but others said, "No, he just looks like him." He said, "I am."

They brought the one who was once blind to the Pharisees. Now Jesus had made clay and opened his eyes on a Sabbath. So then the Pharisees also asked him how he was able to see. He said to them, "He put clay on my eyes, and I washed, and now I can see." So some of the Pharisees said, "This man is not from God, because he does not keep the Sabbath." But others said, "How can a sinful man do such signs?" And there was a division among them. So they said to the blind man again, "What do you have to say about him, since he opened your eyes?" He said, "He is a prophet." They answered and said to him, "You were born totally in sin, and are you trying to teach us?" Then they threw him out.

When Jesus heard that they had thrown him out, he found him and said, "Do you believe in the Son of Man?" He answered and said, "Who is he, sir, that I may believe in him?" Jesus said to him, "You have seen him, and the one speaking with you is he." He said, "I do believe, Lord," and he worshiped him.

MONDAY OF THE FOURTH WEEK OF LENT

First Reading   **Isaiah 65:17-21**

Thus says the LORD:

Lo, I am about to create new heavens and a new earth; the things of the past shall not be remembered or come to mind.

Instead, there shall always be rejoicing and happiness in what I create; for I create Jerusalem to be a joy and its people to be a delight; I will rejoice in Jerusalem and exult in my people.

No longer shall the sound of weeping be heard there, or the sound of crying; No longer shall there be in it an infant who lives but a few days, or an old man who does not round out his full lifetime; He dies a mere youth who reaches but a hundred years, and he who fails of a hundred shall be thought accursed.

They shall live in the houses they build, and eat the fruit of the vineyards they plant.

Responsorial Psalm   **Psalm 30:2 and 4, 5-6, 11-12a and 13b**

R. (2a) I will praise you, Lord, for you have rescued me.

I will extol you, O LORD, for you drew me clear and did not let my enemies rejoice over me. O LORD, you brought me up from the nether world; you preserved me from among those going down into the pit. **R.**

Sing praise to the LORD, you his faithful ones, and give thanks to his holy name. For his anger lasts but a moment; a lifetime, his good will. At nightfall, weeping enters in, but with the dawn, rejoicing. **R.**

"Hear, O LORD, and have pity on me; O LORD, be my helper."
You changed my mourning into dancing; O LORD, my God,
forever will I give you thanks. **R.**

Verse before the Gospel   Amos 5:14

Seek good and not evil so that you may live, and the LORD will be
with you.

Gospel   John 4:43-54

At that time Jesus left [Samaria] for Galilee. For Jesus himself
testified that a prophet has no honor in his native place. When he
came into Galilee, the Galileans welcomed him, since they had
seen all he had done in Jerusalem at the feast; for they themselves
had gone to the feast.

Then he returned to Cana in Galilee, where he had made the water
wine. Now there was a royal official whose son was ill in
Capernaum. When he heard that Jesus had arrived in Galilee from
Judea, he went to him and asked him to come down and heal his
son, who was near death. Jesus said to him, "Unless you people
see signs and wonders, you will not believe." The royal official said
to him, "Sir, come down before my child dies." Jesus said to him,
"You may go; your son will live." The man believed what Jesus said
to him and left. While the man was on his way back, his slaves met
him and told him that his boy would live. He asked them when he
began to recover. They told him, "The fever left him yesterday,
about one in the afternoon." The father realized that just at that
time Jesus had said to him, "Your son will live," and he and his
whole household came to believe. Now this was the second sign
Jesus did when he came to Galilee from Judea.

TUESDAY OF THE FOURTH WEEK OF LENT

First Reading   **Ezekiel 47:1-9, 12**

The angel brought me, Ezekiel, back to the entrance of the temple of the LORD, and I saw water flowing out from beneath the threshold of the temple toward the east, for the façade of the temple was toward the east; the water flowed down from the right side of the temple, south of the altar. He led me outside by the north gate, and around to the outer gate facing the east, where I saw water trickling from the right side. Then when he had walked off to the east with a measuring cord in his hand, he measured off a thousand cubits and had me wade through the water, which was ankle-deep. He measured off another thousand and once more had me wade through the water, which was now knee-deep. Again he measured off a thousand and had me wade; the water was up to my waist. Once more he measured off a thousand, but there was now a river through which I could not wade; for the water had risen so high it had become a river that could not be crossed except by swimming. He asked me, "Have you seen this, son of man?" Then he brought me to the bank of the river, where he had me sit. Along the bank of the river I saw very many trees on both sides. He said to me, "This water flows into the eastern district down upon the Arabah, and empties into the sea, the salt waters, which it makes fresh. Wherever the river flows, every sort of living creature that can multiply shall live, and there shall be abundant fish, for wherever this water comes the sea shall be made fresh. Along both banks of the river, fruit trees of every kind shall grow; their leaves shall not fade, nor their fruit fail. Every month they shall bear fresh fruit, for they shall be watered by the flow from the sanctuary. Their fruit shall serve for food, and their leaves for medicine."

Responsorial Psalm   Psalm 46:2-3, 5-6, 8-9

R. (8) The Lord of hosts is with us; our stronghold is the God of Jacob.

God is our refuge and our strength, an ever-present help in distress. Therefore we fear not, though the earth be shaken and mountains plunge into the depths of the sea. **R.**

There is a stream whose runlets gladden the city of God, the holy dwelling of the Most High. God is in its midst; it shall not be disturbed; God will help it at the break of dawn. **R.**

The LORD of hosts is with us; our stronghold is the God of Jacob. Come! Behold the deeds of the LORD, the astounding things he has wrought on earth. **R.**

Verse before the Gospel   Psalm 51:12a, 14a

A clean heart create for me, O God; give me back the joy of your salvation.

Gospel   John 5:1-16

There was a feast of the Jews, and Jesus went up to Jerusalem. Now there is in Jerusalem at the Sheep Gate a pool called in Hebrew Bethesda, with five porticoes. In these lay a large number of ill, blind, lame, and crippled. One man was there who had been ill for thirty-eight years. When Jesus saw him lying there and knew that he had been ill for a long time, he said to him, "Do you want to be well?" The sick man answered him, "Sir, I have no one to put me into the pool when the water is stirred up; while I am on my way, someone else gets down there before me." Jesus said to him, "Rise, take up your mat, and walk." Immediately the man became well, took up his mat, and walked.

Now that day was a Sabbath. So the Jews said to the man who was cured, "It is the Sabbath, and it is not lawful for you to carry your mat." He answered them, "The man who made me well told me, 'Take up your mat and walk.'" They asked him, "Who is the man who told you, 'Take it up and walk'?" The man who was healed did not know who it was, for Jesus had slipped away, since there was a crowd there. After this Jesus found him in the temple area and said to him, "Look, you are well; do not sin anymore, so that nothing worse may happen to you." The man went and told the Jews that Jesus was the one who had made him well. Therefore, the Jews began to persecute Jesus because he did this on a Sabbath.

WEDNESDAY, MARCH 17, 2021
WEDNESDAY OF THE FOURTH WEEK OF LENT
First Reading   **Isaiah 49:8-15**

Thus says the LORD:

In a time of favor I answer you, on the day of salvation I help you; and I have kept you and given you as a covenant to the people, to restore the land and allot the desolate heritages, saying to the prisoners: Come out! To those in darkness: Show yourselves! Along the ways they shall find pasture, on every bare height shall their pastures be. They shall not hunger or thirst, nor shall the scorching wind or the sun strike them; for he who pities them leads them and guides them beside springs of water. I will cut a road through all my mountains, and make my highways level. See, some shall come from afar, others from the north and the west, and some from the land of Syene. Sing out, O heavens, and rejoice, O earth, break forth into song, you mountains. For the LORD comforts his people and shows mercy to his afflicted.

But Zion said, "The LORD has forsaken me; my Lord has forgotten me." Can a mother forget her infant, be without tenderness for the child of her womb? Even should she forget, I will never forget you.

Responsorial Psalm   Psalm 145:8-9, 13cd-14, 17-18
R. (8a) The Lord is gracious and merciful.

The LORD is gracious and merciful, slow to anger and of great kindness. The LORD is good to all and compassionate toward all his works. **R.**

The LORD is faithful in all his words and holy in all his works. The LORD lifts up all who are falling and raises up all who are bowed down. **R.**

The LORD is just in all his ways and holy in all his works. The LORD is near to all who call upon him, to all who call upon him in truth. **R.**

Verse before the Gospel   John 11:25a, 26

I am the resurrection and the life, says the Lord; whoever believes in me will never die.

Gospel   John 5:17-30

Jesus answered the Jews:

"My Father is at work until now, so I am at work." For this reason they tried all the more to kill him, because he not only broke the

Sabbath but he also called God his own father, making himself equal to God.

Jesus answered and said to them, "Amen, amen, I say to you, the Son cannot do anything on his own, but only what he sees the Father doing; for what he does, the Son will do also. For the Father loves the Son and shows him everything that he himself does, and he will show him greater works than these, so that you may be amazed. For just as the Father raises the dead and gives life, so also does the Son give life to whomever he wishes. Nor does the Father judge anyone, but he has given all judgment to the Son, so that all may honor the Son just as they honor the Father. Whoever does not honor the Son does not honor the Father who sent him.

Amen, amen, I say to you, whoever hears my word and believes in the one who sent me has eternal life and will not come to condemnation, but has passed from death to life.

Amen, amen, I say to you, the hour is coming and is now here when the dead will hear the voice of the Son of God, and those who hear will live. For just as the Father has life in himself, so also he gave to the Son the possession of life in himself. And he gave him power to exercise judgment, because he is the Son of Man.

Do not be amazed at this, because the hour is coming in which all who are in the tombs will hear his voice and will come out, those who have done good deeds to the resurrection of life, but those who have done wicked deeds to the resurrection of condemnation.

"I cannot do anything on my own; I judge as I hear, and my judgment is just, because I do not seek my own will but the will of the one who sent me."

THURSDAY OF THE FOURTH WEEK OF LENT

First Reading **Exodus 32:7-14**

The LORD said to Moses, "Go down at once to your people whom you brought out of the land of Egypt, for they have become depraved. They have soon turned aside from the way I pointed out to them, making for themselves a molten calf and worshiping it, sacrificing to it and crying out, 'This is your God, O Israel, who brought you out of the land of Egypt!' The LORD said to Moses, "I see how stiff-necked this people is. Let me alone, then, that my wrath may blaze up against them to consume them. Then I will make of you a great nation." But Moses implored the LORD, his God, saying, "Why, O LORD, should your wrath blaze up against your own people, whom you brought out of the land of Egypt with such great power and with so strong a hand? Why should the Egyptians say, 'With evil intent he brought them out, that he might kill them in the mountains and exterminate them from the face of the earth'? Let your blazing wrath die down; relent in punishing your people. Remember your servants Abraham, Isaac and Israel, and how you swore to them by your own self, saying, 'I will make your descendants as numerous as the stars in the sky; and all this land that I promised, I will give your descendants as their perpetual heritage.'" So the LORD relented in the punishment he had threatened to inflict on his people.

Responsorial Psalm **Psalm 106:19-20, 21-22, 23**

R. (4a) Remember us, O Lord, as you favor your people.

Our fathers made a calf in Horeb and adored a molten image; they exchanged their glory for the image of a grass-eating bullock. **R.**

They forgot the God who had saved them, who had done great deeds in Egypt, Wondrous deeds in the land of Ham, terrible things at the Red Sea. **R.**

Then he spoke of exterminating them, but Moses, his chosen one, withstood him in the breach to turn back his destructive wrath. **R.**

Verse before the Gospel   John 3:16

God so loved the world that he gave his only-begotten Son, so that everyone who believes in him might have eternal life.

Gospel   John 5:31-47

Jesus said to the Jews:

"If I testify on my own behalf, my testimony is not true. But there is another who testifies on my behalf, and I know that the testimony he gives on my behalf is true. You sent emissaries to John, and he testified to the truth. I do not accept human testimony, but I say this so that you may be saved. He was a burning and shining lamp, and for a while you were content to rejoice in his light. But I have testimony greater than John's. The works that the Father gave me to accomplish, these works that I perform testify on my behalf that the Father has sent me. Moreover, the Father who sent me has testified on my behalf. But you have never heard his voice nor seen his form, and you do not have his word remaining in you, because you do not believe in the one whom he has sent. You search the Scriptures, because you think you have eternal life through them; even they testify on my behalf. But you do not want to come to me to have life. "I do not accept human praise; moreover, I know that you do not have the love of God in you. I came in the name of my Father, but you do not accept me; yet if another comes in his own name, you will accept him. How can you believe, when you accept praise from one another and do not seek the praise that comes from the only God? Do not think that I will accuse you before the Father: the one who will accuse you is Moses, in whom you have placed your hope. For if you had believed Moses, you would have believed me, because he wrote about me. But if you do not believe his writings, how will you believe my words?"

SOLEMNITY OF SAINT JOSEPH, HUSBAND OF THE BLESSED VIRGIN MARY

First Reading   **2 Samuel 7:4-5a, 12-14a, 16**

The LORD spoke to Nathan and said:

"Go, tell my servant David, 'When your time comes and you rest with your ancestors, I will raise up your heir after you, sprung from your loins, and I will make his kingdom firm. It is he who shall build a house for my name. And I will make his royal throne firm forever. I will be a father to him, and he shall be a son to me. Your house and your kingdom shall endure forever before me; your throne shall stand firm forever.'"

Responsorial Psalm   **Psalm 89:2-3, 4-5, 27 and 29**

R. (37) The son of David will live for ever.

The promises of the LORD I will sing forever; through all generations my mouth shall proclaim your faithfulness, for you have said, "My kindness is established forever"; in heaven you have confirmed your faithfulness. **R.**

"I have made a covenant with my chosen one, I have sworn to David my servant: Forever will I confirm your posterity and establish your throne for all generations." **R.**

"He shall say of me, 'You are my father, my God, the Rock, my savior.' Forever I will maintain my kindness toward him, and my covenant with him stands firm." **R.**

Second Reading   Romans 4:13, 16-18, 22

Brothers and sisters:

It was not through the law that the promise was made to Abraham and his descendants that he would inherit the world, but through the righteousness that comes from faith. For this reason, it depends on faith, so that it may be a gift, and the promise may be guaranteed to all his descendants, not to those who only adhere to the law but to those who follow the faith of Abraham, who is the father of all of us, as it is written, *I have made you father of many nations.* He is our father in the sight of God, in whom he believed, who gives life to the dead and calls into being what does not exist. He believed, hoping against hope, that he would become *the father of many nations,* according to what was said, *thus shall your descendants be.* That is why *it was credited to him as righteousness.*

Verse before the Gospel   Psalm 84:5

Blessed are those who dwell in your house, O Lord; they never cease to praise you.

Gospel   Matthew 1:16, 18-21, 24a or Luke 2:41-51a

Matthew 1:16, 18-21, 24a

Jacob was the father of Joseph, the husband of Mary. Of her was born Jesus who is called the Christ. Now this is how the birth of Jesus Christ came about. When his mother Mary was betrothed to Joseph, but before they lived together, she was found with child through the Holy Spirit. Joseph her husband, since he was a righteous man, yet unwilling to expose her to shame, decided to divorce her quietly. Such was his intention when, behold, the angel of the Lord appeared to him in a dream and said, "Joseph, son of David, do not be afraid to take Mary your wife into your home. For it is through the Holy Spirit that this child has been conceived in her. She will bear a son and you are to name him Jesus, because he will save his people from their sins." When Joseph awoke, he did as the angel of the Lord had commanded him and took his wife into his home.

Or:

Luke 2:41-51a

Each year Jesus' parents went to Jerusalem for the feast of Passover, and when he was twelve years old, they went up according to festival custom. After they had completed its days, as they were returning, the boy Jesus remained behind in Jerusalem, but his parents did not know it. Thinking that he was in the caravan, they journeyed for a day and looked for him among their relatives and acquaintances, but not finding him, they returned to Jerusalem to look for him. After three days they found him in the temple, sitting in the midst of the teachers, listening to them and asking them questions, and all who heard him were astounded at his understanding and his answers.

When his parents saw him, they were astonished, and his mother said to him, "Son, why have you done this to us? Your father and I have been looking for you with great anxiety." And he said to them, "Why were you looking for me? Did you not know that I must be in my Father's house?" But they did not understand what he said to them. He went down with them and came to Nazareth, and was obedient to them.

SATURDAY, MARCH 20, 2021
SATURDAY OF THE FOURTH WEEK OF LENT

First Reading   **Jeremiah 11:18-20**

I knew their plot because the LORD informed me; at that time you, O LORD, showed me their doings. Yet I, like a trusting lamb led to slaughter, had not realized that they were hatching plots against me: "Let us destroy the tree in its vigor; let us cut him off from the land of the living, so that his name will be spoken no more." But, you, O LORD of hosts, O just Judge, searcher of mind and heart, Let me witness the vengeance you take on them, for to you I have entrusted my cause!

Responsorial Psalm   **Psalm 7:2-3, 9bc-10, 11-12**

R. (2a) O Lord, my God, in you I take refuge.

O LORD, my God, in you I take refuge; save me from all my pursuers and rescue me, lest I become like the lion's prey, to be torn to pieces, with no one to rescue me. **R.**

Do me justice, O LORD, because I am just, and because of the innocence that is mine. Let the malice of the wicked come to an end, but sustain the just, O searcher of heart and soul, O just God. **R.**

A shield before me is God, who saves the upright of heart; a just judge is God, a God who punishes day by day. **R.**

Verse before the Gospel   Luke 8:15

Blessed are they who have kept the word with a generous heart and yield a harvest through perseverance.

Gospel   John 7:40-53

Some in the crowd who heard these words of Jesus said, "This is truly the Prophet." Others said, "This is the Christ." But others said, "The Christ will not come from Galilee, will he? Does not Scripture say that the Christ will be of David's family and come from Bethlehem, the village where David lived?" So a division occurred in the crowd because of him. Some of them even wanted to arrest him, but no one laid hands on him.

So the guards went to the chief priests and Pharisees, who asked them, "Why did you not bring him?" The guards answered, "Never before has anyone spoken like this man." So the Pharisees answered them, "Have you also been deceived? Have any of the authorities or the Pharisees believed in him? But this crowd, which does not know the law, is accursed." Nicodemus, one of their members who had come to him earlier, said to them, "Does our law condemn a man before it first hears him and finds out what he is doing?" They answered and said to him, "You are not from Galilee also, are you? Look and see that no prophet arises from Galilee." Then each went to his own house.

FIFTH SUNDAY OF LENT

First Reading   **Jeremiah 31:31-34**

The days are coming, says the LORD, when I will make a new covenant with the house of Israel and the house of Judah. It will not be like the covenant I made with their fathers the day I took them by the hand to lead them forth from the land of Egypt; for they broke my covenant, and I had to show myself their master, says the LORD. But this is the covenant that I will make with the house of Israel after those days, says the LORD. I will place my law within them and write it upon their hearts; I will be their God, and they shall be my people. No longer will they have need to teach their friends and relatives how to know the LORD. All, from least to greatest, shall know me, says the LORD, for I will forgive their evildoing and remember their sin no more.

Responsorial Psalm   **Psalm 51:3-4, 12-13, 14-15**

R. (12a) Create a clean heart in me, O God.

Have mercy on me, O God, in your goodness; in the greatness of your compassion wipe out my offense. Thoroughly wash me from my guilt and of my sin cleanse me. **R.**

A clean heart create for me, O God, and a steadfast spirit renew within me. Cast me not out from your presence, and your Holy Spirit take not from me. **R.**

Give me back the joy of your salvation, and a willing spirit sustain in me. I will teach transgressors your ways, and sinners shall return to you. **R.**

Second Reading   **Hebrew 5:7-9**

In the days when Christ Jesus was in the flesh, he offered prayers and supplications with loud cries and tears to the one who was able to save him from death, and he was heard because of his reverence. Son though he was, he learned obedience from what he suffered; and when he was made perfect, he became the source of eternal salvation for all who obey him.

Verse before the Gospel   John 12:26

Whoever serves me must follow me, says the Lord; and where I am, there also will my servant be.

Gospel   John 12:20-33

Some Greeks who had come to worship at the Passover Feast came to Philip, who was from Bethsaida in Galilee, and asked him, "Sir, we would like to see Jesus." Philip went and told Andrew; then Andrew and Philip went and told Jesus. Jesus answered them, "The hour has come for the Son of Man to be glorified. Amen, amen, I say to you, unless a grain of wheat falls to the ground and dies, it remains just a grain of wheat; but if it dies, it produces much fruit. Whoever loves his life loses it, and whoever hates his life in this world will preserve it for eternal life. Whoever serves me must follow me, and where I am, there also will my servant be. The Father will honor whoever serves me. "I am troubled now. Yet what should I say? 'Father, save me from this hour'? But it was for this purpose that I came to this hour. Father, glorify your name." Then a voice came from heaven, "I have glorified it and will glorify it again." The crowd there heard it and said it was thunder; but others said, "An angel has spoken to him." Jesus answered and said, "This voice did not come for my sake but for yours. Now is the time of judgment on this world; now the ruler of this world will be driven out. And when I am lifted up from the earth, I will draw everyone to myself." He said this indicating the kind of death he would die.

MONDAY OF THE FIFTH WEEK OF LENT

<u>**First Reading**</u>   <u>**Daniel 13:1-9, 15-17, 19-30, 33-62 or**</u>

<u>**13:41c-62**</u>

Daniel 13:1-9, 15-17, 19-30, 33-62

In Babylon there lived a man named Joakim, who married a very beautiful and God-fearing woman, Susanna, the daughter of Hilkiah; her pious parents had trained their daughter according to the Law of Moses. Joakim was very rich; he had a garden near his house, and the Jews had recourse to him often because he was the most respected of them all.

That year, two elders of the people were appointed judges, of whom the Lord said, "Wickedness has come out of Babylon: from the elders who were to govern the people as judges." These men, to whom all brought their cases, frequented the house of Joakim. When the people left at noon, Susanna used to enter her husband's garden for a walk. When the old men saw her enter every day for her walk, they began to lust for her. They suppressed their consciences; they would not allow their eyes to look to heaven, and did not keep in mind just judgments.

One day, while they were waiting for the right moment, she entered the garden as usual, with two maids only. She decided to bathe, for the weather was warm. Nobody else was there except the two elders, who had hidden themselves and were watching her.

"Bring me oil and soap," she said to the maids, "and shut the garden doors while I bathe."

As soon as the maids had left, the two old men got up and hurried to her. "Look," they said, "the garden doors are shut, and no one can see us; give in to our desire, and lie with us. If you refuse, we will testify against you that you dismissed your maids because a young man was here with you." "I am completely trapped," Susanna groaned. "If I yield, it will be my death; if I refuse, I cannot escape your power. Yet it is better for me to fall into your power without guilt than to sin before the Lord." Then Susanna shrieked, and the old men also shouted at her, as one of them ran to open the garden doors. When the people in the house heard the cries from the garden, they rushed in by the side gate to see what had happened to her. At the accusations by the old men, the servants felt very much ashamed, for never had any such thing been said about Susanna.

When the people came to her husband Joakim the next day, the two wicked elders also came, fully determined to put Susanna to death. Before all the people they ordered: "Send for Susanna, the daughter of Hilkiah, the wife of Joakim." When she was sent for, she came with her parents, children and all her relatives. All her relatives and the onlookers were weeping.

In the midst of the people the two elders rose up and laid their hands on her head. Through tears she looked up to heaven, for she trusted in the Lord wholeheartedly. The elders made this accusation: "As we were walking in the garden alone, this woman entered with two girls and shut the doors of the garden, dismissing the girls. A young man, who was hidden there, came and lay with her. When we, in a corner of the garden, saw this crime, we ran toward them. We saw them lying together, but the man we could not hold, because he was stronger than we; he opened the doors and ran off. Then we seized her and asked who the young man was, but she refused to tell us. We testify to this." The assembly believed them, since they were elders and judges of the people, and they condemned her to death.

But Susanna cried aloud: "O eternal God, you know what is hidden and are aware of all things before they come to be: you know that they have testified falsely against me. Here I am about to die, though I have done none of the things with which these wicked men have charged me."

The Lord heard her prayer. As she was being led to execution, God stirred up the holy spirit of a young boy named Daniel, and he cried aloud: "I will have no part in the death of this woman." All the people turned and asked him, "What is this you are saying?" He stood in their midst and continued, "Are you such fools, O children of Israel! To condemn a woman of Israel without examination and without clear evidence? Return to court, for they have testified falsely against her." Then all the people returned in haste. To Daniel the elders said, "Come, sit with us and inform us, since God has given you the prestige of old age." But he replied, "Separate these two far from each other that I may examine them." After they were separated one from the other, he called one of them and said: "How you have grown evil with age! Now have your past sins come to term: passing unjust sentences, condemning the innocent, and freeing the guilty, although the Lord says, 'The innocent and the just you shall not put to death.' Now, then, if you were a witness, tell me under what tree you saw them together." "Under a mastic tree," he answered. Daniel replied, "Your fine lie has cost you your head, for the angel of God shall receive the sentence from him and split you in two." Putting him to one side, he ordered the other one to be brought. Daniel said to him, "Offspring of Canaan, not of Judah, beauty has seduced you, lust has subverted your conscience. This is how you acted with the daughters of Israel, and in their fear they yielded to you; but a daughter of Judah did not tolerate your wickedness. Now, then, tell me under what tree you surprised them together." "Under an oak," he said. Daniel replied, "Your fine lie has cost you also your head, for the angel of God waits with a sword to cut you in two so as to make an end of you both."

The whole assembly cried aloud, blessing God who saves those who hope in him. They rose up against the two elders, for by their own words Daniel had convicted them of perjury. According to the Law of Moses, they inflicted on them the penalty they had plotted to impose on their neighbor: they put them to death. Thus was innocent blood spared that day.

Or:

Daniel 13:41c-62

The assembly condemned Susanna to death. But Susanna cried aloud: "O eternal God, you know what is hidden and are aware of all things before they come to be: you know that they have testified falsely against me. Here I am about to die, though I have done none of the things with which these wicked men have charged me."

The Lord heard her prayer. As she was being led to execution, God stirred up the holy spirit of a young boy named Daniel, and he cried aloud: "I will have no part in the death of this woman." All the people turned and asked him, "What is this you are saying?" He stood in their midst and continued, "Are you such fools, O children of Israel! To condemn a woman of Israel without examination and without clear evidence? Return to court, for they have testified falsely against her." Then all the people returned in haste. To Daniel the elders said, "Come, sit with us and inform us, since God has given you the prestige of old age." But he replied, "Separate these two far from each other that I may examine them." After they were separated one from the other, he called one of them and said: "How you have grown evil with age! Now have your past sins come to term: passing unjust sentences, condemning the innocent, and freeing the guilty, although the Lord says, 'The innocent and the just you shall not put to death.' Now, then, if you were a witness, tell me under what tree you saw them together." "Under a mastic tree," he answered. Daniel replied, "Your fine lie has cost you your head, for the angel of God shall receive the sentence from him and split you in two." Putting him to one side, he ordered the other one to be brought. Daniel said to him, "Offspring of Canaan, not of Judah, beauty has seduced you, lust has subverted your conscience. This is how you acted with the daughters of Israel, and in their fear they yielded to you; but a daughter of Judah did not tolerate your wickedness. Now, then, tell me under what tree you surprised them together." "Under an oak," he said. Daniel replied, "Your fine lie has cost you also your head," for the angel of God waits with a sword to cut you in two so as to make an end of you both."

The whole assembly cried aloud, blessing God who saves those who hope in him. They rose up against the two elders, for by their own words Daniel had convicted them of perjury. According to the

Law of Moses, they inflicted on them the penalty they had plotted to impose on their neighbor: they put them to death. Thus was innocent blood spared that day.

Responsorial Psalm   Psalm 23:1-3a, 3b-4, 5, 6

R. (4ab) Even though I walk in the dark valley I fear no evil; for you are at my side.

The LORD is my shepherd; I shall not want. In verdant pastures he gives me repose; beside restful waters he leads me; he refreshes my soul. **R.**

He guides me in right paths for his name's sake. Even though I walk in the dark valley I fear no evil; for you are at my side with your rod and your staff that give me courage. **R.**

You spread the table before me in the sight of my foes; you anoint my head with oil; my cup overflows. **R.**

Only goodness and kindness follow me all the days of my life; and I shall dwell in the house of the LORD for years to come. **R.**

Verse before the Gospel   Ezekiel 33:11

I take no pleasure in the death of the wicked man, says the Lord, but rather in his conversion, that he may live.

Gospel   John 8:1-11

Jesus went to the Mount of Olives. But early in the morning he arrived again in the temple area, and all the people started coming to him, and he sat down and taught them. Then the scribes and the Pharisees brought a woman who had been caught in adultery and made her stand in the middle. They said to him, "Teacher, this woman was caught in the very act of committing adultery. Now in the law, Moses commanded us to stone such women. So what do you say?" They said this to test him, so that they could have some charge to bring against him. Jesus bent down and began to write on the ground with his finger. But when they continued asking him, he straightened up and said to them, "Let the one among you who is without sin be the first to throw a stone at her."

Again he bent down and wrote on the ground. And in response, they went away one by one, beginning with the elders. So he was left alone with the woman before him. Then Jesus straightened up and said to her, "Woman, where are they? Has no one condemned you?" She replied, "No one, sir." Then Jesus said, "Neither do I condemn you. Go, and from now on do not sin anymore."

TUESDAY OF THE FIFTH WEEK OF LENT

First Reading   **Numbers 21:4-9**

From Mount Hor the children of Israel set out on the Red Sea road, to bypass the land of Edom. But with their patience worn out by the journey, the people complained against God and Moses, "Why have you brought us up from Egypt to die in this desert, where there is no food or water? We are disgusted with this wretched food!"

In punishment the LORD sent among the people saraph serpents, which bit the people so that many of them died. Then the people came to Moses and said, "We have sinned in complaining against the LORD and you. Pray the LORD to take the serpents away from us." So Moses prayed for the people, and the LORD said to Moses, "Make a saraph and mount it on a pole, and whoever looks at it after being bitten will live." Moses accordingly made a bronze serpent and mounted it on a pole, and whenever anyone who had been bitten by a serpent looked at the bronze serpent, he lived.

Responsorial Psalm **Psalm 102:2-3, 16-18, 19-21**

R. (2) O Lord, hear my prayer, and let my cry come to you.

O LORD, hear my prayer, and let my cry come to you. Hide not your face from me in the day of my distress. Incline your ear to me; in the day when I call, answer me speedily. **R.**

The nations shall revere your name, O LORD, and all the kings of the earth your glory, When the LORD has rebuilt Zion and appeared in his glory; when he has regarded the prayer of the destitute, and not despised their prayer. **R.**

Let this be written for the generation to come, and let his future creatures praise the LORD: "The LORD looked down from his holy height, from heaven he beheld the earth, to hear the groaning of the prisoners, to release those doomed to die." **R.**

Verse before the Gospel

The seed is the word of God, Christ is the sower; all who come to him will live forever.

Gospel **John 8:21-30**

Jesus said to the Pharisees:

"I am going away and you will look for me, but you will die in your sin. Where I am going you cannot come." So the Jews said, "He is not going to kill himself, is he, because he said, 'Where I am going you cannot come'?" He said to them, "You belong to what is below, I belong to what is above. You belong to this world, but I do not belong to this world. That is why I told you that you will die in your sins. For if you do not believe that I AM, you will die in your sins." So they said to him, "Who are you?" Jesus said to them, "What I told you from the beginning. I have much to say about you in condemnation. But the one who sent me is true, and what I heard from him I tell the world." They did not realize that he was speaking to them of the Father. So Jesus said to them, "When you lift up the Son of Man, then you will realize that I AM, and that I do nothing on my own, but I say only what the Father taught me. The one who sent me is with me. He has not left me alone, because I always do what is pleasing to him." Because he spoke this way, many came to believe in him.

WEDNESDAY OF THE FIFTH WEEK OF LENT

First Reading   **Daniel 3:14-20, 91-92, 95**

King Nebuchadnezzar said:

"Is it true, Shadrach, Meshach, and Abednego, that you will not serve my god, or worship the golden statue that I set up? Be ready now to fall down and worship the statue I had made, whenever you hear the sound of the trumpet, flute, lyre, harp, psaltery, bagpipe, and all the other musical instruments; otherwise, you shall be instantly cast into the white-hot furnace; and who is the God who can deliver you out of my hands?" Shadrach, Meshach, and Abednego answered King Nebuchadnezzar, "There is no need for us to defend ourselves before you in this matter. If our God, whom we serve, can save us from the white-hot furnace and from your hands, O king, may he save us! But even if he will not, know, O king, that we will not serve your god or worship the golden statue that you set up."

King Nebuchadnezzar's face became livid with utter rage against Shadrach, Meshach, and Abednego. He ordered the furnace to be heated seven times more than usual and had some of the strongest men in his army bind Shadrach, Meshach, and Abednego and cast them into the white-hot furnace.

Nebuchadnezzar rose in haste and asked his nobles, "Did we not cast three men bound into the fire?" "Assuredly, O king," they answered. "But," he replied, "I see four men unfettered and unhurt, walking in the fire, and the fourth looks like a son of God." Nebuchadnezzar exclaimed, "Blessed be the God of Shadrach, Meshach, and Abednego, who sent his angel to deliver the servants who trusted in him; they disobeyed the royal command and yielded their bodies rather than serve or worship any god except their own God."

Responsorial Psalm   Daniel 3:52, 53, 54, 55, 56

R. (52b) Glory and praise forever!

Blessed are you, O Lord, the God of our fathers, praiseworthy and exalted above all forever; and blessed is your holy and glorious name, praiseworthy and exalted above all for all ages. R.

Blessed are you in the temple of your holy glory, praiseworthy and exalted above all forever. **R.**

Blessed are you on the throne of your kingdom, praiseworthy and exalted above all forever. **R.**

Blessed are you who look into the depths from your throne upon the cherubim; praiseworthy and exalted above all forever. **R.**

Blessed are you in the firmament of heaven, praiseworthy and glorious forever. **R.**

Verse before the Gospel   Luke 8:15

Blessed are they who have kept the word with a generous heart and yield a harvest through perseverance.

Gospel   John 8:31-42

Jesus said to those Jews who believed in him, "If you remain in my word, you will truly be my disciples, and you will know the truth, and the truth will set you free." They answered him, "We are descendants of Abraham and have never been enslaved to anyone. How can you say, 'You will become free'?" Jesus answered them, "Amen, amen, I say to you, everyone who commits sin is a slave of sin. A slave does not remain in a household forever, but a son always remains. So if the Son frees you, then you will truly be free. I know that you are descendants of Abraham. But you are trying to kill me, because my word has no room among you. I tell you what I have seen in the Father's presence; then do what you have heard from the Father."

They answered and said to him, "Our father is Abraham." Jesus said to them, "If you were Abraham's children, you would be doing the works of Abraham. But now you are trying to kill me, a man who has told you the truth that I heard from God; Abraham did not do this. You are doing the works of your father!" So they said to him, "We were not born of fornication. We have one Father, God." Jesus said to them, "If God were your Father, you would love me, for I came from God and am here; I did not come on my own, but he sent me."

SOLEMNITY OF THE ANNUNCIATION OF THE LORD

First Reading   **Isaiah 7:10-14; 8:10**

The Lord spoke to Ahaz, saying:

Ask for a sign from the Lord, your God; let it be deep as the nether world, or high as the sky! But Ahaz answered, "I will not ask! I will not tempt the Lord!" Then Isaiah said: Listen, O house of David! Is it not enough for you to weary people, must you also weary my God? Therefore the Lord himself will give you this sign: the virgin shall be with child, and bear a son, and shall name him Emmanuel, which means "God is with us!"

Responsorial Psalm   **Psalm 40:7-8a, 8b-9, 10, 11**

R. (8a and 9a) Here I am, Lord; I come to do your will.

Sacrifice or oblation you wished not, but ears open to obedience you gave me. Holocausts or sin-offerings you sought not; then said I, "Behold I come." **R.**

"In the written scroll it is prescribed for me, to do your will, O my God, is my delight, and your law is within my heart!" **R.**

I announced your justice in the vast assembly; I did not restrain my lips, as you, O Lord, know. **R.**

Your justice I kept not hid within my heart; your faithfulness and your salvation I have spoken of; I have made no secret of your kindness and your truth in the vast assembly. **R.**

Second Reading   **Hebrew 10:4-10**

Brothers and sisters:

It is impossible that the blood of bulls and goats take away sins. For this reason, when Christ came into the world, he said:

"Sacrifice and offering you did not desire, but a body you prepared for me; in holocausts and sin offerings you took no delight. Then I said, 'As is written of me in the scroll, behold, I come to do your will, O God.'"

First he says, "Sacrifices and offerings, holocausts and sin offerings, you neither desired nor delighted in." These are offered according to the law. Then he says, "Behold, I come to do your will." He takes away the first to establish the second. By this "will," we have been consecrated through the offering of the Body of Jesus Christ once for all.

Verse before the Gospel   John 1:14ab

The Word of God became flesh and made his dwelling among us; and we saw his glory.

Gospel   Luke 1:26-38

The angel Gabriel was sent from God to a town of Galilee called Nazareth, to a virgin betrothed to a man named Joseph, of the house of David, and the virgin's name was Mary. And coming to her, he said, "Hail, full of grace! The Lord is with you." But she was greatly troubled at what was said and pondered what sort of greeting this might be. Then the angel said to her, "Do not be afraid, Mary, for you have found favor with God. Behold, you will conceive in your womb and bear a son, and you shall name him Jesus. He will be great and will be called Son of the Most High, and the Lord God will give him the throne of David his father, and he will rule over the house of Jacob forever, and of his Kingdom there will be no end." But Mary said to the angel, "How can this be, since I have no relations with a man?" And the angel said to her in reply, "The Holy Spirit will come upon you, and the power of the Most High will overshadow you. Therefore the child to be born will be called holy, the Son of God. And behold, Elizabeth, your relative, has also conceived a son in her old age, and this is the sixth month for her who was called barren; for nothing will be impossible for God." Mary said, "Behold, I am the handmaid of the Lord. May it be done to me according to your word." Then the angel departed from her.

FRIDAY OF THE FIFTH WEEK OF LENT

First Reading   **Jeremiah 20:10-13**

I hear the whisperings of many:

"Terror on every side! Denounce! Let us denounce him!" All those who were my friends are on the watch for any misstep of mine. "Perhaps he will be trapped; then we can prevail, and take our vengeance on him." But the LORD is with me, like a mighty champion: my persecutors will stumble, they will not triumph. In their failure they will be put to utter shame, to lasting, unforgettable confusion. O LORD of hosts, you who test the just, who probe mind and heart, let me witness the vengeance you take on them, for to you I have entrusted my cause. Sing to the LORD, praise the LORD, for he has rescued the life of the poor from the power of the wicked!

Responsorial Psalm   **Psalm 18:2-3a, 3bc-4, 5-6, 7**

R. (7) In my distress I called upon the Lord, and he heard my voice.

I love you, O LORD, my strength, O LORD, my rock, my fortress, my deliverer. **R.**

My God, my rock of refuge, my shield, the horn of my salvation, my stronghold!

Praised be the LORD, I exclaim, and I am safe from my enemies. **R.**

The breakers of death surged round about me, the destroying floods overwhelmed me; the cords of the nether world enmeshed me, the snares of death overtook me. **R.**

In my distress I called upon the LORD and cried out to my God; from his temple he heard my voice, and my cry to him reached his ears. **R.**

Verse before the Gospel   John 6:63c, 68c

Your words, Lord, are Spirit and life; you have the words of everlasting life.

Gospel   John 10:31-42

The Jews picked up rocks to stone Jesus. Jesus answered them, "I have shown you many good works from my Father. For which of these are you trying to stone me?" The Jews answered him, "We are not stoning you for a good work but for blasphemy. You, a man, are making yourself God." Jesus answered them, "Is it not written in your law, 'I said, 'You are gods'"? If it calls them gods to whom the word of God came, and Scripture cannot be set aside, can you say that the one whom the Father has consecrated and sent into the world blasphemes because I said, 'I am the Son of God'? If I do not perform my Father's works, do not believe me; but if I perform them, even if you do not believe me, believe the works, so that you may realize and understand that the Father is in me and I am in the Father." Then they tried again to arrest him; but he escaped from their power. He went back across the Jordan to the place where John first baptized, and there he remained. Many came to him and said, "John performed no sign, but everything John said about this man was true." And many there began to believe in him.

SATURDAY OF THE FIFTH WEEK OF LENT

First Reading   Ezekiel 37:21-28

Thus says the Lord GOD:

I will take the children of Israel from among the nations to which they have come, and gather them from all sides to bring them back to their land. I will make them one nation upon the land, in the mountains of Israel, and there shall be one prince for them all. Never again shall they be two nations, and never again shall they be divided into two kingdoms. No longer shall they defile themselves with their idols, their abominations, and all their transgressions. I will deliver them from all their sins of apostasy, and cleanse them so that they may be my people and I may be their God. My servant David shall be prince over them, and there shall be one shepherd for them all; they shall live by my statutes and carefully observe my decrees. They shall live on the land that I gave to my servant Jacob, the land where their fathers lived; they shall live on it forever, they, and their children, and their children's children, with my servant David their prince forever. I will make with them a covenant of peace; it shall be an everlasting covenant with them, and I will multiply them, and put my

274

sanctuary among them forever. My dwelling shall be with them; I will be their God, and they shall be my people. Thus the nations shall know that it is I, the LORD, who make Israel holy, when my sanctuary shall be set up among them forever.

Responsorial Psalm   Jeremiah 31:10, 11-12abcd, 13

R. (10d) The Lord will guard us, as a shepherd guards his flock.

Hear the word of the LORD, O nations, proclaim it on distant isles, and say: He who scattered Israel, now gathers them together, he guards them as a shepherd his flock. **R.**

The LORD shall ransom Jacob, he shall redeem him from the hand of his conqueror. Shouting, they shall mount the heights of Zion, they shall come streaming to the LORD's blessings: The grain, the wine, and the oil, the sheep and the oxen. **R.**

Then the virgins shall make merry and dance, and young men and old as well. I will turn their mourning into joy, I will console and gladden them after their sorrows. **R.**

Verse before the Gospel   Ezekiel 18:31

Cast away from you all the crimes you have committed, says the LORD, and make for yourselves a new heart and a new spirit.

Gospel   John 11:45-56

Many of the Jews who had come to Mary and seen what Jesus had done began to believe in him. But some of them went to the Pharisees and told them what Jesus had done. So the chief priests and the Pharisees convened the Sanhedrin and said, "What are we going to do? This man is performing many signs. If we leave him alone, all will believe in him, and the Romans will come and take away both our land and our nation." But one of them, Caiaphas, who was high priest that year, said to them, "You know nothing, nor do you consider that it is better for you that one man should die instead of the people, so that the whole nation may not perish." He did not say this on his own, but since he was high priest for that year, he prophesied that Jesus was going to die for the nation, and not only for the nation, but also to gather into one the dispersed children of God. So from that day on they planned to kill him. So Jesus no longer walked about in public among the Jews, but he left for the region near the desert, to a town called Ephraim, and there he remained with his disciples. Now the Passover of the Jews was near, and many went up from the country to Jerusalem before Passover to purify themselves. They looked for Jesus and said to one another as they were in the temple area, "What do you think? That he will not come to the feast?"

SUNDAY, MARCH 28, 2021

PALM SUNDAY OF THE LORD'S PASSION

AT THE PROCESSION WITH PALMS

Gospel   **Mark 11:1-10 or John 12:12-16**

Mark 11:1-10

When Jesus and his disciples drew near to Jerusalem, to Bethphage and Bethany at the Mount of Olives, he sent two of his disciples and said to them, "Go into the village opposite you, and immediately on entering it, you will find a colt tethered on which no one has ever sat. Untie it and bring it here. If anyone should say to you, 'Why are you doing this?' reply, 'The Master has need of it and will send it back here at once.'" So they went off and found a colt tethered at a gate outside on the street, and they untied it. Some of the bystanders said to them, "What are you doing, untying the colt?" They answered them just as Jesus had told them to, and they permitted them to do it. So they brought the colt to Jesus and put their cloaks over it. And he sat on it. Many people spread their cloaks on the road, and others spread leafy branches that they had cut from the fields. Those preceding him as well as those following kept crying out: "Hosanna! Blessed is he who comes in the name of the Lord! Blessed is the kingdom of our father David that is to come! Hosanna in the highest!"

Or:

John 12:12-16

When the great crowd that had come to the feast heard that Jesus was coming to Jerusalem, they took palm branches and went out to meet him, and cried out: "Hosanna! "Blessed is he who comes in the name of the Lord, the king of Israel."

Jesus found an ass and sat upon it, as is written:

Fear no more, O daughter Zion; see, your king comes, seated upon an ass's colt. His disciples did not understand this at first, but when Jesus had been glorified they remembered that these things were written about him and that they had done this for him.

AT THE MASS

First Reading Isaiah 50:4-7

The Lord GOD has given me a well-trained tongue, that I might know how to speak to the weary a word that will rouse them. Morning after morning he opens my ear that I may hear; and I have not rebelled, have not turned back. I gave my back to those who beat me, my cheeks to those who plucked my beard; my face I did not shield from buffets and spitting. The Lord GOD is my help, therefore I am not disgraced; I have set my face like flint, knowing that I shall not be put to shame.

Responsorial Psalm   Psalm 22:8-9, 17-18, 19-20, 23-24

R. (2a) My God, my God, why have you abandoned me?

All who see me scoff at me; they mock me with parted lips, they wag their heads: "He relied on the LORD; let him deliver him, let him rescue him, if he loves him." **R.**

Indeed, many dogs surround me, a pack of evildoers closes in upon me; they have pierced my hands and my feet; I can count all my bones. **R.**

They divide my garments among them, and for my vesture they cast lots. But you, O LORD, be not far from me; O my help, hasten to aid me. **R.**

I will proclaim your name to my brethren; in the midst of the assembly I will praise you: "You who fear the LORD, praise him; all you descendants of Jacob, give glory to him; revere him, all you descendants of Israel!" **R.**

Second Reading   Philippians 2:6-11

Christ Jesus, though he was in the form of God, did not regard equality with God something to be grasped. Rather, he emptied himself, taking the form of a slave, coming in human likeness; and found human in appearance, he humbled himself, becoming obedient to the point of death, even death on a cross. Because of this, God greatly exalted him and bestowed on him the name which is above every name, that at the name of Jesus every knee should bend, of those in heaven and on earth and under the earth, and every tongue confess that Jesus Christ is Lord, to the glory of God the Father.

Verse before the Gospel   Philippians 2:8-9

Christ became obedient to the point of death, even death on a cross. Because of this, God greatly exalted him and bestowed on him the name which is above every name.

Gospel   Mark 14:1—15:47 or Mark 15:1-39

Mark 14:1-15:47

The Passover and the Feast of Unleavened Bread were to take place in two days' time. So the chief priests and the scribes were seeking a way to arrest him by treachery and put him to death. They said, "Not during the festival, for fear that there may be a riot among the people."

When he was in Bethany reclining at table in the house of Simon the leper, a woman came with an alabaster jar of perfumed oil, costly genuine spikenard. She broke the alabaster jar and poured it on his head. There were some who were indignant. "Why has there been this waste of perfumed oil? It could have been sold for more than three hundred days' wages and the money given to the poor." They were infuriated with her. Jesus said, "Let her alone. Why do you make trouble for her? She has done a good thing for me. The poor you will always have with you, and whenever you wish you can do good to them, but you will not always have me. She has done what she could. She has anticipated anointing my body for burial. Amen, I say to you, wherever the gospel is proclaimed to the whole world, what she has done will be told in memory of her."

Then Judas Iscariot, one of the Twelve, went off to the chief priests to hand him over to them. When they heard him they were pleased and promised to pay him money. Then he looked for an opportunity to hand him over.

On the first day of the Feast of Unleavened Bread, when they sacrificed the Passover lamb, his disciples said to him, "Where do you want us to go and prepare for you to eat the Passover?" He sent two of his disciples and said to them, "Go into the city and a man will meet you, carrying a jar of water. Follow him. Wherever he enters, say to the master of the house, 'The Teacher says, "Where is my guest room where I may eat the Passover with my disciples?"' Then he will show you a large upper room furnished and ready. Make the preparations for us there." The disciples then went off, entered the city, and found it just as he had told them; and they prepared the Passover.

When it was evening, he came with the Twelve. And as they reclined at table and were eating, Jesus said, "Amen, I say to you, one of you will betray me, one who is eating with me." They began to be distressed and to say to him, one by one, "Surely it is not I?" He said to them, "One of the Twelve, the one who dips with me into the dish. For the Son of Man indeed goes, as it is written of him, but woe to that man by whom the Son of Man is betrayed. It would be better for that man if he had never been born."

While they were eating, he took bread, said the blessing, broke it, and gave it to them, and said, "Take it; this is my body." Then he took a cup, gave thanks, and gave it to them, and they all drank from it. He said to them, "This is my blood of the covenant, which will be shed for many. Amen, I say to you, I shall not drink again the fruit of the vine until the day when I drink it new in the kingdom of God." Then, after singing a hymn, they went out to the Mount of Olives.

Then Jesus said to them, "All of you will have your faith shaken, for it is written: *I will strike the shepherd, and the sheep will be dispersed.* But after I have been raised up, I shall go before you to Galilee." Peter said to him, "Even though all should have their faith shaken, mine will not be." Then Jesus said to him, "Amen, I say to you, this very night before the cock crows twice you will deny me three times. But he vehemently replied, "Even though I should have to die with you, I will not deny you." And they all spoke similarly.

Then they came to a place named Gethsemane, and he said to his disciples, "Sit here while I pray." He took with him Peter, James, and John, and began to be troubled and distressed. Then he said to them, "My soul is sorrowful even to death. Remain here and keep watch." He advanced a little and fell to the ground and prayed that if it were possible the hour might pass by him; he said, "Abba, Father, all things are possible to you. Take this cup away from me, but not what I will but what you will." When he returned he found them asleep. He said to Peter, "Simon, are you asleep? Could you not keep watch for one hour? Watch and pray that you may not undergo the test. The spirit is willing but the flesh is weak." Withdrawing again, he prayed, saying the same thing. Then he returned once more and found them asleep, for they could not keep their eyes open and did not know what to answer him. He returned a third time and said to them, "Are you still sleeping and taking your rest? It is enough. The hour has come. Behold, the Son of Man is to be handed over to sinners. Get up, let us go. See, my betrayer is at hand."

Then, while he was still speaking, Judas, one of the Twelve, arrived, accompanied by a crowd with swords and clubs who had come from the chief priests, the scribes, and the elders. His betrayer had arranged a signal with them, saying, "The man I shall kiss is the one; arrest him and lead him away securely." He came and immediately went over to him and said, "Rabbi." And he kissed him. At this they laid hands on him and arrested him. One of the bystanders drew his sword, struck the high priest's servant, and cut off his ear. Jesus said to them in reply, "Have you come out as against a robber, with swords and clubs, to seize me? Day after day I was with you teaching in the temple area, yet you did not arrest me; but that the Scriptures may be fulfilled." And they all left him and fled. Now a young man followed him wearing nothing but a linen cloth about his body. They seized him, but he left the cloth behind and ran off naked.

They led Jesus away to the high priest, and all the chief priests and the elders and the scribes came together. Peter followed him at a distance into the high priest's courtyard and was seated with the guards, warming himself at the fire. The chief priests and the entire Sanhedrin kept trying to obtain testimony against Jesus in order to put him to death, but they found none. Many gave false witness against him, but their testimony did not agree. Some took the stand and testified falsely against him, alleging, "We heard him say, 'I will destroy this temple made with hands and within three days I will build another not made with hands.'" Even so their testimony did not agree. The high priest rose before the assembly and questioned Jesus, saying, "Have you no answer? What are these men testifying against you?" But he was silent and answered nothing. Again the high priest asked him and said to him, "Are you the Christ, the son of the Blessed One?" Then Jesus answered, "I am; and 'you will see the Son of Man seated at the right hand of the Power and coming with the clouds of heaven.'" At that the high priest tore his garments and said, "What further need have we of witnesses? You have heard the blasphemy. What do you think?" They all condemned him as deserving to die. Some began to spit on him. They blindfolded him and struck him and said to him, "Prophesy!" And the guards greeted him with blows.

While Peter was below in the courtyard, one of the high priest's maids came along. Seeing Peter warming himself, she looked intently at him and said, "You too were with the Nazarene, Jesus." But he denied it saying, "I neither know nor understand what you are talking about." So he went out into the outer court. Then the cock crowed. The maid saw him and began again to say to the bystanders, "This man is one of them." Once again he denied it. A little later the bystanders said to Peter once more, "Surely you are one of them; for you too are a Galilean." He began to curse and to swear, "I do not know this man about whom you are talking." And immediately a cock crowed a second time. Then Peter remembered the word that Jesus had said to him, "Before the cock crows twice you will deny me three times." He broke down and wept.

As soon as morning came, the chief priests with the elders and the scribes, that is, the whole Sanhedrin held a council. They bound Jesus, led him away, and handed him over to Pilate. Pilate questioned him, "Are you the king of the Jews?" He said to him in reply, "You say so." The chief priests accused him of many things. Again Pilate questioned him, "Have you no answer? See how many things they accuse you of." Jesus gave him no further answer, so that Pilate was amazed.

Now on the occasion of the feast he used to release to them one prisoner whom they requested. A man called Barabbas was then in prison along with the rebels who had committed murder in a rebellion. The crowd came forward and began to ask him to do for them as he was accustomed. Pilate answered, "Do you want me to release to you the king of the Jews?" For he knew that it was out of envy that the chief priests had handed him over. But the chief priests stirred up the crowd to have him release Barabbas for them instead. Pilate again said to them in reply, "Then what do you want me to do with the man you call the king of the Jews?" They shouted again, "Crucify him." Pilate said to them, "Why? What evil has he done?" They only shouted the louder, "Crucify him." So Pilate, wishing to satisfy the crowd, released Barabbas to them and, after he had Jesus scourged, handed him over to be crucified.

The soldiers led him away inside the palace, that is, the praetorium, and assembled the whole cohort. They clothed him in purple and, weaving a crown of thorns, placed it on him. They began to salute him with, "Hail, King of the Jews!" and kept striking his head with a reed and spitting upon him. They knelt before him in homage. And when they had mocked him, they stripped him of the purple cloak, dressed him in his own clothes, and led him out to crucify him.

They pressed into service a passer-by, Simon, a Cyrenian, who was coming in from the country, the father of Alexander and Rufus, to carry his cross.

They brought him to the place of Golgotha — which is translated Place of the Skull —, they gave him wine drugged with myrrh, but he did not take it. Then they crucified him and divided his garments by casting lots for them to see what each should take. It was nine o'clock in the morning when they crucified him. The inscription of the charge against him read, "The King of the Jews." With him they crucified two revolutionaries, one on his right and one on his left. Those passing by reviled him shaking their heads and saying, "Aha! You who would destroy the temple and rebuild it in three days, save yourself by coming down from the cross." Likewise the chief priests, with the scribes, mocked him among themselves and said, "He saved others; he cannot save himself. Let the Christ, the King of Israel, come down now from the cross that we may see and believe." Those who were crucified with him also kept abusing him.

At noon darkness came over the whole land until three in the afternoon. And at three o'clock Jesus cried out in a loud voice, *"Eloi, Eloi, lema sabachthani?"* which is translated, "My God, my God, why have you forsaken me?" Some of the bystanders who heard it said, "Look, he is calling Elijah." One of them ran, soaked a sponge with wine, put it on a reed and gave it to him to drink saying, "Wait, let us see if Elijah comes to take him down." Jesus gave a loud cry and breathed his last.

[Here all kneel and pause for a short time.]

The veil of the sanctuary was torn in two from top to bottom. When the centurion who stood facing him saw how he breathed his last he said, "Truly this man was the Son of God!" There were also women looking on from a distance. Among them were Mary Magdalene, Mary the mother of the younger James and of Joses, and Salome. These women had followed him when he was in

Galilee and ministered to him. There were also many other women who had come up with him to Jerusalem.

When it was already evening, since it was the day of preparation, the day before the sabbath, Joseph of Arimathea, a distinguished member of the council, who was himself awaiting the kingdom of God, came and courageously went to Pilate and asked for the body of Jesus. Pilate was amazed that he was already dead. He summoned the centurion and asked him if Jesus had already died. And when he learned of it from the centurion, he gave the body to Joseph. Having bought a linen cloth, he took him down, wrapped him in the linen cloth, and laid him in a tomb that had been hewn out of the rock. Then he rolled a stone against the entrance to the tomb. Mary Magdalene and Mary the mother of Joses watched where he was laid.

Or:

Mk 15:1-39

As soon as morning came, the chief priests with the elders and the scribes, that is, the whole Sanhedrin held a council. They bound Jesus, led him away, and handed him over to Pilate. Pilate questioned him, "Are you the king of the Jews?" He said to him in reply, "You say so." The chief priests accused him of many things. Again Pilate questioned him, "Have you no answer? See how many things they accuse you of." Jesus gave him no further answer, so that Pilate was amazed.

Now on the occasion of the feast he used to release to them one prisoner whom they requested. A man called Barabbas was then in prison along with the rebels who had committed murder in a rebellion. The crowd came forward and began to ask him to do for them as he was accustomed. Pilate answered, "Do you want me to release to you the king of the Jews?" For he knew that it was out of envy that the chief priests had handed him over. But the chief priests stirred up the crowd to have him release Barabbas for them instead. Pilate again said to them in reply, "Then what do you want me to do with the man you call the king of the Jews?" They shouted again, "Crucify him." Pilate said to them, "Why? What evil has he done?" They only shouted the louder, "Crucify him." So Pilate, wishing to satisfy the crowd, released Barabbas to them and, after he had Jesus scourged, handed him over to be crucified.

The soldiers led him away inside the palace, that is, the praetorium, and assembled the whole cohort. They clothed him in purple and, weaving a crown of thorns, placed it on him. They began to salute him with, "Hail, King of the Jews!" and kept striking his head with a reed and spitting upon him. They knelt before him in homage. And when they had mocked him, they stripped him of the purple cloak, dressed him in his own clothes, and led him out to crucify him.

They pressed into service a passer-by, Simon, a Cyrenian, who was coming in from the country, the father of Alexander and Rufus, to carry his cross.

They brought him to the place of Golgotha —which is translated Place of the Skull — they gave him wine drugged with myrrh, but he did not take it. Then they crucified him and divided his garments by casting lots for them to see what each should take. It was nine o'clock in the morning when they crucified him. The inscription of the charge against him read, "The King of the Jews." With him they crucified two revolutionaries, one on his right and one on his left. Those passing by reviled him, shaking their heads and saying, "Aha! You who would destroy the temple and rebuild it in three days, save yourself by coming down from the cross." Likewise the chief priests, with the scribes, mocked him among themselves and said, "He saved others; he cannot save himself. Let the Christ, the King of Israel, come down now from the cross that we may see and believe." Those who were crucified with him also kept abusing him.

At noon darkness came over the whole land until three in the afternoon. And at three o'clock Jesus cried out in a loud voice, "*Eloi, Eloi, lema sabachthani?*" which is translated, "My God, my God, why have you forsaken me?" Some of the bystanders who heard it said, "Look, he is calling Elijah." One of them ran, soaked a sponge with wine, put it on a reed and gave it to him to drink saying, "Wait, let us see if Elijah comes to take him down." Jesus gave a loud cry and breathed his last.

[Here all kneel and pause for a short time.]

The veil of the sanctuary was torn in two from top to bottom. When the centurion who stood facing him saw how he breathed his last he said, "Truly this man was the Son of God!"

MONDAY OF HOLY WEEK

First Reading   **Isaiah 42:1-7**

Here is my servant whom I uphold, my chosen one with whom I am pleased, upon whom I have put my Spirit; he shall bring forth justice to the nations, not crying out, not shouting, not making his voice heard in the street. A bruised reed he shall not break, and a smoldering wick he shall not quench, until he establishes justice on the earth; the coastlands will wait for his teaching. Thus says

God, the LORD, who created the heavens and stretched them out, who spreads out the earth with its crops, Who gives breath to its people and spirit to those who walk on it: I, the LORD, have called you for the victory of justice, I have grasped you by the hand; I formed you, and set you as a covenant of the people, a light for the nations, To open the eyes of the blind, to bring out prisoners from confinement, and from the dungeon, those who live in darkness.

Responsorial Psalm   Psalm 27:1, 2, 3, 13-14

R. (1a) The Lord is my light and my salvation.

The LORD is my light and my salvation; whom should I fear? The LORD is my life's refuge; of whom should I be afraid? **R.**

When evildoers come at me to devour my flesh, my foes and my enemies themselves stumble and fall. **R.**

Though an army encamp against me, my heart will not fear; though war be waged upon me, even then will I trust. **R.**

I believe that I shall see the bounty of the LORD in the land of the living. Wait for the LORD with courage; be stouthearted, and wait for the LORD. **R.**

Verse before the Gospel

Hail to you, our King; you alone are compassionate with our faults.

Gospel   John 12:1-11

Six days before Passover Jesus came to Bethany, where Lazarus was, whom Jesus had raised from the dead. They gave a dinner for him there, and Martha served, while Lazarus was one of those reclining at table with him. Mary took a liter of costly perfumed oil made from genuine aromatic nard and anointed the feet of Jesus and dried them with her hair; the house was filled with the fragrance of the oil. Then Judas the Iscariot, one of his disciples, and the one who would betray him, said, "Why was this oil not sold for three hundred days' wages and given to the poor?" He said this not because he cared about the poor but because he was a thief and held the money bag and used to steal the contributions. So Jesus said, "Leave her alone. Let her keep this for the day of my burial. You always have the poor with you, but you do not always have me." The large crowd of the Jews found out that he was there and came, not only because of him, but also to see Lazarus, whom he had raised from the dead. And the chief priests plotted to kill Lazarus too, because many of the Jews were turning away and believing in Jesus because of him.

TUESDAY, MARCH 30, 2021

TUESDAY OF HOLY WEEK

First Reading   **Isaiah 49:1-6**

Hear me, O islands, listen, O distant peoples. The LORD called me from birth, from my mother's womb he gave me my name. He made of me a sharp-edged sword and concealed me in the shadow of his arm. He made me a polished arrow, in his quiver he hid me. You are my servant, he said to me, Israel, through whom I show my glory. Though I thought I had toiled in vain, and for nothing, uselessly, spent my strength, yet my reward is with the LORD, my recompense is with my God. For now the LORD has spoken who formed me as his servant from the womb, That Jacob may be brought back to him and Israel gathered to him; and I am made glorious in the sight of the LORD, and my God is now my strength! It is too little, he says, for you to be my servant, to raise up the tribes of Jacob, and restore the survivors of Israel; I will make you a light to the nations, that my salvation may reach to the ends of the earth.

Responsorial Psalm   Psalm 71:1-2, 3-4a, 5ab-6ab, 15 and 17

R. (15ab) I will sing of your salvation.
In you, O LORD, I take refuge; let me never be put to shame. In your justice rescue me, and deliver me; incline your ear to me, and save me. **R.**

Be my rock of refuge, a stronghold to give me safety, for you are my rock and my fortress. O my God, rescue me from the hand of the wicked. **R.**
For you are my hope, O LORD; my trust, O God, from my youth. On you I depend from birth; from my mother's womb you are my strength. **R.**
My mouth shall declare your justice, day by day your salvation. O God, you have taught me from my youth, and till the present I proclaim your wondrous deeds. **R.**

Verse before the Gospel

Hail to you, our King, obedient to the Father; you were led to your crucifixion like a gentle lamb to the slaughter.

Gospel   John 13:21-33, 36-38

Reclining at table with his disciples, Jesus was deeply troubled and testified, "Amen, amen, I say to you, one of you will betray me." The disciples looked at one another, at a loss as to whom he meant. One of his disciples, the one whom Jesus loved, was reclining at Jesus' side. So Simon Peter nodded to him to find out whom he meant. He leaned back against Jesus' chest and said to him, "Master, who is it?" Jesus answered, "It is the one to whom I hand the morsel after I have dipped it." So he dipped the morsel and took it and handed it to Judas, son of Simon the Iscariot. After Judas took the morsel, Satan entered him. So Jesus said to him, "What you are going to do, do quickly." Now none of those reclining at table realized why he said this to him. Some thought that since Judas kept the money bag, Jesus had told him, "Buy what we need for the feast," or to give something to the poor. So Judas took the morsel and left at once. And it was night.

When he had left, Jesus said, "Now is the Son of Man glorified, and God is glorified in him. If God is glorified in him, God will also glorify him in himself, and he will glorify him at once. My children, I will be with you only a little while longer. You will look for me, and as I told the Jews, 'Where I go you cannot come,' so now I say it to you." Simon Peter said to him, "Master, where are you going?" Jesus answered him, "Where I am going, you cannot follow me now, though you will follow later." Peter said to him, "Master, why can I not follow you now? I will lay down my life for you." Jesus answered, "Will you lay down your life for me? Amen, amen, I say to you, the cock will not crow before you deny me three times."

WEDNESDAY OF HOLY WEEK

First Reading   Isaiah 50:4-9a

The Lord GOD has given me a well-trained tongue, that I might know how to speak to the weary a word that will rouse them.

Morning after morning he opens my ear that I may hear; And I have not rebelled, have not turned back. I gave my back to those who beat me, my cheeks to those who plucked my beard; my face I did not shield from buffets and spitting. The Lord GOD is my help, therefore I am not disgraced; I have set my face like flint, knowing that I shall not be put to shame. He is near who upholds my right; if anyone wishes to oppose me, let us appear together. Who disputes my right? Let him confront me. See, the Lord GOD is my help; who will prove me wrong?

Responsorial Psalm   Psalm 69:8-10, 21-22, 31 and 33-34

R. (14c) Lord, in your great love, answer me.

For your sake I bear insult, and shame covers my face. I have become an outcast to my brothers, a stranger to my mother's sons, because zeal for your house consumes me, and the insults of those who blaspheme you fall upon me. **R.**

Insult has broken my heart, and I am weak, I looked for sympathy, but there was none; for consolers, not one could I find. Rather they put gall in my food, and in my thirst they gave me vinegar to drink. **R.**

I will praise the name of God in song, and I will glorify him with thanksgiving: "See, you lowly ones, and be glad; you who seek God, may your hearts revive! For the LORD hears the poor, and his own who are in bonds he spurns not." **R.**

Verse before the Gospel

Hail to you, our King; you alone are compassionate with our errors.

Or:

Hail to you, our King, obedient to the Father; you were led to your crucifixion like a gentle lamb to the slaughter.

Gospel   Matthew 26:14-25

One of the Twelve, who was called Judas Iscariot, went to the chief priests and said, "What are you willing to give me if I hand him over to you?" They paid him thirty pieces of silver, and from that time on he looked for an opportunity to hand him over.

On the first day of the Feast of Unleavened Bread, the disciples approached Jesus and said, "Where do you want us to prepare for you to eat the Passover?" He said, "Go into the city to a certain man and tell him, 'The teacher says, my appointed time draws near; in your house I shall celebrate the Passover with my disciples.'" The disciples then did as Jesus had ordered, and prepared the Passover.

When it was evening, he reclined at table with the Twelve. And while they were eating, he said, "Amen, I say to you, one of you will betray me." Deeply distressed at this, they began to say to him one after another, "Surely it is not I, Lord?" He said in reply, "He who has dipped his hand into the dish with me is the one who will betray me. The Son of Man indeed goes, as it is written of him, but woe to that man by whom the Son of Man is betrayed. It would be better for that man if he had never been born." Then Judas, his betrayer, said in reply, "Surely it is not I, Rabbi?" He answered, "You have said so."

THURSDAY, APRIL 1, 2021

HOLY THURSDAY

(Chrism Mass and Evening Mass of the Lord's Supper)

HOLY THURSDAY: CHRISM MASS

First Reading   Isaiah 61:1-3a, 6a, 8b-9

The Spirit of the Lord GOD is upon me, because the LORD has anointed me; He has sent me to bring glad tidings to the lowly, to heal the brokenhearted, to proclaim liberty to the captives and release to the prisoners, to announce a year of favor from the LORD and a day of vindication by our God, to comfort all who mourn; To place on those who mourn in Zion a diadem instead of ashes, To give them oil of gladness in place of mourning, a glorious mantle instead of a listless spirit. You yourselves shall be named priests of the LORD, ministers of our God shall you be called. I will give them their recompense faithfully, a lasting covenant I will make with them. Their descendants shall be renowned among the nations, and their offspring among the peoples; all who see them shall acknowledge them as a race the LORD has blessed.

Responsorial Psalm   Psalm 89:21-22, 25 and 27

R. (2) For ever I will sing the goodness of the Lord.

"I have found David, my servant; with my holy oil I have anointed him. That my hand may always be with him; and that my arm may make him strong." R.

"My faithfulness and my mercy shall be with him; and through my name shall his horn be exalted. He shall say of me, 'You are my father, my God, the Rock, my savior!'" **R.**

Second Reading   Revelation 1:5-8

[Grace to you and peace] from Jesus Christ, who is the faithful witness, the firstborn of the dead and ruler of the kings of the earth. To him who loves us and has freed us from our sins by his Blood, who has made us into a Kingdom, priests for his God and Father, to him be glory and power forever and ever. Amen.

Behold, he is coming amid the clouds, and every eye will see him, even those who pierced him. All the peoples of the earth will lament him. Yes. Amen.

"I am the Alpha and the Omega," says the Lord God, "the one who is and who was and who is to come, the Almighty."

Verse before the Gospel   Isaiah 61:1 (cited in Luke 4:18)

The Spirit of the LORD is upon me; for he has sent me to bring glad tidings to the poor.

Gospel   Luke 4:16-21

Jesus came to Nazareth, where he had grown up, and went according to his custom into the synagogue on the Sabbath day. He stood up to read and was handed a scroll of the prophet Isaiah. He unrolled the scroll and found the passage where it was written:
The Spirit of the Lord is upon me, because he has anointed me to bring glad tidings to the poor. He has sent me to proclaim liberty to captives and recovery of sight to the blind, to let the oppressed go free, and to proclaim a year acceptable to the Lord.

Rolling up the scroll, he handed it back to the attendant and sat down, and the eyes of all in the synagogue looked intently at him. He said to them, "Today this Scripture passage is fulfilled in your hearing."

HOLY THURSDAY: EVENING MASS OF THE LORD'S SUPPER

First Reading   **Exodus 12:1-8, 11-14**

The LORD said to Moses and Aaron in the land of Egypt,

"This month shall stand at the head of your calendar; you shall reckon it the first month of the year. Tell the whole community of Israel: On the tenth of this month every one of your families must procure for itself a lamb, one apiece for each household. If a family is too small for a whole lamb, it shall join the nearest household in procuring one and shall share in the lamb in proportion to the number of persons who partake of it. The lamb must be a year-old male and without blemish. You may take it from either the sheep or the goats. You shall keep it until the fourteenth day of this month, and then, with the whole assembly of Israel present, it shall be slaughtered during the evening twilight. They shall take some of its blood and apply it to the two doorposts and the lintel of every house in which they partake of the lamb. That same night they shall eat its roasted flesh with unleavened bread and bitter herbs.

"This is how you are to eat it: with your loins girt, sandals on your feet and your staff in hand, you shall eat like those who are in flight. It is the Passover of the LORD. For on this same night I will go through Egypt, striking down every firstborn of the land, both man and beast, and executing judgment on all the gods of Egypt—

I, the LORD! But the blood will mark the houses where you are. Seeing the blood, I will pass over you; thus, when I strike the land of Egypt, no destructive blow will come upon you.

"This day shall be a memorial feast for you, which all your generations shall celebrate with pilgrimage to the LORD, as a perpetual institution."

Responsorial Psalm   Psalm 116:12-13, 15-16bc, 17-18.

R. (1 Cor 10:16) Our blessing-cup is a communion with the Blood of Christ.

How shall I make a return to the LORD for all the good he has done for me? The cup of salvation I will take up, and I will call upon the name of the LORD. **R.**

Precious in the eyes of the LORD is the death of his faithful ones. I am your servant, the son of your handmaid; you have loosed my bonds. **R.**

To you will I offer sacrifice of thanksgiving, and I will call upon the name of the LORD. My vows to the LORD I will pay in the presence of all his people. **R.**

Second Reading   1 Corinthians 11:23-26

Brothers and sisters:

I received from the Lord what I also handed on to you, that the Lord Jesus, on the night he was handed over, took bread, and, after he had given thanks, broke it and said, "This is my body that is for you. Do this in remembrance of me."

In the same way also the cup, after supper, saying, "This cup is the new covenant in my blood. Do this, as often as you drink it, in remembrance of me." For as often as you eat this bread and drink the cup, you proclaim the death of the Lord until he comes.

Verse before the Gospel   John 13:34

I give you a new commandment, says the Lord: love one another as I have loved you.

Gospel   John 13:1-15

Before the feast of Passover, Jesus knew that his hour had come to pass from this world to the Father. He loved his own in the world and he loved them to the end. The devil had already induced Judas, son of Simon the Iscariot, to hand him over.

So, during supper, fully aware that the Father had put everything into his power and that he had come from God and was returning to God, he rose from supper and took off his outer garments. He took a towel and tied it around his waist. Then he poured water into a basin and began to wash the disciples' feet and dry them with the towel around his waist. He came to Simon Peter, who said to him, "Master, are you going to wash my feet?" Jesus answered and said to him, "What I am doing, you do not understand now, but you will understand later." Peter said to him, "You will never wash my feet." Jesus answered him, "Unless I wash you, you will have no inheritance with me." Simon Peter said to him, "Master, then not only my feet, but my hands and head as well." Jesus said to him, "Whoever has bathed has no need except to have his feet washed, for he is clean all over; so you are clean, but not all." For he knew who would betray him; for this reason, he said, "Not all of you are clean." So when he had washed their feet and put his garments back on and reclined at table again, he said to them, "Do you realize what I have done for you? You call me 'teacher' and 'master,' and rightly so, for indeed I am. If I, therefore, the master and teacher, have washed your feet, you ought to wash one another's feet. I have given you a model to follow, so that as I have done for you, you should also do."

GOOD FRIDAY OF THE LORD'S PASSION

First Reading   **Isaiah 52:13-53:12**

See, my servant shall prosper, he shall be raised high and greatly exalted. Even as many were amazed at him so marred was his look beyond human semblance and his appearance beyond that of the sons of man so shall he startle many nations, because of him kings shall stand speechless; for those who have not been told shall see, those who have not heard shall ponder it.

Who would believe what we have heard? To whom has the arm of the LORD been revealed? He grew up like a sapling before him, like a shoot from the parched earth; there was in him no stately bearing to make us look at him, nor appearance that would attract us to him. He was spurned and avoided by people, a man of suffering, accustomed to infirmity, one of those from whom people hide their faces, spurned, and we held him in no esteem.

Yet it was our infirmities that he bore, our sufferings that he endured, while we thought of him as stricken, as one smitten by God and afflicted. But he was pierced for our offenses, crushed for our sins; upon him was the chastisement that makes us whole, by his stripes we were healed. We had all gone astray like sheep, each following his own way; but the LORD laid upon him the guilt of us all. Though he was harshly treated, he submitted and opened not his mouth; like a lamb led to the slaughter or a sheep before the shearers, he was silent and opened not his mouth. Oppressed and condemned, he was taken away, and who would have thought any more of his destiny? When he was cut off from the land of the living, and smitten for the sin of his people, a grave was assigned him among the wicked and a burial place with evildoers, though he had done no wrong nor spoken any falsehood. But the LORD was pleased to crush him in infirmity.

If he gives his life as an offering for sin, he shall see his descendants in a long life, and the will of the LORD shall be accomplished through him. Because of his affliction he shall see the light in fullness of days; through his suffering, my servant shall justify many, and their guilt he shall bear. Therefore I will give him his portion among the great, and he shall divide the spoils with the mighty, because he surrendered himself to death and was counted among the wicked; and he shall take away the sins of many, and win pardon for their offenses.

Responsorial Psalm   Psalm 31:2, 6, 12-13, 15-
16, 17, 25

R. (Lk 23:46) Father, into your hands I commend my spirit.
In you, O LORD, I take refuge; let me never be put to shame. In your justice rescue me. Into your hands I commend my spirit; you will redeem me, O LORD, O faithful God. **R.**
For all my foes I am an object of reproach, a laughingstock to my neighbors, and a dread to my friends; they who see me abroad flee from me. I am forgotten like the unremembered dead; I am like a dish that is broken. **R.**

But my trust is in you, O LORD; I say, "You are my God. In your hands is my destiny; rescue me from the clutches of my enemies and my persecutors." **R.** Father, into your hands I commend my spirit. Let your face shine upon your servant; save me in your kindness. Take courage and be stouthearted, all you who hope in the LORD. **R.**

Second Reading   Hebrews 4:14-16; 5:7-9

Brothers and sisters:

Since we have a great high priest who has passed through the heavens, Jesus, the Son of God, let us hold fast to our confession. For we do not have a high priest who is unable to sympathize with our weaknesses, but one who has similarly been tested in every way, yet without sin. So let us confidently approach the throne of grace to receive mercy and to find grace for timely help.

In the days when Christ was in the flesh, he offered prayers and supplications with loud cries and tears to the one who was able to save him from death, and he was heard because of his reverence. Son though he was, he learned obedience from what he suffered; and when he was made perfect, he became the source of eternal salvation for all who obey him.

Verse before the Gospel   Philippians 2:8-9

Christ became obedient to the point of death, even death on a cross. Because of this, God greatly exalted him and bestowed on him the name which is above every other name.

Gospel   John 18:1-19:42

Jesus went out with his disciples across the Kidron valley to where there was a garden, into which he and his disciples entered. Judas his betrayer also knew the place, because Jesus had often met there with his disciples. So Judas got a band of soldiers and guards from the chief priests and the Pharisees and went there with lanterns, torches, and weapons. Jesus, knowing everything that was going to happen to him, went out and said to them, "Whom are you looking for?" They answered him, "Jesus the Nazorean." He said to them, "I AM." Judas his betrayer was also with them. When he said to them, "I AM, "they turned away and fell to the ground. So he again asked them, "Whom are you looking for?" They said, "Jesus the Nazorean." Jesus answered, "I told you that I AM. So if you are looking for me, let these men go." This was to fulfill what he had said, "I have not lost any of those you gave me." Then Simon Peter, who had a sword, drew it, struck the high priest's slave, and cut off his right ear. The slave's name was Malchus. Jesus said to Peter, "Put your sword into its scabbard. Shall I not drink the cup that the Father gave me?"

So the band of soldiers, the tribune, and the Jewish guards seized Jesus, bound him, and brought him to Annas first. He was the father-in-law of Caiaphas, who was high priest that year. It was Caiaphas who had counseled the Jews that it was better that one man should die rather than the people.

Simon Peter and another disciple followed Jesus. Now the other disciple was known to the high priest, and he entered the courtyard of the high priest with Jesus. But Peter stood at the gate outside. So the other disciple, the acquaintance of the high priest, went out and spoke to the gatekeeper and brought Peter in. Then the maid who was the gatekeeper said to Peter, "You are not one of this man's disciples, are you?" He said, "I am not." Now the slaves and the guards were standing around a charcoal fire that they had made, because it was cold, and were warming themselves. Peter was also standing there keeping warm.

The high priest questioned Jesus about his disciples and about his doctrine. Jesus answered him, "I have spoken publicly to the world. I have always taught in a synagogue or in the temple area where all the Jews gather, and in secret I have said nothing. Why ask me? Ask those who heard me what I said to them. They know what I said." When he had said this, one of the temple guards standing there struck Jesus and said, "Is this the way you answer the high priest?" Jesus answered him, "If I have spoken wrongly, testify to the wrong; but if I have spoken rightly, why do you strike me?" Then Annas sent him bound to Caiaphas the high priest.

Now Simon Peter was standing there keeping warm. And they said to him, "You are not one of his disciples, are you?" He denied it and said, "I am not." One of the slaves of the high priest, a relative of the one whose ear Peter had cut off, said, "Didn't I see you in the garden with him?" Again Peter denied it. And immediately the cock crowed.

Then they brought Jesus from Caiaphas to the praetorium. It was morning. And they themselves did not enter the praetorium, in order not to be defiled so that they could eat the Passover. So Pilate came out to them and said, "What charge do you bring against this man?" They answered and said to him, "If he were not a criminal, we would not have handed him over to you." At this, Pilate said to them, "Take him yourselves, and judge him according to your law." The Jews answered him, "We do not have the right to execute anyone, "in order that the word of Jesus might be fulfilled that he said indicating the kind of death he would die. So Pilate went back into the praetorium and summoned Jesus and said to him, "Are you the King of the Jews?" Jesus answered, "Do you say this on your own or have others told you about me?" Pilate answered, "I am not a Jew, am I? Your own nation and the chief priests handed you over to me. What have you done?" Jesus answered, "My kingdom does not belong to this world. If my kingdom did belong to this world, my attendants would be fighting to keep me from being handed over to the Jews. But as it is, my kingdom is not here." So Pilate said to him, "Then you are a king?" Jesus answered, "You say I am a king. For this I was born and for this I came into the world, to testify to the truth. Everyone who belongs to the truth listens to my voice." Pilate said to him, "What is truth?" When he had said this, he again went out to the Jews and said to them, "I find no guilt in him. But you have a custom that I release one prisoner to you at Passover. Do you want me to release to you the King of the Jews?" They cried out again, "Not this one but Barabbas!" Now Barabbas was a revolutionary.

Then Pilate took Jesus and had him scourged. And the soldiers wove a crown out of thorns and placed it on his head, and clothed him in a purple cloak, and they came to him and said, "Hail, King of the Jews!" And they struck him repeatedly. Once more Pilate went out and said to them, "Look, I am bringing him out to you, so that you may know that I find no guilt in him." So Jesus came out, wearing the crown of thorns and the purple cloak. And he said to them, Behold, the man!" When the chief priests and the guards saw him they cried out, "Crucify him, crucify him!" Pilate said to them, "Take him yourselves and crucify him.

I find no guilt in him." The Jews answered, "We have a law, and according to that law he ought to die, because he made himself the Son of God." Now when Pilate heard this statement, he became even more afraid, and went back into the praetorium and said to Jesus, "Where are you from?" Jesus did not answer him. So Pilate said to him, "Do you not speak to me? Do you not know that I have power to release you and I have power to crucify you?" Jesus answered him, "You would have no power over me if it had not been given to you from above. For this reason the one who handed me over to you has the greater sin." Consequently, Pilate tried to release him; but the Jews cried out, "If you release him, you are not a Friend of Caesar. Everyone who makes himself a king opposes Caesar."

When Pilate heard these words he brought Jesus out and seated him on the judge's bench in the place called Stone Pavement, in Hebrew, Gabbatha. It was preparation day for Passover, and it was about noon. And he said to the Jews, "Behold, your king!" They cried out, "Take him away, take him away! Crucify him!" Pilate said to them, "Shall I crucify your king?" The chief priests answered, "We have no king but Caesar." Then he handed him over to them to be crucified. So they took Jesus, and, carrying the cross himself, he went out to what is called the Place of the Skull, in Hebrew, Golgotha. There they crucified him, and with him two others, one on either side, with Jesus in the middle. Pilate also had an inscription written and put on the cross. It read, "Jesus the Nazorean, the King of the Jews." Now many of the Jews read this inscription, because the place where Jesus was crucified was near the city; and it was written in Hebrew, Latin, and Greek. So the chief priests of the Jews said to Pilate, "Do not write 'The King of the Jews,' but that he said, 'I am the King of the Jews'." Pilate answered, "What I have written, I have written."

When the soldiers had crucified Jesus, they took his clothes and divided them into four shares, a share for each soldier. They also took his tunic, but the tunic was seamless, woven in one piece from the top down. So they said to one another, "Let's not tear it, but cast lots for it to see whose it will be, " in order that the passage of Scripture might be fulfilled that says:

They divided my garments among them, and for my vesture they cast lots. This is what the soldiers did.

Standing by the cross of Jesus were his mother and his mother's sister, Mary the wife of Clopas, and Mary of Magdala. When Jesus saw his mother and the disciple there whom he loved he said to his mother, "Woman, behold, your son." Then he said to the disciple, "Behold, your mother." And from that hour the disciple took her into his home. After this, aware that everything was now finished, in order that the Scripture might be fulfilled, Jesus said, "I thirst." There was a vessel filled with common wine. So they put a sponge soaked in wine on a sprig of hyssop and put it up to his mouth. When Jesus had taken the wine, he said, "It is finished." And bowing his head, he handed over the spirit.

[Here all kneel and pause for a short time.]

Now since it was preparation day, in order that the bodies might not remain on the cross on the Sabbath, for the Sabbath day of that week was a solemn one, the Jews asked Pilate that their legs be broken and that they be taken down. So the soldiers came and broke the legs of the first and then of the other one who was crucified with Jesus. But when they came to Jesus and saw that he was already dead, they did not break his legs, but one soldier thrust his lance into his side, and immediately blood and water flowed out.

An eyewitness has testified, and his testimony is true; he knows that he is speaking the truth, so that you also may come to believe. For this happened so that the Scripture passage might be fulfilled: *Not a bone of it will be broken.*

And again another passage says: *They will look upon him whom they have pierced.*

After this, Joseph of Arimathea, secretly a disciple of Jesus for fear of the Jews, asked Pilate if he could remove the body of Jesus. And Pilate permitted it. So he came and took his body. Nicodemus, the one who had first come to him at night, also came bringing a mixture of myrrh and aloes weighing about one hundred pounds. They took the body of Jesus and bound it with burial cloths along with the spices, according to the Jewish burial custom. Now in the place where he had been crucified there was a garden, and in the garden a new tomb, in which no one had yet been buried. So they laid Jesus there because of the Jewish preparation day; for the tomb was close by.

HOLY SATURDAY: AT THE EASTER VIGIL IN THE HOLY NIGHT OF EASTER

First Reading   Genesis 1:1-2:2 or Genesis 1:1, 26-31a

Genesis 1:1-2:2

In the beginning, when God created the heavens and the earth, the earth was a formless wasteland, and darkness covered the abyss, while a mighty wind swept over the waters.

Then God said, "Let there be light," and there was light. God saw how good the light was. God then separated the light from the darkness. God called the light "day," and the darkness he called "night." Thus evening came, and morning followed—the first day.

Then God said, "Let there be a dome in the middle of the waters, to separate one body of water from the other." And so it happened: God made the dome, and it separated the water above the dome from the water below it. God called the dome "the sky." Evening came, and morning followed—the second day.

Then God said, "Let the water under the sky be gathered into a single basin, so that the dry land may appear." And so it happened: the water under the sky was gathered into its basin, and the dry land appeared. God called the dry land "the earth," and the basin of the water he called "the sea." God saw how good it was. Then God said, "Let the earth bring forth vegetation: every kind of plant that bears seed and every kind of fruit tree on earth that bears fruit with its seed in it." And so it happened: the earth brought forth every kind of plant that bears seed and every kind of fruit tree on earth that bears fruit with its seed in it. God saw how good it was. Evening came, and morning followed—the third day.

Then God said: "Let there be lights in the dome of the sky, to separate day from night. Let them mark the fixed times, the days and the years, and serve as luminaries in the dome of the sky, to shed light upon the earth." And so it happened: God made the two great lights, the greater one to govern the day, and the lesser one to govern the night; and he made the stars. God set them in the dome of the sky, to shed light upon the earth, to govern the day and the night, and to separate the light from the darkness. God saw how good it was. Evening came, and morning followed—the fourth day.

Then God said, "Let the water teem with an abundance of living creatures, and on the earth let birds fly beneath the dome of the sky." And so it happened: God created the great sea monsters and all kinds of swimming creatures with which the water teems, and all kinds of winged birds. God saw how good it was, and God blessed them, saying, "Be fertile, multiply, and fill the water of the seas; and let the birds multiply on the earth." Evening came, and morning followed—the fifth day.

Then God said, "Let the earth bring forth all kinds of living creatures: cattle, creeping things, and wild animals of all kinds." And so it happened: God made all kinds of wild animals, all kinds of cattle, and all kinds of creeping things of the earth. God saw how good it was. Then God said: "Let us make man in our image, after our likeness. Let them have dominion over the fish of the sea, the birds of the air, and the cattle, and over all the wild animals and all the creatures that crawl on the ground." God created man in his image; in the image of God he created him; male and female he created them. God blessed them, saying: "Be fertile and multiply; fill the earth and subdue it. Have dominion over the fish of the sea, the birds of the air, and all the living things that move on the earth." God also said: "See, I give you every seed-bearing plant all over the earth and every tree that has seed-bearing fruit on it to be your food; and to all the animals of the land, all the birds of the air, and all the living creatures that crawl on the ground, I give all the green plants for food." And so it happened. God looked at everything he had made, and he found it very good.

Evening came, and morning followed—the sixth day. Thus the heavens and the earth and all their array were completed.

Since on the seventh day God was finished with the work he had been doing, he rested on the seventh day from all the work he had undertaken.

Or:

Genesis 1:1, 26-31a

In the beginning, when God created the heavens and the earth, God said: "Let us make man in our image, after our likeness. Let them have dominion over the fish of the sea, the birds of the air, and the cattle, and over all the wild animals and all the creatures that crawl on the ground." God created man in his image; in the image of God he created him; male and female he created them. God blessed them, saying: "Be fertile and multiply; fill the earth and subdue it. Have dominion over the fish of the sea, the birds of the air, and all the living things that move on the earth."

God also said: "See, I give you every seed-bearing plant all over the earth and every tree that has seed-bearing fruit on it to be your food; and to all the animals of the land, all the birds of the air, and all the living creatures that crawl on the ground, I give all the green plants for food." And so it happened. God looked at everything he had made, and found it very good.

Responsorial Psalm   Psalm 104:1-2, 5-6, 10, 12, 13-14, 24, 35

R. (30) Lord, send out your Spirit, and renew the face of the earth.

Bless the LORD, O my soul! O LORD, my God, you are great indeed! You are clothed with majesty and glory, robed in light as with a cloak. **R.**

You fixed the earth upon its foundation, not to be moved forever; with the ocean, as with a garment, you covered it; above the mountains the waters stood. **R.**

You send forth springs into the watercourses that wind among the mountains. Beside them the birds of heaven dwell; from among the branches they send forth their song. **R.**

You water the mountains from your palace; the earth is replete with the fruit of your works. You raise grass for the cattle, and vegetation for man's use, Producing bread from the earth. **R.**

How manifold are your works, O LORD! In wisdom you have wrought them all—the earth is full of your creatures. Bless the LORD, O my soul! **R.**

Or:
Psalm 33:4-5, 6-7, 12-13, 20 and 22
R. (5b) The earth is full of the goodness of the Lord.
Upright is the word of the LORD, and all his works are trustworthy. He loves justice and right; of the kindness of the LORD the earth is full. **R.**

By the word of the LORD the heavens were made; by the breath of his mouth all their host. He gathers the waters of the sea as in a flask; in cellars he confines the deep. **R.**

Blessed the nation whose God is the LORD, the people he has chosen for his own inheritance. From heaven the LORD looks down; he sees all mankind. **R.**

Our soul waits for the LORD, who is our help and our shield. May your kindness, O LORD, be upon us who have put our hope in you. **R.**

<u>**Second Reading**</u>   **Genesis 22:1-18 or 22:1-2, 9a, 10-13, 15-18**

Genesis 22:1-18

God put Abraham to the test. He called to him, "Abraham!" "Here I am," he replied. Then God said: "Take your son Isaac, your only one, whom you love, and go to the land of Moriah. There you shall offer him up as a holocaust on a height that I will point out to you." Early the next morning Abraham saddled his donkey, took with him his son Isaac and two of his servants as well, and with the wood that he had cut for the holocaust, set out for the place of which God had told him.

On the third day Abraham got sight of the place from afar. Then he said to his servants: "Both of you stay here with the donkey, while the boy and I go on over yonder. We will worship and then come back to you." Thereupon Abraham took the wood for the holocaust and laid it on his son Isaac's shoulders, while he himself carried the fire and the knife. As the two walked on together, Isaac spoke to his father Abraham: "Father!" Isaac said. "Yes, son, " he replied. Isaac continued, "Here are the fire and the wood, but where is the sheep for the holocaust?" "Son," Abraham answered, "God himself will provide the sheep for the holocaust." Then the two continued going forward.

When they came to the place of which God had told him, Abraham built an altar there and arranged the wood on it. Next he tied up his son Isaac, and put him on top of the wood on the altar. Then he reached out and took the knife to slaughter his son. But the LORD's messenger called to him from heaven, "Abraham, Abraham!" "Here I am!" he answered. "Do not lay your hand on the boy," said the messenger. "Do not do the least thing to him. I know now how devoted you are to God, since you did not withhold from me your own beloved son." As Abraham looked about, he spied a ram caught by its horns in the thicket. So he went and took the ram and offered it up as a holocaust in place of his son. Abraham named the site Yahweh-yireh; hence people now say, "On the mountain the LORD will see."

Again the LORD's messenger called to Abraham from heaven and said: "I swear by myself, declares the LORD, that because you acted as you did in not withholding from me your beloved son, I will bless you abundantly and make your descendants as countless as the stars of the sky and the sands of the seashore; your descendants shall take possession of the gates of their enemies, and in your descendants all the nations of the earth shall find blessing-- all this because you obeyed my command."

Or:
Genesis 22:1-2, 9a, 10-13, 15-18

God put Abraham to the test. He called to him, "Abraham!" "Here I am," he replied. Then God said: "Take your son Isaac, your only one, whom you love, and go to the land of Moriah. There you shall offer him up as a holocaust on a height that I will point out to you."

When they came to the place of which God had told him, Abraham built an altar there and arranged the wood on it. Then he reached out and took the knife to slaughter his son. But the LORD's messenger called to him from heaven, "Abraham, Abraham!" "Here I am," he answered. "Do not lay your hand on the boy, "said the messenger. "Do not do the least thing to him. I know now how devoted you are to God, since you did not withhold from me your own beloved son." As Abraham looked about, he spied a ram caught by its horns in the thicket. So he went and took the ram and offered it up as a holocaust in place of his son.

Again the LORD's messenger called to Abraham from heaven and said: "I swear by myself, declares the LORD, that because you acted as you did in not withholding from me your beloved son, I will bless you abundantly and make your descendants as countless as the stars of the sky and the sands of the seashore; your descendants shall take possession of the gates of their enemies, and in your descendants all the nations of the earth shall find blessing-- all this because you obeyed my command."

Responsorial Psalm   Psalm 16:5, 8, 9-10, 11

R. (1) You are my inheritance, O Lord.

O LORD, my allotted portion and my cup, you it is who hold fast my lot. I set the LORD ever before me; with him at my right hand I shall not be disturbed. **R.**

Therefore my heart is glad and my soul rejoices, my body, too, abides in confidence; because you will not abandon my soul to the netherworld, nor will you suffer your faithful one to undergo corruption. **R.**

You will show me the path to life, fullness of joys in your presence, the delights at your right hand forever. **R.**

Third Reading   Exodus 14:15-15:1

The LORD said to Moses, "Why are you crying out to me? Tell the Israelites to go forward. And you, lift up your staff and, with hand outstretched over the sea, split the sea in two, that the Israelites may pass through it on dry land. But I will make the Egyptians so obstinate that they will go in after them. Then I will receive glory through Pharaoh and all his army, his chariots and charioteers. The Egyptians shall know that I am the LORD, when I receive glory through Pharaoh and his chariots and charioteers."

The angel of God, who had been leading Israel's camp, now moved and went around behind them. The column of cloud also, leaving the front, took up its place behind them, so that it came between the camp of the Egyptians and that of Israel. But the cloud now became dark, and thus the night passed without the rival camps coming any closer together all night long. Then Moses stretched out his hand over the sea, and the LORD swept the sea with a strong east wind throughout the night and so turned it into dry land. When the water was thus divided, the Israelites marched into the midst of the sea on dry land, with the water like a wall to their right and to their left.

The Egyptians followed in pursuit; all Pharaoh's horses and chariots and charioteers went after them right into the midst of the sea. In the night watch just before dawn the LORD cast through the column of the fiery cloud upon the Egyptian force a glance that threw it into a panic; and he so clogged their chariot wheels that they could hardly drive. With that the Egyptians sounded the retreat before Israel, because the LORD was fighting for them against the Egyptians.

Then the LORD told Moses, "Stretch out your hand over the sea, that the water may flow back upon the Egyptians, upon their chariots and their charioteers." So Moses stretched out his hand over the sea, and at dawn the sea flowed back to its normal depth. The Egyptians were fleeing head on toward the sea, when the LORD hurled them into its midst. As the water flowed back, it covered the chariots and the charioteers of Pharaoh's whole army which had followed the Israelites into the sea. Not a single one of them escaped. But the Israelites had marched on dry land through the midst of the sea, with the water like a wall to their right and to their left. Thus the LORD saved Israel on that day from the power of the Egyptians. When Israel saw the Egyptians lying dead on the seashore and beheld the great power that the LORD had shown against the Egyptians, they feared the LORD and believed in him and in his servant Moses.

Then Moses and the Israelites sang this song to the LORD: I will sing to the LORD, for he is gloriously triumphant; horse and chariot he has cast into the sea.

Responsorial Psalm   Exodus 15:1-2, 3-4, 5-6, 17-18
R. (1b) Let us sing to the Lord; he has covered himself in glory.

I will sing to the LORD, for he is gloriously triumphant; horse and chariot he has cast into the sea. My strength and my courage is the LORD, and he has been my savior. He is my God, I praise him; the God of my father, I extol him. **R.**

The LORD is a warrior, LORD is his name! Pharaoh's chariots and army he hurled into the sea; the elite of his officers were submerged in the Red Sea. **R.**

The flood waters covered them, they sank into the depths like a stone. Your right hand, O LORD, magnificent in power, your right hand, O LORD, has shattered the enemy. **R.**

You brought in the people you redeemed and planted them on the mountain of your inheritance the place where you made your seat, O LORD, the sanctuary, LORD, which your hands established. The LORD shall reign forever and ever. **R.**

Fourth Reading   Isaiah 54:5-14

The One who has become your husband is your Maker; his name is the LORD of hosts; your redeemer is the Holy One of Israel, called God of all the earth. The LORD calls you back, like a wife forsaken and grieved in spirit, a wife married in youth and then cast off, says your God. For a brief moment I abandoned you, but with great tenderness I will take you back. In an outburst of wrath, for a moment I hid my face from you; but with enduring love I take pity on you, says the LORD, your redeemer. This is for me like the days of Noah, when I swore that the waters of Noah should never again deluge the earth; so I have sworn not to be angry with you, or to rebuke you. Though the mountains leave their place and the hills be shaken, my love shall never leave you nor my covenant of peace be shaken, says the LORD, who has mercy on you. O afflicted one, storm-battered and unconsoled, I lay your pavements in carnelians, and your foundations in sapphires; I will make your battlements of rubies, your gates of carbuncles, and all your walls of precious stones. All your children shall be taught by the LORD, and great shall be the peace of your children. In justice shall you be established, far from the fear of oppression, where destruction cannot come near you.

Responsorial Psalm   Psalm 30:2, 4, 5-6, 11-12, 13

R. (2a) I will praise you, Lord, for you have rescued me.

I will extol you, O LORD, for you drew me clear and did not let my enemies rejoice over me. O LORD, you brought me up from the netherworld; you preserved me from among those going down into the pit. **R.**

Sing praise to the LORD, you his faithful ones, and give thanks to his holy name. For his anger lasts but a moment; a lifetime, his good will. At nightfall, weeping enters in, but with the dawn, rejoicing. **R.**

Hear, O LORD, and have pity on me; O LORD, be my helper. You changed my mourning into dancing; O LORD, my God, forever will I give you thanks. **R.**

Fifth Reading   Isaiah 55:1-11

Thus says the LORD:

All you who are thirsty, come to the water! You who have no money, come, receive grain and eat; come, without paying and without cost, drink wine and milk! Why spend your money for what is not bread, your wages for what fails to satisfy? Heed me, and you shall eat well, you shall delight in rich fare. Come to me heedfully, listen, that you may have life. I will renew with you the everlasting covenant, the benefits assured to David. As I made him a witness to the peoples, a leader and commander of nations, so shall you summon a nation you knew not, and nations that knew you not shall run to you, because of the LORD, your God, the Holy One of Israel, who has glorified you.

Seek the LORD while he may be found, call him while he is near. Let the scoundrel forsake his way, and the wicked man his thoughts; let him turn to the LORD for mercy; to our God, who is generous in forgiving. For my thoughts are not your thoughts, nor are your ways my ways, says the LORD. As high as the heavens are above the earth, so high are my ways above your ways and my thoughts above your thoughts.

For just as from the heavens the rain and snow come down and do not return there till they have watered the earth, making it fertile and fruitful, giving seed to the one who sows and bread to the one who eats, so shall my word be that goes forth from my mouth; my word shall not return to me void, but shall do my will, achieving the end for which I sent it.

Responsorial Psalm   Isaiah 12:2-3, 4, 5-6

R. (3) You will draw water joyfully from the springs of salvation.

God indeed is my savior; I am confident and unafraid. My strength and my courage is the LORD, and he has been my savior. With joy you will draw water at the fountain of salvation. **R.**

Give thanks to the LORD, acclaim his name; among the nations make known his deeds, proclaim how exalted is his name. **R.**

Sing praise to the LORD for his glorious achievement; let this be known throughout all the earth. Shout with exultation, O city of Zion, for great in your midst is the Holy One of Israel! **R.**

Sixth Reading   Baruch 3:9-15, 32-4:4

Hear, O Israel, the commandments of life:

listen, and know prudence! How is it, Israel, that you are in the land of your foes, grown old in a foreign land, defiled with the dead, accounted with those destined for the netherworld? You have forsaken the fountain of wisdom! Had you walked in the way of God, you would have dwelt in enduring peace. Learn where prudence is, where strength, where understanding; that you may know also where are length of days, and life, where light of the eyes, and peace. Who has found the place of wisdom, who has entered into her treasuries?

The One who knows all things knows her; he has probed her by his knowledge — The One who established the earth for all time, and filled it with four-footed beasts; he who dismisses the light, and it departs, calls it, and it obeys him trembling; before whom the stars at their posts shine and rejoice; when he calls them, they answer, "Here we are!" shining with joy for their Maker. Such is our God; no other is to be compared to him: he has traced out the whole way of understanding, and has given her to Jacob, his servant, to Israel, his beloved son.

Since then she has appeared on earth, and moved among people. She is the book of the precepts of God, the law that endures forever; all who cling to her will live, but those will die who forsake her. Turn, O Jacob, and receive her: walk by her light toward splendor. Give not your glory to another, your privileges to an alien race. Blessed are we, O Israel; for what pleases God is known to us!

Responsorial Psalm   **Psalm 19:8, 9, 10, 11**

R. (John 6:68c) Lord, you have the words of everlasting life.

The law of the LORD is perfect, refreshing the soul; the decree of the LORD is trustworthy, giving wisdom to the simple. **R.**

The precepts of the LORD are right, rejoicing the heart; the command of the LORD is clear, enlightening the eye. **R.**

The fear of the LORD is pure, enduring forever; the ordinances of the LORD are true, all of them just. **R.**

They are more precious than gold, than a heap of purest gold; sweeter also than syrup or honey from the comb. **R.**

Seventh Reading   Ezra 36:16-17a, 18-28

The word of the LORD came to me, saying: Son of man, when the house of Israel lived in their land, they defiled it by their conduct and deeds. Therefore I poured out my fury upon them because of the blood that they poured out on the ground, and because they defiled it with idols. I scattered them among the nations, dispersing them over foreign lands; according to their conduct and deeds I judged them. But when they came among the nations wherever they came, they served to profane my holy name, because it was said of them: "These are the people of the LORD, yet they had to leave their land." So I have relented because of my holy name which the house of Israel profaned among the nations where they came. Therefore say to the house of Israel: Thus says the Lord GOD:

Not for your sakes do I act, house of Israel, but for the sake of my holy name, which you profaned among the nations to which you came. I will prove the holiness of my great name, profaned among the nations, in whose midst you have profaned it. Thus the nations shall know that I am the LORD, says the Lord GOD, when in their sight I prove my holiness through you. For I will take you away from among the nations, gather you from all the foreign lands, and bring you back to your own land. I will sprinkle clean water upon you to cleanse you from all your impurities, and from all your idols I will cleanse you. I will give you a new heart and place a new spirit within you, taking from your bodies your stony hearts and giving you natural hearts. I will put my spirit within you and make you live by my statutes, careful to observe my decrees. You shall live in the land I gave your fathers; you shall be my people, and I will be your God.

Responsorial Psalm   Psalm 42:3, 5; 43:3, 4

[When baptism is celebrated]

R. (42:2) Like a deer that longs for running streams, my soul longs for you, my God.

Athirst is my soul for God, the living God. When shall I go and behold the face of God? **R**

I went with the throng and led them in procession to the house of God, amid loud cries of joy and thanksgiving, with the multitude keeping festival. **R.**

Send forth your light and your fidelity; they shall lead me on and bring me to your holy mountain, to your dwelling-place. **R.**

Then will I go in to the altar of God, the God of my gladness and joy; then will I give you thanks upon the harp, O God, my God! **R.**

Or

Isaiah 12:2-3, 4bcd, 5-6

[When baptism is not celebrated]

323

R. (3) You will draw water joyfully from the springs of salvation.

God indeed is my savior; I am confident and unafraid. My strength and my courage is the LORD, and he has been my savior. With joy you will draw water at the fountain of salvation. **R.**

Give thanks to the LORD, acclaim his name; among the nations make known his deeds, proclaim how exalted is his name. **R.**

Sing praise to the LORD for his glorious achievement; let this be known throughout all the earth. Shout with exultation, O city of Zion, for great in your midst is the Holy One of Israel! **R.**

Or

Psalm 51:12-13, 14-15, 18-19

[When baptism is not celebrated]

R. (12a) Create a clean heart in me, O God.

A clean heart create for me, O God, and a steadfast spirit renew within me. Cast me not out from your presence, and your Holy Spirit take not from me. **R.**

Give me back the joy of your salvation, and a willing spirit sustain in me. I will teach transgressors your ways, and sinners shall return to you. **R.**

For you are not pleased with sacrifices; should I offer a holocaust, you would not accept it. My sacrifice, O God, is a contrite spirit; a heart contrite and humbled, O God, you will not spurn. **R.**

Epistle   **Romans 6:3-11**

Brothers and sisters:

Are you unaware that we who were baptized into Christ Jesus were baptized into his death? We were indeed buried with him through baptism into death, so that, just as Christ was raised from the dead by the glory of the Father, we too might live in newness of life.

For if we have grown into union with him through a death like his, we shall also be united with him in the resurrection. We know that our old self was crucified with him, so that our sinful body might be done away with, that we might no longer be in slavery to sin. For a dead person has been absolved from sin. If, then, we have died with Christ, we believe that we shall also live with him. We know that Christ, raised from the dead, dies no more; death no longer has power over him. As to his death, he died to sin once and for all; as to his life, he lives for God. Consequently, you too must think of yourselves as being dead to sin and living for God in Christ Jesus.

Responsial Psalm   Psalm 118:1-2, 16-17, 22-23
R. Alleluia, alleluia, alleluia.

Give thanks to the LORD, for he is good, for his mercy endures forever. Let the house of Israel say, "His mercy endures forever."
R.

The right hand of the LORD has struck with power; the right hand of the LORD is exalted. I shall not die, but live, and declare the works of the LORD. **R.**

The stone the builders rejected has become the cornerstone. By the LORD has this been done; it is wonderful in our eyes. **R.**

Gospel   Mark 16:1-7

When the Sabbath was over, Mary Magdalene, Mary, the mother of James, and Salome bought spices so that they might go and anoint him. Very early when the sun had risen, on the first day of the week, they came to the tomb. They were saying to one another, "Who will roll back the stone for us from the entrance to the tomb? When they looked up, they saw that the stone had been rolled back; it was very large.

On entering the tomb they saw a young man sitting on the right side, clothed in a white robe, and they were utterly amazed. He said to them, "Do not be amazed! You seek Jesus of Nazareth, the crucified. He has been raised; he is not here. Behold the place where they laid him. But go and tell his disciples and Peter, 'He is going before you to Galilee; there you will see him, as he told you.'"

EASTER SUNDAY
THE RESURRECTION OF THE LORD

First Reading   **Acts 10:34a, 37-43**

Peter proceeded to speak and said:

"You know what has happened all over Judea, beginning in Galilee after the baptism that John preached, how God anointed Jesus of Nazareth with the Holy Spirit and power. He went about doing good and healing all those oppressed by the devil, for God was with him. We are witnesses of all that he did both in the country of the Jews and in Jerusalem. They put him to death by hanging him on a tree. This man God raised on the third day and granted that he be visible, not to all the people, but to us, the witnesses chosen by God in advance, who ate and drank with him after he rose from the dead. He commissioned us to preach to the people and testify that he is the one appointed by God as judge of the living and the dead. To him all the prophets bear witness, that everyone who believes in him will receive forgiveness of sins through his name."

Responsorial Psalm   Psalm 118:1-2, 16-17, 22-23

R. (24) This is the day the Lord has made; let us rejoice and be glad.

Or:

R. Alleluia.

Give thanks to the LORD, for he is good, for his mercy endures forever. Let the house of Israel say, "His mercy endures forever."
R.

"The right hand of the LORD has struck with power; the right hand of the LORD is exalted. I shall not die, but live, and declare the works of the LORD." **R.**

The stone which the builders rejected has become the cornerstone. By the LORD has this been done; it is wonderful in our eyes. **R.**

Second Reading   Col 3:1-4 or 1 Cor 5:6b-8

Colossians 3:1-4

Brothers and sisters:

If then you were raised with Christ, seek what is above, where Christ is seated at the right hand of God. Think of what is above, not of what is on earth. For you have died, and your life is hidden with Christ in God. When Christ your life appears, then you too will appear with him in glory.

Or:

1 Corinthians 5:6b-8

Brothers and sisters:

Do you not know that a little yeast leavens all the dough? Clear out the old yeast, so that you may become a fresh batch of dough, inasmuch as you are unleavened. For our paschal lamb, Christ, has been sacrificed. Therefore, let us celebrate the feast, not with the old yeast, the yeast of malice and wickedness, but with the unleavened bread of sincerity and truth.

Sequence   Victimae Paschali Laudes

Christians, to the Paschal Victim
  Offer your thankful praises!
A Lamb the sheep redeems;
  Christ, who only is sinless,
  Reconciles sinners to the Father.
Death and life have contended in that combat stupendous:
  The Prince of life, who died, reigns immortal.
Speak, Mary, declaring
  What you saw, wayfaring.
"The tomb of Christ, who is living,
  The glory of Jesus' resurrection;
bright angels attesting,
  The shroud and napkin resting.
Yes, Christ my hope is arisen;
  to Galilee he goes before you."
Christ indeed from death is risen, our new life obtaining.
  Have mercy, victor King, ever reigning!
  Amen. Alleluia.

Alleluia   1 Corinthian 5:7b-8a

R. Alleluia, alleluia.

Christ, our paschal lamb, has been sacrificed; let us then feast with joy in the Lord. **R.**

Gospel   John 20:1-9

On the first day of the week, Mary of Magdala came to the tomb early in the morning, while it was still dark, and saw the stone removed from the tomb. So she ran and went to Simon Peter and to the other disciple whom Jesus loved, and told them, "They have taken the Lord from the tomb, and we don't know where they put him." So Peter and the other disciple went out and came to the tomb. They both ran, but the other disciple ran faster than Peter and arrived at the tomb first; he bent down and saw the burial cloths there, but did not go in.

When Simon Peter arrived after him, he went into the tomb and saw the burial cloths there, and the cloth that had covered his head, not with the burial cloths but rolled up in a separate place. Then the other disciple also went in, the one who had arrived at the tomb first, and he saw and believed. For they did not yet understand the Scripture that he had to rise from the dead.

MONDAY IN THE OCTAVE OF EASTER

First Reading   Acts 2:14, 22-33

On the day of Pentecost, Peter stood up with the Eleven, raised his voice, and proclaimed: "You who are Jews, indeed all of you staying in Jerusalem. Let this be known to you, and listen to my words. "You who are children of Israel, hear these words. Jesus the Nazorean was a man commended to you by God with mighty deeds, wonders, and signs, which God worked through him in your midst, as you yourselves know. This man, delivered up by the set plan and foreknowledge of God, you killed, using lawless men to crucify him. But God raised him up, releasing him from the throes of death, because it was impossible for him to be held by it. For David says of him:

I saw the Lord ever before me, with him at my right hand I shall not be disturbed. Therefore my heart has been glad and my tongue has exulted; my flesh, too, will dwell in hope, because you will not abandon my soul to the nether world, nor will you suffer your holy one to see corruption. You have made known to me the paths of life; you will fill me with joy in your presence.

My brothers, one can confidently say to you about the patriarch David that he died and was buried, and his tomb is in our midst to this day. But since he was a prophet and knew that God had sworn an oath to him that he would set one of his descendants upon his throne, he foresaw and spoke of the resurrection of the Christ, that neither was he abandoned to the netherworld nor did his flesh see corruption. God raised this Jesus; of this we are all witnesses. Exalted at the right hand of God, he poured forth the promise of the Holy Spirit that he received from the Father, as you both see and hear."

Responsorial Psalm   Psalm 16:1-2a and 5, 7-8, 9-10, 11
R. (1) Keep me safe, O God; you are my hope.
Or:
R. Alleluia.

Keep me, O God, for in you I take refuge; I say to the LORD, "My Lord are you." O LORD, my allotted portion and my cup, you it is who hold fast my lot. **R.**

I bless the LORD who counsels me; even in the night my heart exhorts me. I set the LORD ever before me; with him at my right hand I shall not be disturbed. **R.**

Therefore my heart is glad and my soul rejoices, my body, too, abides in confidence; because you will not abandon my soul to the nether world, nor will you suffer your faithful one to undergo corruption. **R.**

You will show me the path to life, fullness of joys in your presence, the delights at your right hand forever. **R.**

Alleluia   Psalm 118:24

R. Alleluia, alleluia.

This is the day the LORD has made; let us be glad and rejoice in it. **R.**

Gospel   Matthew 28:8-15

Mary Magdalene and the other Mary went away quickly from the tomb, fearful yet overjoyed, and ran to announce the news to his disciples. And behold, Jesus met them on their way and greeted them. They approached, embraced his feet, and did him homage. Then Jesus said to them, "Do not be afraid. Go tell my brothers to go to Galilee, and there they will see me."

While they were going, some of the guard went into the city and told the chief priests all that had happened. The chief priests assembled with the elders and took counsel; then they gave a large sum of money to the soldiers, telling them, "You are to say, 'His disciples came by night and stole him while we were asleep.' And if this gets to the ears of the governor, we will satisfy him and keep you out of trouble." The soldiers took the money and did as they were instructed. And this story has circulated among the Jews to the present day.

TUESDAY, APRIL 6, 2021
TUESDAY IN THE OCTAVE OF EASTER

First Reading   **Acts 2: 36-41**

On the day of Pentecost, Peter said to the Jewish people, "Let the whole house of Israel know for certain that God has made him both Lord and Christ, this Jesus whom you crucified." Now when they heard this, they were cut to the heart, and they asked Peter and the other Apostles, "What are we to do, my brothers?" Peter said to them, "Repent and be baptized, every one of you, in the name of Jesus Christ, for the forgiveness of your sins; and you will receive the gift of the Holy Spirit. For the promise is made to you and to your children and to all those far off, whomever the Lord our God will call." He testified with many other arguments, and was exhorting them, "Save yourselves from this corrupt generation." Those who accepted his message were baptized, and about three thousand persons were added that day.

Responsorial Psalm   **Psalm 33:4-5, 18-19, 20 and 22**

R. (5b) The earth is full of the goodness of the Lord.

Or:

R. Alleluia.

Upright is the word of the LORD, and all his works are trustworthy. He loves justice and right; of the kindness of the LORD the earth is full. **R.**

See, the eyes of the LORD are upon those who fear him, upon those who hope for his kindness, to deliver them from death and preserve them in spite of famine. **R.**

Our soul waits for the LORD, who is our help and our shield. May your kindness, O LORD, be upon us who have put our hope in you. **R.**

Alleluia   Psalm 118:24

R. Alleluia, alleluia.

This is the day the LORD has made; let us be glad and rejoice in it.
R.

Gospel   John 20:11-18

Mary Magdalene stayed outside the tomb weeping. And as she wept, she bent over into the tomb and saw two angels in white sitting there, one at the head and one at the feet where the Body of Jesus had been. And they said to her, "Woman, why are you weeping?" She said to them, "They have taken my Lord, and I don't know where they laid him."

When she had said this, she turned around and saw Jesus there, but did not know it was Jesus. Jesus said to her, "Woman, why are you weeping? Whom are you looking for?" She thought it was the gardener and said to him, "Sir, if you carried him away, tell me where you laid him, and I will take him."

Jesus said to her, "Mary!" She turned and said to him in Hebrew, "Rabbouni," which means Teacher. Jesus said to her, "Stop holding on to me, for I have not yet ascended to the Father. But go to my brothers and tell them, 'I am going to my Father and your Father, to my God and your God.'" Mary went and announced to the disciples, "I have seen the Lord," and then reported what he had told her.

WEDNESDAY IN THE OCTAVE OF EASTER

First Reading _____ Acts 3:1-10

Peter and John were going up to the temple area for the three o'clock hour of prayer. And a man crippled from birth was carried and placed at the gate of the temple called "the Beautiful Gate" every day to beg for alms from the people who entered the temple. When he saw Peter and John about to go into the temple, he asked for alms. But Peter looked intently at him, as did John, and said, "Look at us." He paid attention to them, expecting to receive something from them. Peter said, "I have neither silver nor gold, but what I do have I give you: in the name of Jesus Christ the Nazorean, rise and walk." Then Peter took him by the right hand and raised him up, and immediately his feet and ankles grew strong. He leaped up, stood, and walked around, and went into the temple with them, walking and jumping and praising God. When all the people saw him walking and praising God, they recognized him as the one who used to sit begging at the Beautiful Gate of the temple, and they were filled with amazement and astonishment at what had happened to him.

Responsorial Psalm Psalm 105:1-2, 3-4, 6-7, 8-9
R. (3b) Rejoice, O hearts that seek the Lord.

Or:

R. Alleluia.

Give thanks to the LORD, invoke his name; make known among the nations his deeds. Sing to him, sing his praise, proclaim all his wondrous deeds. **R.**

Glory in his holy name; rejoice, O hearts that seek the LORD! Look to the LORD in his strength; seek to serve him constantly. **R.**

You descendants of Abraham, his servants, sons of Jacob, his chosen ones!

He, the LORD, is our God; throughout the earth his judgments prevail. **R.**

He remembers forever his covenant which he made binding for a thousand generations which he entered into with Abraham and by his oath to Isaac. **R.**

Alleluia	Psalm 118:24

R. Alleluia, alleluia.

This is the day the LORD has made; let us be glad and rejoice in it. **R.**

Gospel	Luke 24:13-35

That very day, the first day of the week, two of Jesus' disciples were going to a village seven miles from Jerusalem called Emmaus, and they were conversing about all the things that had occurred. And it happened that while they were conversing and debating, Jesus himself drew near and walked with them, but their eyes were prevented from recognizing him. He asked them, "What are you discussing as you walk along?" They stopped, looking downcast. One of them, named Cleopas, said to him in reply, "Are you the only visitor to Jerusalem who does not know of the things that have taken place there in these days?" And he replied to them, "What sort of things?" They said to him, "The things that happened to Jesus the Nazarene, who was a prophet mighty in deed and word before God and all the people, how our chief priests and rulers both handed him over to a sentence of death and crucified him. But we were hoping that he would be the one to redeem Israel; and besides all this, it is now the third day since this took place. Some women from our group, however, have astounded us: they were at the tomb early in the morning and did not find his Body; they came back and reported that they had indeed seen a vision of angels who announced that he was alive. Then some of those with us went to the tomb and found things just as the women had described, but him they did not see." And he said to them, "Oh, how foolish you are! How slow of heart to believe all that the prophets spoke! Was it not necessary that the Christ should suffer these things and enter into his glory?" Then beginning with Moses and all the prophets, he interpreted to them what referred to him in all the Scriptures.

As they approached the village to which they were going, he gave the impression that he was going on farther. But they urged him, "Stay with us, for it is nearly evening and the day is almost over." So he went in to stay with them. And it happened that, while he was with them at table, he took bread, said the blessing, broke it, and gave it to them. With that their eyes were opened and they recognized him, but he vanished from their sight. Then they said to each other, "Were not our hearts burning within us while he spoke to us on the way and opened the Scriptures to us?"

So they set out at once and returned to Jerusalem where they found gathered together the Eleven and those with them who were saying, "The Lord has truly been raised and has appeared to Simon!" Then the two recounted what had taken place on the way and how he was made known to them in the breaking of the bread.

THURSDAY IN THE OCTAVE OF EASTER

First Reading   **Acts 3:11-26**

As the crippled man who had been cured clung to Peter and John, all the people hurried in amazement toward them in the portico called "Solomon's Portico." When Peter saw this, he addressed the people, "You children of Israel, why are you amazed at this, and why do you look so intently at us as if we had made him walk by our own power or piety? The God of Abraham, the God of Isaac, and the God of Jacob, the God of our fathers, has glorified his servant Jesus whom you handed over and denied in Pilate's presence, when he had decided to release him. You denied the Holy and Righteous One and asked that a murderer be released to you. The author of life you put to death, but God raised him from the dead; of this we are witnesses. And by faith in his name, this man, whom you see and know, his name has made strong, and the faith that comes through it has given him this perfect health, in the presence of all of you. Now I know, brothers and sisters, that you acted out of ignorance, just as your leaders did; but God has thus brought to fulfillment what he had announced beforehand through the mouth of all the prophets, that his Christ would suffer. Repent, therefore, and be converted, that your sins may be wiped away, and that the Lord may grant you times of   refreshment and send you the Christ already appointed for you, Jesus, whom heaven must receive until the times of universal restoration of which God spoke through the mouth of his holy prophets from of old. For Moses said:

A prophet like me will the Lord, your God, raise up for you from among your own kin; to him you shall listen in all that he may say to you. Everyone who does not listen to that prophet will be cut off from the people.

"Moreover, all the prophets who spoke, from Samuel and those afterwards, also announced these days. You are the children of the prophets and of the covenant that God made with your ancestors when he said to Abraham, *in your offspring all the families of the earth shall be blessed.* For you first, God raised up his servant and sent him to bless you by turning each of you from your evil ways."

Responsorial Psalm   Psalm 8:2ab and 5, 6-7, 8-9

R. (2ab) O Lord, our God, how wonderful your name in all the earth!

Or:

R. Alleluia.

O LORD, our Lord, how glorious is your name over all the earth!
What is man that you should be mindful of him, or the son of man that you should care for him? **R.**

You have made him little less than the angels, and crowned him with glory and honor. You have given him rule over the works of your hands, putting all things under his feet. **R.**

All sheep and oxen, yes, and the beasts of the field, the birds of the air, the fishes of the sea, and whatever swims the paths of the seas. **R.**

Alleluia   **Psalm 118:24**

R. Alleluia, alleluia.

This is the day the LORD has made; let us be glad and rejoice in it.

R.

Gospel   Luke 24:35-48

The disciples of Jesus recounted what had taken place along the way, and how they had come to recognize him in the breaking of bread. While they were still speaking about this, he stood in their midst and said to them, "Peace be with you." But they were startled and terrified and thought that they were seeing a ghost. Then he said to them, "Why are you troubled? And why do questions arise in your hearts? Look at my hands and my feet, that it is I myself. Touch me and see, because a ghost does not have flesh and bones as you can see I have." And as he said this, he showed them his hands and his feet. While they were still incredulous for joy and were amazed, he asked them, "Have you anything here to eat?" They gave him a piece of baked fish; he took it and ate it in front of them. He said to them, "These are my words that I spoke to you while I was still with you, that everything written about me in the Law of Moses and in the prophets and psalms must be fulfilled." Then he opened their minds to understand the Scriptures. And he said to them, "Thus it is written that the Christ would suffer and rise from the dead on the third day and that repentance, for the forgiveness of sins, would be preached in his name to all the nations, beginning from Jerusalem. You are witnesses of these things."

FRIDAY IN THE OCTAVE OF EASTER

First Reading   **Acts 4:1-12**

After the crippled man had been cured, while Peter and John were still speaking to the people, the priests, the captain of the temple guard, and the Sadducees confronted them, disturbed that they were teaching the people and proclaiming in Jesus the resurrection of the dead. They laid hands on Peter and John and put them in custody until the next day, since it was already evening. But many of those who heard the word came to believe and the number of men grew to about five thousand.

On the next day, their leaders, elders, and scribes were assembled in Jerusalem, with Annas the high priest, Caiaphas, John, Alexander, and all who were of the high-priestly class. They brought them into their presence and questioned them, "By what power or by what name have you done this?" Then Peter, filled with the Holy Spirit, answered them, "Leaders of the people and elders: If we are being examined today about a good deed done to a cripple, namely, by what means he was saved, then all of you and all the people of Israel should know that it was in the name of Jesus Christ the Nazorean whom you crucified, whom God raised from the dead; in his name this man stands before you healed. *He is the stone rejected by you, the builders, which has become the cornerstone.* There is no salvation through anyone else, nor is there any other name under heaven given to the human race by which we are to be saved."

Responsorial Psalm   **Psalm 118:1-2 and 4, 22-24, 25-27a**

R. (22) The stone rejected by the builders has become the cornerstone.

Or:

R. Alleluia.

Give thanks to the LORD, for he is good, for his mercy endures forever. Let the house of Israel say, "His mercy endures forever." Let those who fear the LORD say, "His mercy endures forever." **R.** The stone which the builders rejected has become the cornerstone. By the LORD has this been done; it is wonderful in our eyes. This is the day the LORD has made; let us be glad and rejoice in it. **R.** O LORD, grant salvation! O LORD, grant prosperity! Blessed is he who comes in the name of the LORD; we bless you from the house of the LORD. The LORD is God, and he has given us light. **R.**

Alleluia   **Psalm 118:24**

R. Alleluia, alleluia.

This is the day the LORD has made; let us be glad and rejoice in it. **R.**

Gospel   **John 21:1-14**

Jesus revealed himself again to his disciples at the Sea of Tiberias. He revealed himself in this way. Together were Simon Peter, Thomas called Didymus, Nathanael from Cana in Galilee, Zebedee's sons, and two others of his disciples. Simon Peter said to them, "I am going fishing." They said to him, "We also will come with you." So they went out and got into the boat, but that night they caught nothing. When it was already dawn, Jesus was standing on the shore; but the disciples did not realize that it was Jesus. Jesus said to them, "Children, have you caught anything to eat?" They answered him, "No." So he said to them, "Cast the net over the right side of the boat and you will find something." So they cast it, and were not able to pull it in because of the number of fish. So the disciple whom Jesus loved said to Peter, "It is the Lord." When Simon Peter heard that it was the Lord, he tucked in his garment, for he was lightly clad, and jumped into the sea.

The other disciples came in the boat, for they were not far from shore, only about a hundred yards, dragging the net with the fish. When they climbed out on shore, they saw a charcoal fire with fish on it and bread. Jesus said to them, "Bring some of the fish you just caught." So Simon Peter went over and dragged the net ashore full of one hundred fifty-three large fish. Even though there were so many, the net was not torn. Jesus said to them, "Come, have breakfast." And none of the disciples dared to ask him, "Who are you?" because they realized it was the Lord. Jesus came over and took the bread and gave it to them, and in like manner the fish. This was now the third time Jesus was revealed to his disciples after being raised from the dead.

SATURDAY, APRIL 10, 2021

SATURDAY IN THE OCTAVE OF EASTER

First Reading   **Acts 4:13-21**

Observing the boldness of Peter and John and perceiving them to be uneducated, ordinary men, the leaders, elders, and scribes were amazed, and they recognized them as the companions of Jesus. Then when they saw the man who had been cured standing there with them, they could say nothing in reply. So they ordered them to leave the Sanhedrin, and conferred with one another, saying, "What are we to do with these men? Everyone living in Jerusalem knows that a remarkable sign was done through them, and we cannot deny it. But so that it may not be spread any further among the people, let us give them a stern warning never again to speak to anyone in this name." So they called them back and ordered them not to speak or teach at all in the name of Jesus. Peter and John, however, said to them in reply, "Whether it is right in the sight of God for us to obey you rather than God, you be the judges. It is impossible for us not to speak about what we have seen and heard." After threatening them further, they released them, finding no way to punish them, on account of the people who were all praising God for what had happened.

Responsorial Psalm   Psalm 118:1 and 14-15ab, 16-18, 19-21

R. (21a) I will give thanks to you, for you have answered me.

Or:

R. Alleluia.

Give thanks to the LORD, for he is good, for his mercy endures forever. My strength and my courage is the LORD, and he has been my savior. The joyful shout of victory in the tents of the just. R.

"The right hand of the LORD is exalted; the right hand of the LORD has struck with power." I shall not die, but live, and declare the works of the LORD. Though the LORD has indeed chastised me, yet he has not delivered me to death. R.

Open to me the gates of justice; I will enter them and give thanks to the LORD. This is the gate of the LORD; the just shall enter it. I will give thanks to you, for you have answered me and have been my savior. **R.**

Alleluia   Psalm 118:24

R. Alleluia, alleluia.

This is the day the LORD has made; let us be glad and rejoice in it. **R.**

Gospel   Mark 16:9-15

When Jesus had risen, early on the first day of the week, he appeared first to Mary Magdalene, out of whom he had driven seven demons. She went and told his companions who were mourning and weeping. When they heard that he was alive and had been seen by her, they did not believe.

After this he appeared in another form to two of them walking along on their way to the country. They returned and told the others; but they did not believe them either.

But later, as the Eleven were at table, he appeared to them and rebuked them for their unbelief and hardness of heart because they had not believed those who saw him after he had been raised. He said to them, "Go into the whole world and proclaim the Gospel to every creature."

SUNDAY, APRIL 11, 2021

SECOND SUNDAY OF EASTER

First Reading   Acts 4:32-35

The community of believers was of one heart and mind, and no one claimed that any of his possessions was his own, but they had everything in common. With great power the apostles bore witness to the resurrection of the Lord Jesus, and great favor was accorded them all.

There was no needy person among them, for those who owned property or houses would sell them, bring the proceeds of the sale, and put them at the feet of the apostles, and they were distributed to each according to need.

Responsorial Psalm   Psalm 118:2-4, 13-15, 22-24

R. (1) Give thanks to the LORD, for he is good, his love is everlasting.

Or:

R. Alleluia.

Let the house of Israel say, "His mercy endures forever." Let the house of Aaron say, "His mercy endures forever." Let those who fear the LORD say, "His mercy endures forever." **R.**

I was hard pressed and was falling, but the LORD helped me. My strength and my courage is the LORD, and he has been my savior. The joyful shout of victory in the tents of the just: **R.**

The stone which the builders rejected has become the cornerstone. By the LORD has this been done; it is wonderful in our eyes. This is the day the LORD has made; let us be glad and rejoice in it. **R.**

Second Reading   1 John 5:1-6

Beloved:

Everyone who believes that Jesus is the Christ is begotten by God, and everyone who loves the Father loves also the one begotten by him. In this way we know that we love the children of God when we love God and obey his commandments. For the love of God is this, that we keep his commandments. And his commandments are not burdensome, for whoever is begotten by God conquers the world. And the victory that conquers the world is our faith. Who indeed is the victor over the world but the one who believes that Jesus is the Son of God? This is the one who came through water and blood, Jesus Christ, not by water alone, but by water and blood. The Spirit is the one that testifies, and the Spirit is truth.

Alleluia   John 20:29
R. Alleluia, alleluia.

You believe in me, Thomas, because you have seen me, says the Lord; blessed are they who have not seen me, but still believe! **R.**

Gospel   John 20:19-31
On the evening of that first day of the week, when the doors were locked, where the disciples were, for fear of the Jews, Jesus came and stood in their midst and said to them, "Peace be with you." When he had said this, he showed them his hands and his side. The disciples rejoiced when they saw the Lord. Jesus said to them again, "Peace be with you. As the Father has sent me, so I send you." And when he had said this, he breathed on them and said to them, "Receive the Holy Spirit. Whose sins you forgive are forgiven them, and whose sins you retain are retained."

Thomas, called Didymus, one of the Twelve, was not with them when Jesus came. So the other disciples said to him, "We have seen the Lord." But he said to them, "Unless I see the mark of the nails in his hands and put my finger into the nailmarks and put my hand into his side, I will not believe."

Now a week later his disciples were again inside and Thomas was with them. Jesus came, although the doors were locked, and stood in their midst and said, "Peace be with you." Then he said to Thomas, "Put your finger here and see my hands, and bring your hand and put it into my side, and do not be unbelieving, but believe." Thomas answered and said to him, "My Lord and my God!" Jesus said to him, "Have you come to believe because you have seen me? Blessed are those who have not seen and have believed."

Now, Jesus did many other signs in the presence of his disciples that are not written in this book. But these are written that you may come to believe that Jesus is the Christ, the Son of God, and that through this belief you may have life in his name.

MONDAY OF THE SECOND WEEK OF EASTER

First Reading   **Acts 4:23-31**

After their release Peter and John went back to their own people and reported what the chief priests and elders had told them. And when they heard it, they raised their voices to God with one accord and said, "Sovereign Lord, maker of heaven and earth and the sea and all that is in them, you said by the Holy Spirit through the mouth of our father David, your servant:

Why did the Gentiles rage and the peoples entertain folly? The kings of the earth took their stand and the princes gathered together against the Lord and against his anointed.

Indeed they gathered in this city against your holy servant Jesus whom you anointed, Herod and Pontius Pilate, together with the

Gentiles and the peoples of Israel, to do what your hand and your will had long ago planned to take place.

And now, Lord, take note of their threats, and enable your servants to speak your word with all boldness, as you stretch forth your hand to heal, and signs and wonders are done through the name of your holy servant Jesus." As they prayed, the place where they were gathered shook, and they were all filled with the Holy Spirit and continued to speak the word of God with boldness.

Responsorial Psalm   Psalm 2:1-3, 4-7a, 7b-9
R. (11d) Blessed are all who take refuge in the Lord.
Or:
R. Alleluia.

Why do the nations rage and the peoples utter folly? The kings of the earth rise up, and the princes conspire together against the LORD and against his anointed: "Let us break their fetters and cast their bonds from us!" **R.**

He who is throned in heaven laughs; the LORD derides them. Then in anger he speaks to them; he terrifies them in his wrath: "I myself have set up my king on Zion, my holy mountain." I will proclaim the decree of the LORD. **R.**

The LORD said to me, "You are my Son; this day I have begotten you. Ask of me and I will give you the nations for an inheritance and the ends of the earth for your possession. You shall rule them with an iron rod; you shall shatter them like an earthen dish." **R.**

Alleluia   Colossians 3:1
R. Alleluia, alleluia.

If then you were raised with Christ, seek what is above, where Christ is seated at the right hand of God. **R.**

Gospel John 3:1-8

There was a Pharisee named Nicodemus, a ruler of the Jews. He came to Jesus at night and said to him, "Rabbi, we know that you are a teacher who has come from God, for no one can do these signs that you are doing unless God is with him." Jesus answered and said to him, "Amen, amen, I say to you, unless one is born from above, he cannot see the Kingdom of God."

Nicodemus said to him, "How can a man once grown old be born again? Surely he cannot reenter his mother's womb and be born again, can he?" Jesus answered, "Amen, amen, I say to you, unless one is born of water and Spirit he cannot enter the Kingdom of God. What is born of flesh is flesh and what is born of spirit is spirit. Do not be amazed that I told you, 'You must be born from above.' The wind blows where it wills, and you can hear the sound it makes, but you do not know where it comes from or where it goes; so it is with everyone who is born of the Spirit."

TUESDAY, APRIL 13, 2021
TUESDAY OF THE SECOND WEEK OF EASTER

First Reading Acts 4:32-37

The community of believers was of one heart and mind, and no one claimed that any of his possessions was his own, but they had everything in common. With great power the Apostles bore witness to the resurrection of the Lord Jesus, and great favor was accorded them all. There was no needy person among them, for those who owned property or houses would sell them, bring the proceeds of the sale, and put them at the feet of the Apostles, and they were distributed to each according to need. Thus Joseph, also named by the Apostles Barnabas (which is translated son of encouragement"), a Levite, a Cypriot by birth, sold a piece of property that he owned, then brought the money and put it at the feet of the Apostles.

Responsorial Psalm   Psalm 93:1ab, 1cd-2, 5

R. (1a) The Lord is king; he is robed in majesty.
Or:
R. Alleluia.

The LORD is king, in splendor robed; robed is the LORD and girt about with strength. **R.**

And he has made the world firm, not to be moved. Your throne stands firm from of old; from everlasting you are, O LORD. **R.**

Your decrees are worthy of trust indeed: holiness befits your house, O LORD, for length of days. **R.**

Alleluia   John 3:14-15

R. Alleluia, alleluia.

The Son of Man must be lifted up, so that everyone who believes in him may have eternal life. **R.**

Gospel   John 3:7b-15

Jesus said to Nicodemus:

"'You must be born from above.' The wind blows where it wills, and you can hear the sound it makes, but you do not know where it comes from or where it goes; so it is with everyone who is born of the Spirit." Nicodemus answered and said to him, 'How can this happen?"

Jesus answered and said to him, "You are the teacher of Israel and you do not understand this? Amen, amen, I say to you, we speak of what we know and we testify to what we have seen, but you people do not accept our testimony. If I tell you about earthly things and you do not believe, how will you believe if I tell you about heavenly things? No one has gone up to heaven except the one who has come down from heaven, the Son of Man. And just as Moses lifted up the serpent in the desert, so must the Son of Man be lifted up, so that everyone who believes in him may have eternal life."

WEDNESDAY OF THE SECOND WEEK OF EASTER

First Reading   **Acts 5:17-26**

The high priest rose up and all his companions, that is, the party of the Sadducees, and, filled with jealousy, laid hands upon the Apostles and put them in the public jail. But during the night, the angel of the Lord opened the doors of the prison, led them out, and said, "Go and take your place in the temple area, and tell the people everything about this life." When they heard this, they went to the temple early in the morning and taught. When the high priest and his companions arrived, they convened the Sanhedrin, the full senate of the children of Israel, and sent to the jail to have them brought in. But the court officers who went did not find them in the prison, so they came back and reported, "We found the jail securely locked and the guards stationed outside the doors, but when we opened them, we found no one inside." When the captain of the temple guard and the chief priests heard this report, they were at a loss about them, as to what this would come to. Then someone came in and reported to them, "The men whom you put in prison are in the temple area and are teaching the people." Then the captain and the court officers went and brought them, but without force, because they were afraid of being stoned by the people.

Responsorial Psalm   Psalm 34:2-3, 4-5, 6-7, 8-9

R. (7a) The Lord hears the cry of the poor.

Or:

R. Alleluia.

I will bless the LORD at all times; his praise shall be ever in my mouth. Let my soul glory in the LORD; the lowly will hear me and be glad. **R.**

Glorify the LORD with me, let us together extol his name. I sought the LORD, and he answered me and delivered me from all my fears. **R.**

Look to him that you may be radiant with joy, and your faces may not blush with shame. When the poor one called out, the LORD heard, and from all his distress he saved him. **R.**

The angel of the LORD encamps around those who fear him, and delivers them. Taste and see how good the LORD is; blessed the man who takes refuge in him. **R.**

Alleluia   John 3:16

R. Alleluia, alleluia.

God so love the world that he gave his only-begotten Son, so that everyone who believes in him might have eternal life. **R.**

Gospel   **John 3:16-21**

God so loved the world that he gave his only-begotten Son, so that everyone who believes in him might not perish but might have eternal life. For God did not send his Son into the world to condemn the world, but that the world might be saved through him. Whoever believes in him will not be condemned, but whoever does not believe has already been condemned, because he has not believed in the name of the only-begotten Son of God. And this is the verdict, that the light came into the world, but people preferred darkness to light, because their works were evil. For everyone who does wicked things hates the light and does not come toward the light, so that his works might not be exposed. But whoever lives the truth comes to the light, so that his works may be clearly seen as done in God.

THURSDAY, APRIL 15, 2021

THURSDAY OF THE SECOND WEEK OF EASTER

First Reading   **Acts 5:27-33**

When the court officers had brought the Apostles in and made them stand before the Sanhedrin, the high priest questioned them, "We gave you strict orders did we not, to stop teaching in that name. Yet you have filled Jerusalem with your teaching and want to bring this man's blood upon us." But Peter and the Apostles said in reply, "We must obey God rather than men. The God of our ancestors raised Jesus, though you had him killed by hanging him on a tree. God exalted him at his right hand as leader and savior to grant Israel repentance and forgiveness of sins. We are witnesses of these things, as is the Holy Spirit whom God has given to those who obey him." When they heard this, they became infuriated and wanted to put them to death.

R. (7a) The Lord hears the cry of the poor.
Or:
R. Alleluia.
I will bless the LORD at all times; his praise shall be ever in my mouth. Taste and see how good the LORD is; blessed the man who takes refuge in him. **R.**
The LORD confronts the evildoers, to destroy remembrance of them from the earth. When the just cry out, the LORD hears them, and from all their distress he rescues them. **R.**
The LORD is close to the brokenhearted; and those who are crushed in spirit he saves. Many are the troubles of the just man, but out of them all the LORD delivers him. **R.**

Alleluia   **John 20:29**
R. Alleluia, alleluia.
You believe in me, Thomas, because you have seen me, says the Lord; blessed are those who have not seen, but still believe! **R.**

Gospel   **John 3:31-36**
The one who comes from above is above all. The one who is of the earth is earthly and speaks of earthly things. But the one who comes from heaven is above all. He testifies to what he has seen and heard, but no one accepts his testimony. Whoever does accept his testimony certifies that God is trustworthy. For the one whom God sent speaks the words of God. He does not ration his gift of

the Spirit. The Father loves the Son and has given everything over to him. Whoever believes in the Son has eternal life, but whoever disobeys the Son will not see life, but the wrath of God remains upon him.

FRIDAY OF THE SECOND WEEK OF EASTER

First Reading   **Acts 5:34-42**

A Pharisee in the Sanhedrin named Gamaliel, a teacher of the law, respected by all the people, stood up, ordered the Apostles to be put outside for a short time, and said to the Sanhedrin, "Fellow children of Israel, be careful what you are about to do to these men. Some time ago, Theudas appeared, claiming to be someone important, and about four hundred men joined him, but he was killed, and all those who were loyal to him were disbanded and came to nothing. After him came Judas the Galilean at the time of the census. He also drew people after him, but he too perished and all who were loyal to him were scattered. So now I tell you, have nothing to do with these men, and let them go. For if this endeavor or this activity is of human origin, it will destroy itself. But if it comes from God, you will not be able to destroy them; you may even find yourselves fighting against God."

They were persuaded by him. After recalling the Apostles, they had them flogged, ordered them to stop speaking in the name of Jesus, and dismissed them. So they left the presence of the Sanhedrin, rejoicing that they had been found worthy to suffer dishonor for the sake of the name. And all day long, both at the temple and in their homes, they did not stop teaching and proclaiming the Christ, Jesus.

Responsorial Psalm   **Psalm 27:1, 4, 13-14**

R. (4abc) One thing I seek: to dwell in the house of the Lord.

Or:

R. Alleluia.

The LORD is my light and my salvation; whom should I fear? The LORD is my life's refuge; of whom should I be afraid? **R.**

One thing I ask of the LORD this I seek: To dwell in the house of the LORD all the days of my life, that I may gaze on the loveliness of the LORD and contemplate his temple. **R.**

I believe that I shall see the bounty of the LORD in the land of the living. Wait for the LORD with courage; be stouthearted, and wait for the LORD. **R.**

Alleluia   **Matthew 4:4b**

R. Alleluia, alleluia.

One does not live on bread alone, but on every word that comes forth from the mouth of God. **R.**

Gospel   **John 6:1-15**

Jesus went across the Sea of Galilee. A large crowd followed him, because they saw the signs he was performing on the sick. Jesus went up on the mountain, and there he sat down with his disciples. The Jewish feast of Passover was near. When Jesus raised his eyes and saw that a large crowd was coming to him, he said to Philip, "Where can we buy enough food for them to eat?" He said this to test him, because he himself knew what he was going to do. Philip answered him, "Two hundred days' wages worth of food would not be enough for each of them to have a little." One of his disciples, Andrew, the brother of Simon Peter, said to him, "There is a boy here who has five barley loaves and two fish; but what good are these for so many?" Jesus said, "Have the people recline."

Now there was a great deal of grass in that place. So the men reclined, about five thousand in number. Then Jesus took the loaves, gave thanks, and distributed them to those who were reclining, and also as much of the fish as they wanted. When they had had their fill, he said to his disciples, "Gather the fragments left over, so that nothing will be wasted." So they collected them, and filled twelve wicker baskets with fragments from the five barley loaves that had been more than they could eat. When the people saw the sign he had done, they said, "This is truly the Prophet, the one who is to come into the world." Since Jesus knew that they were going to come and carry him off to make him king, he withdrew again to the mountain alone.

SATURDAY, APRIL 17, 2021

SATURDAY OF THE SECOND WEEK OF EASTER

First Reading   **Acts 6:1-7**

As the number of disciples continued to grow, the Hellenists complained against the Hebrews because their widows were being neglected in the daily distribution. So the Twelve called together the community of the disciples and said, "It is not right for us to neglect the word of God to serve at table. Brothers, select from among you seven reputable men, filled with the Spirit and wisdom, whom we shall appoint to this task, whereas we shall devote ourselves to prayer and to the ministry of the word." The proposal was acceptable to the whole community, so they chose

Stephen, a man filled with faith and the Holy Spirit, also Philip, Prochorus, Nicanor, Timon, Parmenas, and Nicholas of Antioch, a convert to Judaism. They presented these men to the Apostles who prayed and laid hands on them. The word of God continued to spread, and the number of the disciples in Jerusalem increased greatly; even a large group of priests were becoming obedient to the faith.

Responsorial Psalm   Psalm 33:1-2, 4-5, 18-19

R. (22) Lord, let your mercy be on us, as we place our trust in you.

Or:

R. Alleluia.

Exult, you just, in the LORD; praise from the upright is fitting.
Give thanks to the LORD on the harp; with the ten-stringed lyre chant his praises. **R.**
Upright is the word of the LORD, and all his works are trustworthy. He loves justice and right; of the kindness of the LORD the earth is full. **R.**
See, the eyes of the LORD are upon those who fear him, upon those who hope for his kindness, to deliver them from death and preserve them in spite of famine. **R.**

Alleluia

R. Alleluia, alleluia.

Christ is risen, who made all things; he has shown mercy on all people. **R.**

Gospel   John 6:16-21

When it was evening, the disciples of Jesus went down to the sea, embarked in a boat, and went across the sea to Capernaum. It had already grown dark, and Jesus had not yet come to them. The sea was stirred up because a strong wind was blowing. When they had rowed about three or four miles, they saw Jesus walking on the sea and coming near the boat, and they began to be afraid. But he said to them, "It is I. Do not be afraid." They wanted to take him into the boat, but the boat immediately arrived at the shore to which they were heading.

THIRD SUNDAY OF EASTER

First Reading   **Acts 3:13-15, 17-19**

Peter said to the people:

"The God of Abraham, the God of Isaac, and the God of Jacob, the God of our fathers, has glorified his servant Jesus, whom you handed over and denied in Pilate's presence when he had decided to release him. You denied the Holy and Righteous One and asked that a murderer be released to you. The author of life you put to death, but God raised him from the dead; of this we are witnesses. Now I know, brothers, that you acted out of ignorance, just as your leaders did; but God has thus brought to fulfillment what he had announced beforehand through the mouth of all the prophets, that his Christ would suffer. Repent, therefore, and be converted, that your sins may be wiped away."

Responsorial Psalm   **Psalm 4:2, 4, 7-8, 9**

R. (7a) Lord, let your face shine on us.

Or:

R. Alleluia.

When I call, answer me, O my just God, you who relieve me when I am in distress; have pity on me, and hear my prayer! **R.**

Know that the LORD does wonders for his faithful one; the LORD will hear me when I call upon him. **R.**

O LORD, let the light of your countenance shine upon us! You put gladness into my heart. **R.**

As soon as I lie down, I fall peacefully asleep, for you alone, O LORD, bring security to my dwelling. **R.**

Second Reading   1 John 2:1-5a

My children, I am writing this to you so that you may not commit sin. But if anyone does sin, we have an Advocate with the Father, Jesus Christ the righteous one. He is expiation for our sins, and not for our sins only but for those of the whole world. The way we may be sure that we know him is to keep his commandments. Those who say, "I know him," but do not keep his commandments are liars, and the truth is not in them. But whoever keeps his word, the love of God is truly perfected in him

Alleluia   Luke 24:32

R. Alleluia, alleluia.

Lord Jesus, open the Scriptures to us; make our hearts burn while you speak to us. **R.**

Gospel   Luke 24:35-48

The two disciples recounted what had taken place on the way, and how Jesus was made known to them in the breaking of bread.

While they were still speaking about this, he stood in their midst and said to them, "Peace be with you." But they were startled and terrified and thought that they were seeing a ghost. Then he said to them, "Why are you troubled? And why do questions arise in your hearts? Look at my hands and my feet, that it is I myself. Touch me and see, because a ghost does not have flesh and bones as you can see I have." And as he said this, he showed them his hands and his feet. While they were still incredulous for joy and were amazed, he asked them, "Have you anything here to eat?" They gave him a piece of baked fish; he took it and ate it in front of them.

He said to them, "These are my words that I spoke to you while I was still with you, that everything written about me in the Law of Moses and in the prophets and psalms must be fulfilled." Then he opened their minds to understand the Scriptures. And he said to them, "Thus it is written that the Christ would suffer and rise from the dead on the third day and that repentance, for the forgiveness of sins, would be preached in his name to all the nations, beginning from Jerusalem. You are witnesses of these things."

MONDAY, APRIL 19, 2021

MONDAY OF THE THIRD WEEK OF EASTER

First Reading   **Acts 6:8-15**

Stephen, filled with grace and power, was working great wonders and signs among the people. Certain members of the so-called Synagogue of Freedmen, Cyreneans, and Alexandrians, and people from Cilicia and Asia, came forward and debated with Stephen, but they could not withstand the wisdom and the Spirit with which he spoke. Then they instigated some men to say, "We have heard him speaking blasphemous words against Moses and God." They stirred up the people, the elders, and the scribes, accosted him, seized him, and brought him before the Sanhedrin. They presented false witnesses who testified, "This man never stops saying things against this holy place and the law. For we have heard him claim that this Jesus the Nazorean will destroy this place and change the customs that Moses handed down to us." All those who sat in the Sanhedrin looked intently at him and saw that his face was like the face of an angel.

Responsorial Psalm   Psalm 119:23-24, 26-27, 29-30

R. (1ab) Blessed are they who follow the law of the Lord!
Or:
R. Alleluia.

Though princes meet and talk against me, your servant meditates on your statutes. Yes, your decrees are my delight; they are my counselors. **R.**

I declared my ways, and you answered me; teach me your statutes. Make me understand the way of your precepts, and I will meditate on your wondrous deeds. **R.**

Remove from me the way of falsehood, and favor me with your law. The way of truth I have chosen; I have set your ordinances before me. **R.**

Alleluia   Matthew 4:4b

R. Alleluia, alleluia.

One does not live on bread alone but on every word that comes forth from the mouth of God. **R.**

Gospel   John 6:22-29

[After Jesus had fed the five thousand men, his disciples saw him walking on the sea.] The next day, the crowd that remained across the sea saw that there had been only one boat there, and that Jesus had not gone along with his disciples in the boat, but only his disciples had left. Other boats came from Tiberias near the place where they had eaten the bread when the Lord gave thanks. When the crowd saw that neither Jesus nor his disciples were there, they themselves got into boats and came to Capernaum looking for Jesus. And when they found him across the sea they said to him, "Rabbi, when did you get here?" Jesus answered them and said, "Amen, amen, I say to you, you are looking for me not because you saw signs but because you ate the loaves and were filled. Do not work for food that perishes but for the food that endures for eternal life, which the Son of Man will give you. For on him the Father, God, has set his seal." So they said to him, "What can we do to accomplish the works of God?" Jesus answered and said to them, "This is the work of God, that you believe in the one he sent."

TUESDAY OF THE THIRD WEEK OF EASTER

First Reading   **Acts 7:51—8:1a**

Stephen said to the people, the elders, and the scribes:

"You stiff-necked people, uncircumcised in heart and ears, you always oppose the Holy Spirit; you are just like your ancestors. Which of the prophets did your ancestors not persecute? They put to death those who foretold the coming of the righteous one, whose betrayers and murderers you have now become. You received the law as transmitted by angels, but you did not observe it."

When they heard this, they were infuriated, and they ground their teeth at him. But Stephen, filled with the Holy Spirit, looked up intently to heaven and saw the glory of God and Jesus standing at the right hand of God, and Stephen said, "Behold, I see the heavens opened and the Son of Man standing at the right hand of God." But they cried out in a loud voice, covered their ears, and rushed upon him together. They threw him out of the city, and began to stone him. The witnesses laid down their cloaks at the feet of a young man named Saul. As they were stoning Stephen, he called out, "Lord Jesus, receive my spirit." Then he fell to his knees and cried out in a loud voice, "Lord, do not hold this sin against them"; and when he said this, he fell asleep. Now Saul was consenting to his execution.

Responsorial Psalm   **Psalm31:3cd-4, 6 and 7b and 8a, 17 and 21ab**

R. (6a) Into your hands, O Lord, I commend my spirit.
Or:
R. Alleluia.

Be my rock of refuge, a stronghold to give me safety. You are my rock and my fortress; for your name's sake you will lead and guide me. **R.**

Into your hands I commend my spirit; you will redeem me, O LORD, O faithful God. My trust is in the LORD; I will rejoice and be glad of your mercy. **R.**

Let your face shine upon your servant; save me in your kindness. You hide them in the shelter of your presence from the plottings of men. **R.**

Alleluia   John 6:35ab
R. Alleluia, alleluia.
I am the bread of life, says the Lord; whoever comes to me will never hunger. **R.**

Gospel   John 6:30-35
The crowd said to Jesus: "What sign can you do, that we may see and believe in you? What can you do? Our ancestors ate manna in the desert, as it is written: *"He gave them bread from heaven to eat."*

So Jesus said to them, "Amen, amen, I say to you, it was not Moses who gave the bread from heaven; my Father gives you the true bread from heaven. For the bread of God is that which comes down from heaven and gives life to the world." So they said to Jesus, "Sir, give us this bread always." Jesus said to them, "I am the bread of life; whoever comes to me will never hunger, and whoever believes in me will never thirst."

WEDNESDAY, APRIL 21, 2021
WEDNESDAY OF THE THIRD WEEK OF EASTER
First Reading   Acts 8:1b-8
There broke out a severe persecution of the Church in Jerusalem, and all were scattered throughout the countryside of Judea and Samaria, except the Apostles. Devout men buried Stephen and made a loud lament over him. Saul, meanwhile, was trying to

destroy the Church; entering house after house and dragging out men and women, he handed them over for imprisonment.

Now those who had been scattered went about preaching the word. Thus Philip went down to the city of Samaria and proclaimed the Christ to them. With one accord, the crowds paid attention to what was said by Philip when they heard it and saw the signs he was doing. For unclean spirits, crying out in a loud voice, came out of many possessed people, and many paralyzed and crippled people were cured. There was great joy in that city.

Responsorial Psalm   Psalm 66:1-3a, 4-5, 6-7a

R. (1) Let all the earth cry out to God with joy.

Or:

R. Alleluia.

Shout joyfully to God, all the earth, sing praise to the glory of his name; proclaim his glorious praise. Say to God, "How tremendous are your deeds!" **R.**

"Let all on earth worship and sing praise to you, sing praise to your name!" Come and see the works of God, his tremendous deeds among the children of Adam. **R.**

He has changed the sea into dry land; through the river they passed on foot; therefore let us rejoice in him. He rules by his might forever. **R.**

Alleluia   John 6:40

R. Alleluia, alleluia.

Everyone who believes in the Son has eternal life, and I shall raise him up on the last day, says the Lord. **R.**

Jesus said to the crowds,

"I am the bread of life; whoever comes to me will never hunger, and whoever believes in me will never thirst. But I told you that although you have seen me, you do not believe. Everything that the Father gives me will come to me, and I will not reject anyone who comes to me, because I came down from heaven not to do my own will but the will of the one who sent me. And this is the will of the one who sent me, that I should not lose anything of what he gave me, but that I should raise it on the last day. For this is the will of my Father, that everyone who sees the Son and believes in him may have eternal life, and I shall raise him on the last day."

THURSDAY, APRIL 22, 2021

THURSDAY OF THE THIRD WEEK OF EASTER

First Reading   **Acts 8:26-40**

The angel of the Lord spoke to Philip, "Get up and head south on the road that goes down from Jerusalem to Gaza, the desert route." So he got up and set out. Now there was an Ethiopian eunuch, a court official of the Candace, that is, the queen of the Ethiopians, in charge of her entire treasury, who had come to Jerusalem to worship, and was returning home. Seated in his chariot, he was reading the prophet Isaiah. The Spirit said to Philip, "Go and join up with that chariot." Philip ran up and heard him reading Isaiah the prophet and said, "Do you understand what you are reading?" He replied, "How can I, unless someone instructs me?" So he invited Philip to get in and sit with him. This was the Scripture passage he was reading:

Like a sheep he was led to the slaughter, and as a lamb before its shearer is silent, so he opened not his mouth. In his humiliation justice was denied him. Who will tell of his posterity? For his life is taken from the earth.

Then the eunuch said to Philip in reply, "I beg you, about whom is the prophet saying this? About himself, or about someone else?" Then Philip opened his mouth and, beginning with this Scripture passage, he proclaimed Jesus to him. As they traveled along the road they came to some water, and the eunuch said, "Look, there is water. What is to prevent my being baptized?" Then he ordered the chariot to stop, and Philip and the eunuch both went down into the water, and he baptized him. When they came out of the water, the Spirit of the Lord snatched Philip away, and the eunuch saw him no more, but continued on his way rejoicing. Philip came to Azotus, and went about proclaiming the good news to all the towns until he reached Caesarea.

Responsorial Psalm   **Psalm 66:8-9, 16-17, 20**

R. (1) Let all the earth cry out to God with joy.

Or:

R. Alleluia.

Bless our God, you peoples, loudly sound his praise; He has given life to our souls, and has not let our feet slip. **R.**

Hear now, all you who fear God, while I declare what he has done for me. When I appealed to him in words, praise was on the tip of my tongue. **R.**

Blessed be God who refused me not my prayer or his kindness! **R.**

Alleluia   **John 6:51**

R. Alleluia, alleluia.

I am the living bread that came down from heaven, says the Lord;
whoever eats this bread will live forever. **R.**

Gospel   John 6:44-51

Jesus said to the crowds:

"No one can come to me unless the Father who sent me draw him,
and I will raise him on the last day. It is written in the prophets:
They shall all be taught by God.

Everyone who listens to my Father and learns from him comes to
me. Not that anyone has seen the Father except the one who is
from God; he has seen the Father. Amen, amen, I say to you,
whoever believes has eternal life. I am the bread of life. Your
ancestors ate the manna in the desert, but they died; this is the
bread that comes down from heaven so that one may eat it and not
die. I am the living bread that came down from heaven; whoever
eats this bread will live forever; and the bread that I will give is my
Flesh for the life of the world."

FRIDAY, APRIL 23, 2021

FRIDAY OF THE THIRD WEEK OF EASTER

First Reading   Acts 9:1-20

Saul, still breathing murderous threats against the disciples of the
Lord, went to the high priest and asked him for letters to the
synagogues in Damascus, that, if he should find any men or
women who belonged to the Way, he might bring them back to
Jerusalem in chains. On his journey, as he was nearing Damascus,
a light from the sky suddenly flashed around him. He fell to the
ground and heard a voice saying to him, "Saul, Saul, why are you

persecuting me?" He said, "Who are you, sir?" The reply came, "I am Jesus, whom you are persecuting. Now get up and go into the city and you will be told what you must do." The men who were traveling with him stood speechless, for they heard the voice but could see no one. Saul got up from the ground, but when he opened his eyes he could see nothing; so they led him by the hand and brought him to Damascus. For three days he was unable to see, and he neither ate nor drank.

There was a disciple in Damascus named Ananias, and the Lord said to him in a vision, "Ananias." He answered, "Here I am, Lord." The Lord said to him, "Get up and go to the street called Straight and ask at the house of Judas for a man from Tarsus named Saul. He is there praying, and in a vision he has seen a man named Ananias come in and lay his hands on him, that he may regain his sight." But Ananias replied, "Lord, I have heard from many sources about this man, what evil things he has done to your holy ones in Jerusalem. And here he has authority from the chief priests to imprison all who call upon your name." But the Lord said to him, "Go, for this man is a chosen instrument of mine to carry my name before Gentiles, kings, and children of Israel, and I will show him what he will have to suffer for my name." So Ananias went and entered the house; laying his hands on him, he said, "Saul, my brother, the Lord has sent me, Jesus who appeared to you on the way by which you came, that you may regain your sight and be filled with the Holy Spirit." Immediately things like scales fell from his eyes and he regained his sight. He got up and was baptized, and when he had eaten, he recovered his strength. He stayed some days with the disciples in Damascus, and he began at once to proclaim Jesus in the synagogues, that he is the Son of God.

R. (Mark 16:15) Go out to all the world and tell the Good News.

Or:

R. Alleluia.

Praise the LORD, all you nations; glorify him, all you peoples! **R.**

For steadfast is his kindness toward us, and the fidelity of the LORD endures forever. **R.**

R. Alleluia, alleluia.

Whoever eats my Flesh and drinks my Blood, remains in me and I in him, says the Lord. **R.**

The Jews quarreled among themselves, saying, "How can this man give us his Flesh to eat?" Jesus said to them, "Amen, amen, I say to you, unless you eat the Flesh of the Son of Man and drink his Blood, you do not have life within you. Whoever eats my Flesh and drinks my Blood has eternal life, and I will raise him on the last day. For my Flesh is true food, and my Blood is true drink. Whoever eats my Flesh and drinks my Blood remains in me and I in him. Just as the living Father sent me and I have life because of the Father, so also the one who feeds on me will have life because of me. This is the bread that came down from heaven. Unlike your ancestors who ate and still died, whoever eats this bread will live forever." These things he said while teaching in the synagogue in Capernaum.

SATURDAY OF THE THIRD WEEK OF EASTER

First Reading   **Acts 9:31-42**

The Church throughout all Judea, Galilee, and Samaria was at peace. She was being built up and walked in the fear of the Lord, and with the consolation of the Holy Spirit she grew in numbers.

As Peter was passing through every region, he went down to the holy ones living in Lydda. There he found a man named Aeneas, who had been confined to bed for eight years, for he was paralyzed. Peter said to him, "Aeneas, Jesus Christ heals you. Get up and make your bed." He got up at once. And all the inhabitants of Lydda and Sharon saw him, and they turned to the Lord.

Now in Joppa there was a disciple named Tabitha (which translated is Dorcas). She was completely occupied with good deeds and almsgiving. Now during those days she fell sick and died, so after washing her, they laid her out in a room upstairs. Since Lydda was near Joppa, the disciples, hearing that Peter was there, sent two men to him with the request, "Please come to us without delay." So Peter got up and went with them. When he arrived, they took him to the room upstairs where all the widows came to him weeping and showing him the tunics and cloaks that Dorcas had made while she was with them. Peter sent them all out and knelt down and prayed. Then he turned to her body and said, "Tabitha, rise up." She opened her eyes, saw Peter, and sat up. He gave her his hand and raised her up, and when he had called the holy ones and the widows, he presented her alive. This became known all over Joppa, and many came to believe in the Lord.

Responsorial Psalm   Psalm 116:12-13, 14-15, 16-17

R. (12) How shall I make a return to the Lord for all the good he has done for me?
Or:
R. Alleluia.

How shall I make a return to the LORD for all the good he has done for me? The cup of salvation I will take up, and I will call upon the name of the LORD **R.**

My vows to the LORD I will pay in the presence of all his people. Precious in the eyes of the LORD is the death of his faithful ones. **R.**

O LORD, I am your servant; I am your servant, the son of your handmaid; you have loosed my bonds. To you will I offer sacrifice of thanksgiving, and I will call upon the name of the LORD. **R.**

Alleluia   John 6:63c, 68c

R. Alleluia, alleluia.

Your words, Lord, are Spirit and life; you have the words of everlasting life. **R.**

Gospel   John 6:60-69

Many of the disciples of Jesus who were listening said, "This saying is hard; who can accept it?" Since Jesus knew that his disciples were murmuring about this, he said to them, "Does this shock you? What if you were to see the Son of Man ascending to where he was before? It is the Spirit that gives life, while the flesh is of no avail. The words I have spoken to you are Spirit and life. But there are some of you who do not believe." Jesus knew from the beginning the ones who would not believe and the one who would betray him. And he said, "For this reason I have told you that no one can come to me unless it is granted him by my Father." As a result of this, many of his disciples returned to their former way of life and no longer walked with him. Jesus then said to the Twelve, "Do you also want to leave?" Simon Peter answered him, "Master, to whom shall we go? You have the words of eternal life. We have come to believe and are convinced that you are the Holy One of God."

FOURTH SUNDAY OF EASTER

First Reading   Acts 4:8-12

Peter, filled with the Holy Spirit, said:

"Leaders of the people and elders: If we are being examined today about a good deed done to a cripple, namely, by what means he was saved, then all of you and all the people of Israel should know that it was in the name of Jesus Christ the Nazorean whom you crucified, whom God raised from the dead; in his name this man stands before you healed. He is *the stone rejected by you, the builders, which has become the cornerstone.*

There is no salvation through anyone else, nor is there any other name under heaven given to the human race by which we are to be saved."

Responsorial Psalm   Psalm 118:1, 8-9, 21-23, 26, 28, 29

R. (22) The stone rejected by the builders has become the cornerstone.

Or:

R. Alleluia.

Give thanks to the LORD, for he is good, for his mercy endures forever. It is better to take refuge in the LORD than to trust in man. It is better to take refuge in the LORD than to trust in princes. **R.**

I will give thanks to you, for you have answered me and have been my savior. The stone which the builders rejected has become the cornerstone. By the LORD has this been done; it is wonderful in our eyes. **R.**

Blessed is he who comes in the name of the LORD; we bless you from the house of the LORD. I will give thanks to you, for you have answered me and have been my savior. Give thanks to the LORD, for he is good; for his kindness endures forever. **R.**

Second Reading   1 John 3:1-2

Beloved:

See what love the Father has bestowed on us that we may be called the children of God. Yet so we are. The reason the world does not know us is that it did not know him. Beloved, we are God's children now; what we shall be has not yet been revealed. We do know that when it is revealed we shall be like him, for we shall see him as he is.

Alleluia   John 10:14

R. Alleluia, alleluia.

I am the good shepherd, says the Lord; I know my sheep, and mine know me. **R.**

Gospel   John 10:11-18

Jesus said:

"I am the good shepherd. A good shepherd lays down his life for the sheep. A hired man, who is not a shepherd and whose sheep are not his own, sees a wolf coming and leaves the sheep and runs away, and the wolf catches and scatters them. This is because he works for pay and has no concern for the sheep. I am the good shepherd, and I know mine and mine know me, just as the Father knows me and I know the Father; and I will lay down my life for the sheep. I have other sheep that do not belong to this fold. These also I must lead, and they will hear my voice, and there will be one flock, one shepherd. This is why the Father loves me, because I lay down my life in order to take it up again. No one takes it from me, but I lay it down on my own. I have power to lay it down, and power to take it up again. This command I have received from my Father."

MONDAY, APRIL 26, 2021

MONDAY OF THE FOURTH WEEK OF EASTER

First Reading   Acts 11:1-18

The Apostles and the brothers who were in Judea heard that the Gentiles too had accepted the word of God. So when Peter went up to Jerusalem the circumcised believers confronted him, saying, 'You entered the house of uncircumcised people and ate with them." Peter began and explained it to them step by step, saying, "I was at prayer in the city of Joppa when in a trance I had a vision, something resembling a large sheet coming down, lowered from the sky by its four corners, and it came to me. Looking intently into it, I observed and saw the four-legged animals of the earth, the wild beasts, the reptiles, and the birds of the sky. I also heard a voice say to me, 'Get up, Peter. Slaughter and eat.' But I said, 'certainly not, sir, because nothing profane or unclean has ever entered my mouth.' But a second time a voice from heaven answered, 'What God has made clean, you are not to call profane.' This happened three times, and then everything was drawn up again into the sky. Just then three men appeared at the house where we were, who had been sent to me from Caesarea. The Spirit told me to accompany them without discriminating. These six brothers also went with me, and we entered the man's house. He related to us how he had seen the angel standing in his house, saying, 'Send someone to Joppa and summon Simon, who is called Peter, who will speak words to you by which you and all your household will be saved.' As I began to speak, the Holy Spirit fell upon them as it had upon us at the beginning, and I remembered the word of the Lord, how he had said, 'John baptized with water but you will be baptized with the Holy Spirit.' If then God gave them the same gift he gave to us when we came to believe in the Lord Jesus Christ, who was I to be able to hinder God?" When they heard this, they stopped objecting and glorified God, saying, "God has then granted life-giving repentance to the Gentiles too."

Responsorial Psalm   **Psalm 42:2-3; 43:3, 4**

R. (3a) Athirst is my soul for the living God.
Or:
R. Alleluia.

As the hind longs for the running waters, so my soul longs for you, O God. Athirst is my soul for God, the living God. When shall I go and behold the face of God? **R.**

Send forth your light and your fidelity; they shall lead me on and bring me to your holy mountain, to your dwelling-place. **R.**

Then will I go in to the altar of God, the God of my gladness and joy; then will I give you thanks upon the harp, O God, my God! **R.**

Alleluia   John 10:14

R. Alleluia, alleluia.

I am the good shepherd, says the Lord; I know my sheep, and mine know me. **R.**

Gospel   John 10:1-10

Jesus said:

"Amen, amen, I say to you, whoever does not enter a sheepfold through the gate but climbs over elsewhere is a thief and a robber. But whoever enters through the gate is the shepherd of the sheep. The gatekeeper opens it for him, and the sheep hear his voice, as the shepherd calls his own sheep by name and leads them out. When he has driven out all his own, he walks ahead of them, and the sheep follow him, because they recognize his voice. But they will not follow a stranger; they will run away from him, because they do not recognize the voice of strangers." Although Jesus used this figure of speech, the Pharisees did not realize what he was trying to tell them.

So Jesus said again, "Amen, amen, I say to you, I am the gate for the sheep. All who came before me are thieves and robbers, but the sheep did not listen to them. I am the gate. Whoever enters through me will be saved, and will come in and go out and find pasture. A thief comes only to steal and slaughter and destroy; I came so that they might have life and have it more abundantly."

TUESDAY OF THE FOURTH WEEK OF EASTER

First Reading   **Acts 11:19-26**

Those who had been scattered by the persecution that arose because of Stephen went as far as Phoenicia, Cyprus, and Antioch, preaching the word to no one but Jews. There were some Cypriots and Cyrenians among them, however, who came to Antioch and began to speak to the Greeks as well, proclaiming the Lord Jesus. The hand of the Lord was with them and a great number who believed turned to the Lord. The news about them reached the ears of the Church in Jerusalem, and they sent Barnabas to go to Antioch. When he arrived and saw the grace of God, he rejoiced and encouraged them all to remain faithful to the Lord in firmness of heart, for he was a good man, filled with the Holy Spirit and faith. And a large number of people was added to the Lord. Then he went to Tarsus to look for Saul, and when he had found him he brought him to Antioch. For a whole year they met with the Church and taught a large number of people, and it was in Antioch that the disciples were first called Christians.

Responsorial Psalm   **Psalm 87:1b-3, 4-5, 6-7**

R. (117:1a) All you nations, praise the Lord.
Or:
R. Alleluia.

His foundation upon the holy mountains the LORD loves: The gates of Zion, more than any dwelling of Jacob. Glorious things are said of you, O city of God! **R.**

I tell of Egypt and Babylon among those who know the LORD; Of Philistia, Tyre, Ethiopia: "This man was born there." And of Zion they shall say: "One and all were born in her; and he who has established her is the Most High LORD." **R.**

They shall note, when the peoples are enrolled: "This man was born there." And all shall sing, in their festive dance: "My home is within you." **R.**

Alleluia   John 10:27

R. Alleluia, alleluia.

My sheep hear my voice, says the Lord; I know them, and they follow me. **R.**

Gospel   John 10:22-30

The feast of the Dedication was taking place in Jerusalem. It was winter. And Jesus walked about in the temple area on the Portico of Solomon. So the Jews gathered around him and said to him, "How long are you going to keep us in suspense? If you are the Christ, tell us plainly." Jesus answered them, "I told you and you do not believe. The works I do in my Father's name testify to me. But you do not believe, because you are not among my sheep. My sheep hear my voice; I know them, and they follow me. I give them eternal life, and they shall never perish. No one can take them out of my hand. My Father, who has given them to me, is greater than all, and no one can take them out of the Father's hand. The Father and I are one."

WEDNESDAY OF THE FOURTH WEEK OF EASTER

First Reading   **Acts 12:24-13:5a**

The word of God continued to spread and grow. After Barnabas and Saul completed their relief mission, they returned to Jerusalem, taking with them John, who is called Mark.

Now there were in the Church at Antioch prophets and teachers: Barnabas, Symeon who was called Niger, Lucius of Cyrene, Manaen who was a close friend of Herod the tetrarch, and Saul. While they were worshiping the Lord and fasting, the Holy Spirit said, "Set apart for me Barnabas and Saul for the work to which I have called them." Then, completing their fasting and prayer, they laid hands on them and sent them off.

So they, sent forth by the Holy Spirit, went down to Seleucia and from there sailed to Cyprus. When they arrived in Salamis, they proclaimed the word of God in the Jewish synagogues.

Responsorial Psalm   **Psalm 67:2-3, 5, 6 and 8**

R. (4) O God, let all the nations praise you!

Or:

R. Alleluia.

May God have pity on us and bless us; may he let his face shine upon us. So may your way be known upon earth; among all nations, your salvation. **R.**

May the nations be glad and exult because you rule the peoples in equity; the nations on the earth you guide. **R.**

May the peoples praise you, O God; may all the peoples praise you! May God bless us, and may all the ends of the earth fear him! **R.**

Alleluia   John 8:12

R. Alleluia, alleluia.

I am the light of the world, says the Lord; whoever follows me will
have the light of life. **R.**

Gospel   John 12:44-50

Jesus cried out and said, "Whoever believes in me believes not
only in me but also in the one who sent me, and whoever sees me
sees the one who sent me. I came into the world as light, so that
everyone who believes in me might not remain in darkness. And if
anyone hears my words and does not observe them, I do not
condemn him, for I did not come to condemn the world but to save
the world. Whoever rejects me and does not accept my words has
something to judge him: the word that I spoke, it will condemn
him on the last day, because I did not speak on my own, but the
Father who sent me commanded me what to say and speak. And I
know that his commandment is eternal life. So what I say, I say as
the Father told me."

THURSDAY, APRIL 29, 2021

MEMORIAL OF SAINT CATHERINE OF SIENA, VIRGIN
AND DOCTOR OF THE CHURCH

First Reading   Acts 13:13-25

From Paphos, Paul and his companions set sail and arrived at
Perga in Pamphylia. But John left them and returned to
Jerusalem. They continued on from Perga and reached Antioch in
Pisidia. On the Sabbath they entered into the synagogue and took
their seats. After the reading of the law and the prophets, the

synagogue officials sent word to them, "My brothers, if one of you has a word of exhortation for the people, please speak."

So Paul got up, motioned with his hand, and said, "Fellow children of Israel and you others who are God-fearing, listen. The God of this people Israel chose our ancestors and exalted the people during their sojourn in the land of Egypt. With uplifted arm he led them out, and for about forty years he put up with them in the desert. When he had destroyed seven nations in the land of Canaan, he gave them their land as an inheritance at the end of about four hundred and fifty years. After these things he provided judges up to Samuel the prophet. Then they asked for a king. God gave them Saul, son of Kish, a man from the tribe of Benjamin, for forty years. Then he removed him and raised up David as their king; of him he testified, *I have found David, son of Jesse, a man after my own heart; he will carry out my every wish.*

From this man's descendants God, according to his promise, has brought to Israel a savior, Jesus. John heralded his coming by proclaiming a baptism of repentance to all the people of Israel; and as John was completing his course, he would say, 'What do you suppose that I am? I am not he. Behold, one is coming after me; I am not worthy to unfasten the sandals of his feet.'"

Responsorial Psalm   Psalm 89:2-3, 21-22, 25 and 27
R. (2) For ever I will sing the goodness of the Lord.
Or:
R. Alleluia.

The favors of the LORD I will sing forever; through all generations my mouth shall proclaim your faithfulness. For you have said, "My kindness is established forever"; in heaven you have confirmed your faithfulness. **R.**

"I have found David, my servant; with my holy oil I have anointed him, that my hand may be always with him, and that my arm may make him strong." **R.**

"My faithfulness and my mercy shall be with him, and through my name shall his horn be exalted. He shall say of me, 'You are my father, my God, the Rock, my savior.'" **R.**

Alleluia   Revelation 1:5ab
R. Alleluia, alleluia.

Jesus Christ, you are the faithful witness, the firstborn of the dead, you have loved us and freed us from our sins by your Blood. **R.**

Gospel   John 13:16-20

When Jesus had washed the disciples' feet, he said to them: "Amen, amen, I say to you, no slave is greater than his master nor any messenger greater than the one who sent him. If you understand this, blessed are you if you do it. I am not speaking of all of you. I know those whom I have chosen. But so that the Scripture might be fulfilled, *the one who ate my food has raised his heel against me.* From now on I am telling you before it happens, so that when it happens you may believe that I AM. Amen, amen, I say to you, whoever receives the one I send receives me, and whoever receives me receives the one who sent me."

FRIDAY OF THE FOURTH WEEK OF EASTER
First Reading   Acts 13:26-33

When Paul came to Antioch in Pisidia, he said in the synagogue: "My brothers, children of the family of Abraham, and those others among you who are God-fearing, to us this word of salvation has been sent. The inhabitants of Jerusalem and their leaders failed to recognize him, and by condemning him they fulfilled the oracles of the prophets that are read Sabbath after Sabbath. For even though they found no grounds for a death sentence, they asked Pilate to have him put to death, and when they had accomplished all that was written about him, they took him down from the tree and placed him in a tomb. But God raised him from the dead, and for many days he appeared to those who had come up with him from Galilee to Jerusalem. These are now his witnesses before the people. We ourselves are proclaiming this good news to you that what God promised our fathers he has brought to fulfillment for us, their children, by raising up Jesus, as it is written in the second psalm, *You are my Son; this day I have begotten you.*"

Responsorial Psalm   **Psalm 2:6-7, 8-9, 10-11ab**

R. (7bc) You are my Son; this day I have begotten you.

Or:

R. Alleluia.

"I myself have set up my king on Zion, my holy mountain." I will proclaim the decree of the LORD: The LORD said to me, "You are my Son; this day I have begotten you." **R.**

"Ask of me and I will give you the nations for an inheritance and the ends of the earth for your possession. You shall rule them with an iron rod; you shall shatter them like an earthen dish." **R.**

And now, O kings, give heed; take warning, you rulers of the earth. Serve the LORD with fear, and rejoice before him; with trembling rejoice. **R.**

Alleluia   John 14:6

R. Alleluia, alleluia.

I am the way and the truth and the life, says the Lord; no one comes to the Father except through me. **R.**

Gospel   John 14:1-6

Jesus said to his disciples:

"Do not let your hearts be troubled. You have faith in God; have faith also in me. In my Father's house there are many dwelling places. If there were not, would I have told you that I am going to prepare a place for you? And if I go and prepare a place for you, I will come back again and take you to myself, so that where I am you also may be. Where I am going you know the way." Thomas said to him, "Master, we do not know where you are going; how can we know the way?" Jesus said to him, "I am the way and the truth and the life. No one comes to the Father except through me."

SATURDAY, MAY 1, 2021

SATURDAY OF THE FOURTH WEEK OF EASTER

First Reading   **Acts 13:44-52**

On the following Sabbath almost the whole city gathered to hear the word of the Lord. When the Jews saw the crowds, they were filled with jealousy and with violent abuse contradicted what Paul said. Both Paul and Barnabas spoke out boldly and said, "It was necessary that the word of God be spoken to you first, but since you reject it and condemn yourselves as unworthy of eternal life, we now turn to the Gentiles. For so the Lord has commanded us, *I have made you a light to the Gentiles, that you may be an instrument of salvation to the ends of the earth.*"

The Gentiles were delighted when they heard this and glorified the word of the Lord. All who were destined for eternal life came to believe, and the word of the Lord continued to spread through the whole region.

The Jews, however, incited the women of prominence who were worshipers and the leading men of the city, stirred up a persecution against Paul and Barnabas, and expelled them from their territory. So they shook the dust from their feet in protest against them and went to Iconium. The disciples were filled with joy and the Holy Spirit.

Responsorial Psalm   **Psalm 98:1, 2-3ab, 3cd-4**

R. (3cd) All the ends of the earth have seen the saving power of God.

Or:

R. Alleluia.

Sing to the LORD a new song, for he has done wondrous deeds;

His right hand has won victory for him, his holy arm. **R.**

The LORD has made his salvation known: in the sight of the

nations he has revealed his justice. He has remembered his

kindness and his faithfulness toward the house of Israel. **R.**

All the ends of the earth have seen the salvation by our God. Sing

joyfully to the LORD, all you lands; break into song; sing praise. **R.**

Alleluia   John 8:31b-32

R. Alleluia, alleluia.

If you remain in my word, you will truly be my disciples, and you

will know the truth, says the Lord. **R.**

Gospel   John 14:7-14

Jesus said to his disciples:

"If you know me, then you will also know my Father. From now on
you do know him and have seen him." Philip said to Jesus,
"Master, show us the Father, and that will be enough for us." Jesus
said to him, "Have I been with you for so long a time and you still
do not know me, Philip? Whoever has seen me has seen the
Father. How can you say, 'Show us the Father'? Do you not believe
that I am in the Father and the Father is in me? The words that I
speak to you I do not speak on my own. The Father who dwells in
me is doing his works. Believe me that I am in the Father and the
Father is in me, or else, believe because of the works themselves.
Amen, amen, I say to you, whoever believes in me will do the
works that I do, and will do greater ones than these, because I am
going to the Father. And whatever you ask in my name, I will do,

so that the Father may be glorified in the Son. If you ask anything of me in my name, I will do it."

FIFTH SUNDAY OF EASTER

First Reading   **Acts 9:26-31**

When Saul arrived in Jerusalem he tried to join the disciples, but they were all afraid of him, not believing that he was a disciple. Then Barnabas took charge of him and brought him to the apostles, and he reported to them how he had seen the Lord, and that he had spoken to him, and how in Damascus he had spoken out boldly in the name of Jesus. He moved about freely with them in Jerusalem, and spoke out boldly in the name of the Lord. He also spoke and debated with the Hellenists, but they tried to kill him. And when the brothers learned of this, they took him down to Caesarea and sent him on his way to Tarsus.

The church throughout all Judea, Galilee, and Samaria was at peace. It was being built up and walked in the fear of the Lord, and with the consolation of the Holy Spirit it grew in numbers.

Responsorial Psalm   **Psalm 22:26-27, 28, 30, 31-32**

R. (26a) I will praise you, Lord, in the assembly of your people.

Or:

R. Alleluia.

I will fulfill my vows before those who fear the LORD. The lowly shall eat their fill; they who seek the LORD shall praise him: "May your hearts live forever!" **R.**

All the ends of the earth shall remember and turn to the LORD; all the families of the nations shall bow down before him. **R.**

To him alone shall bow down all who sleep in the earth; before him shall bend all who go down into the dust. **R.**

And to him my soul shall live; my descendants shall serve him. Let the coming generation be told of the LORD that they may proclaim to a people yet to be born the justice he has shown. **R.**

Second Reading   1 John 3:18-24

Children, let us love not in word or speech but in deed and truth.

Now this is how we shall know that we belong to the truth and reassure our hearts before him in whatever our hearts condemn, for God is greater than our hearts and knows everything.

Beloved, if our hearts do not condemn us, we have confidence in God and receive from him whatever we ask, because we keep his commandments and do what pleases him. And his commandment is this: we should believe in the name of his Son, Jesus Christ, and love one another just as he commanded us. Those who keep his commandments remain in him, and he in them, and the way we know that he remains in us is from the Spirit he gave us.

Alleluia   John 15:4a, 5b
R. Alleluia, alleluia.

Remain in me as I remain in you, says the Lord. Whoever remains in me will bear much fruit. **R.**

Gospel   John 15:1-8

Jesus said to his disciples:

"I am the true vine, and my Father is the vine grower. He takes away every branch in me that does not bear fruit, and every one that does he prunes so that it bears more fruit. You are already pruned because of the word that I spoke to you. Remain in me, as I remain in you. Just as a branch cannot bear fruit on its own unless it remains on the vine, so neither can you unless you remain in me. I am the vine, you are the branches. Whoever remains in me and I in him will bear much fruit, because without me you can do nothing. Anyone who does not remain in me will be thrown out like a branch and wither; people will gather them and throw them into a fire and they will be burned. If you remain in me and my words remain in you, ask for whatever you want and it will be done for you. By this is my Father glorified, that you bear much fruit and become my disciples."

MONDAY, MAY 3, 2021

FEAST OF SAINTS PHILIP AND JAMES, APOSTLES

First Reading   **1 Corinthians 15:1-8**

I am reminding you, brothers and sisters, of the Gospel I preached to you, which you indeed received and in which you also stand. Through it you are also being saved, if you hold fast to the word I preached to you, unless you believed in vain. For I handed on to you as of first importance what I also received: that Christ died for our sins in accordance with the Scriptures; that he was buried; that he was raised on the third day in accordance with the Scriptures; that he appeared to Cephas, then to the Twelve. After that, he appeared to more than five hundred brothers and sisters at once, most of whom are still living, though some have fallen asleep. After that he appeared to James, then to all the Apostles. Last of all, as to one born abnormally, he appeared to me.

Responsorial Psalm   Psalm 19:2-3, 4-5

R. (5) Their message goes out through all the earth.
Or:
R. Alleluia.

The heavens declare the glory of God; and the firmament proclaims his handiwork. Day pours out the word to day; and night to night imparts knowledge. **R.**

Not a word nor a discourse whose voice is not heard; through all the earth their voice resounds, and to the ends of the world, their message. **R.**

Alleluia   John 14:6b, 9c

R. Alleluia, alleluia.

I am the way, the truth, and the life, says the Lord; Philip, whoever has seen me has seen the Father.

Gospel   John 14:6-14

Jesus said to Thomas,

"I am the way and the truth and the life. No one comes to the Father except through me. If you know me, then you will also know my Father. From now on you do know him and have seen him." Philip said to him, "Master, show us the Father, and that will be enough for us." Jesus said to him, "Have I been with you for so long a time and you still do not know me, Philip? Whoever has seen me has seen the Father. How can you say, 'Show us the Father'? Do you not believe that I am in the Father and the Father is in me? The words that I speak to you I do not speak on my own. The Father who dwells in me is doing his works. Believe me that I am in the Father and the Father is in me, or else, believe because of the works themselves. Amen, amen, I say to you, whoever believes in me will do the works that I do, and will do greater ones than these, because I am going to the Father. And whatever you ask in my name, I will do, so that the Father may be glorified in the Son. If you ask anything of me in my name, I will do it."

TUESDAY OF THE FIFTH WEEK OF EASTER

First Reading   **Acts 14:19-28**

In those days, some Jews from Antioch and Iconium arrived and won over the crowds. They stoned Paul and dragged him out of the city, supposing that he was dead. But when the disciples gathered around him, he got up and entered the city. On the following day he left with Barnabas for Derbe.

After they had proclaimed the good news to that city and made a considerable number of disciples, they returned to Lystra and to Iconium and to Antioch. They strengthened the spirits of the disciples and exhorted them to persevere in the faith, saying, "It is necessary for us to undergo many hardships to enter the Kingdom of God." They appointed presbyters for them in each Church and, with prayer and fasting, commended them to the Lord in whom they had put their faith.

Then they traveled through Pisidia and reached Pamphylia. After proclaiming the word at Perga they went down to Attalia. From there they sailed to Antioch, where they had been commended to the grace of God for the work they had now accomplished. And when they arrived, they called the Church together and reported what God had done with them and how he had opened the door of faith to the Gentiles. Then they spent no little time with the disciples.

Responsorial Psalm   Psalm 145:10-11, 12-13ab, 21
R. (12) Your friends make known, O Lord, the glorious splendor of your kingdom.
Or:
R. Alleluia.
Let all your works give you thanks, O LORD, and let your faithful ones bless you. Let them discourse of the glory of your kingdom and speak of your might. **R.**
Making known to men your might and the glorious splendor of your kingdom. Your kingdom is a kingdom for all ages, and your dominion endures through all generations. **R.**
May my mouth speak the praise of the LORD, and may all flesh bless his holy name forever and ever. **R.**

Alleluia   Luke 24:46, 26
R. Alleluia, alleluia.
Christ had to suffer and to rise from the dead, and so enter into his glory. **R.**

Gospel   John 14:27-31a
Jesus said to his disciples:
"Peace I leave with you; my peace I give to you. Not as the world gives do I give it to you. Do not let your hearts be troubled or afraid. You heard me tell you, 'I am going away and I will come

back to you.' If you loved me, you would rejoice that I am going to the Father; for the Father is greater than I. And now I have told you this before it happens, so that when it happens you may believe. I will no longer speak much with you, for the ruler of the world is coming. He has no power over me, but the world must know that I love the Father and that I do just as the Father has commanded me."

WEDNESDAY, MAY 5, 2021

WEDNESDAY OF THE FIFTH WEEK OF EASTER

First Reading   **Acts 15:1-6**

Some who had come down from Judea were instructing the brothers, "Unless you are circumcised according to the Mosaic practice, you cannot be saved." Because there arose no little dissension and debate by Paul and Barnabas with them, it was decided that Paul, Barnabas, and some of the others should go up to Jerusalem to the Apostles and presbyters about this question. They were sent on their journey by the Church, and passed through Phoenicia and Samaria telling of the conversion of the Gentiles, and brought great joy to all the brethren. When they arrived in Jerusalem, they were welcomed by the Church, as well as by the Apostles and the presbyters, and they reported what God had done with them. But some from the party of the Pharisees who had become believers stood up and said, "It is necessary to circumcise them and direct them to observe the Mosaic Law." The Apostles and the presbyters met together to see about this matter.

Responsorial Psalm   **Psalm 122:1-2, 3-4ab, 4cd-5**

R. (1) Let us go rejoicing to the house of the Lord.

Or:

R. Alleluia.

I rejoiced because they said to me, "We will go up to the house of the LORD." And now we have set foot within your gates, O Jerusalem. **R.**

Jerusalem, built as a city with compact unity. To it the tribes go up, the tribes of the LORD. **R.**

According to the decree for Israel, to give thanks to the name of the LORD. In it are set up judgment seats, seats for the house of David. **R.**

Alleluia   John 15:4a, 5b

R. Alleluia, alleluia.

Remain in me, as I remain in you, says the Lord; whoever remains in me will bear much fruit. **R.**

Gospel   John 15:1-8

Jesus said to his disciples:

"I am the true vine, and my Father is the vine grower. He takes away every branch in me that does not bear fruit, and everyone that does he prunes so that it bears more fruit. You are already pruned because of the word that I spoke to you. Remain in me, as I remain in you. Just as a branch cannot bear fruit on its own unless it remains on the vine, so neither can you unless you remain in me. I am the vine, you are the branches. Whoever remains in me and I in him will bear much fruit, because without me you can do nothing. Anyone who does not remain in me will be thrown out like a branch and wither; people will gather them and throw them into a fire and they will be burned. If you remain in me and my words remain in you, ask for whatever you want and it will be done for you. By this is my Father glorified, that you bear much fruit and become my disciples."

THURSDAY OF THE FIFTH WEEK OF EASTER

First Reading   **Acts 15:7-21**

After much debate had taken place, Peter got up and said to the Apostles and the presbyters, "My brothers, you are well aware that from early days God made his choice among you that through my mouth the Gentiles would hear the word of the Gospel and believe. And God, who knows the heart, bore witness by granting them the Holy Spirit just as he did us. He made no distinction between us and them, for by faith he purified their hearts. Why, then, are you now putting God to the test by placing on the shoulders of the disciples a yoke that neither our ancestors nor we have been able to bear? On the contrary, we believe that we are saved through the grace of the Lord Jesus, in the same way as they." The whole assembly fell silent, and they listened while Paul and Barnabas described the signs and wonders God had worked among the Gentiles through them.

After they had fallen silent, James responded, "My brothers, listen to me. Symeon has described how God first concerned himself with acquiring from among the Gentiles a people for his name. The words of the prophets agree with this, as is written:

After this I shall return and rebuild the fallen hut of David; from its ruins I shall rebuild it and raise it up again, so that the rest of humanity may seek out the Lord, even all the Gentiles on whom my name is invoked. Thus says the Lord who accomplishes these things, known from of old.

It is my judgment, therefore, that we ought to stop troubling the Gentiles who turn to God, but tell them by letter to avoid pollution from idols, unlawful marriage, the meat of strangled animals, and blood. For Moses, for generations now, has had those who proclaim him in every town, as he has been read in the synagogues every Sabbath."

Responsorial Psalm   Psalm 96:1-2a, 2b-3, 10

R. (3) Proclaim God's marvelous deeds to all the nations.
Or:
R. Alleluia.

Sing to the LORD a new song; sing to the LORD, all you lands.
Sing to the LORD; bless his name. **R.**

Announce his salvation, day after day. Tell his glory among the nations; among all peoples, his wondrous deeds. **R.**

Say among the nations: The LORD is king. He has made the world firm, not to be moved; he governs the peoples with equity. **R.**

Alleluia   John 10:27

R. Alleluia, alleluia.

My sheep hear my voice, says the Lord; I know them, and they follow me.

Gospel   John 15:9-11

Jesus said to his disciples:

"As the Father loves me, so I also love you. Remain in my love. If you keep my commandments, you will remain in my love, just as I have kept my Father's commandments and remain in his love.

"I have told you this so that my joy might be in you and your joy might be complete."

FRIDAY OF THE FIFTH WEEK OF EASTER

First Reading   **Acts 15:22-31**

The Apostles and presbyters, in agreement with the whole Church, decided to choose representatives and to send them to Antioch with Paul and Barnabas. The ones chosen were Judas, who was called Barsabbas, and Silas, leaders among the brothers. This is the letter delivered by them: "The Apostles and the presbyters, your brothers, to the brothers in Antioch, Syria, and Cilicia of Gentile origin: greetings. Since we have heard that some of our number who went out without any mandate from us have upset you with their teachings and disturbed your peace of mind, we have with one accord decided to choose representatives and to send them to you along with our beloved Barnabas and Paul, who have dedicated their lives to the name of our Lord Jesus Christ. So we are sending Judas and Silas who will also convey this same message by word of mouth: 'It is the decision of the Holy Spirit and of us not to place on you any burden beyond these necessities, namely, to abstain from meat sacrificed to idols, from blood, from meats of strangled animals, and from unlawful marriage. If you keep free of these, you will be doing what is right. Farewell.'"

And so they were sent on their journey. Upon their arrival in Antioch they called the assembly together and delivered the letter. When the people read it, they were delighted with the exhortation.

Responsorial Psalm   Psalm 57:8-9, 10 and 12

R. (10a) I will give you thanks among the peoples, O Lord.

Or:

R. Alleluia.

My heart is steadfast, O God; my heart is steadfast; I will sing and chant praise.

Awake, O my soul; awake, lyre and harp! I will wake the dawn. **R.**

I will give thanks to you among the peoples, O LORD, I will chant your praise among the nations. For your mercy towers to the heavens, and your faithfulness to the skies. Be exalted above the heavens, O God; above all the earth be your glory! **R.**

Alleluia   John 15:15b

R. Alleluia, alleluia.

I call you my friends, says the Lord, for I have made known to you all that the Father has told me. **R.**

Gospel   John 15:12-17

Jesus said to his disciples:

"This is my commandment: love one another as I love you. No one has greater love than this, to lay down one's life for one's friends. You are my friends if you do what I command you. I no longer call you slaves, because a slave does not know what his master is doing. I have called you friends, because I have told you everything

I have heard from my Father. It was not you who chose me, but I who chose you and appointed you to go and bear fruit that will remain, so that whatever you ask the Father in my name he may give you. This I command you: love one another."

SATURDAY OF THE FIFTH WEEK OF EASTER

First Reading   **Acts 16:1-10**

Paul reached also Derbe and Lystra where there was a disciple named Timothy, the son of a Jewish woman who was a believer, but his father was a Greek. The brothers in Lystra and Iconium spoke highly of him, and Paul wanted him to come along with him. On account of the Jews of that region, Paul had him circumcised, for they all knew that his father was a Greek. As they traveled from city to city, they handed on to the people for observance the decisions reached by the Apostles and presbyters in Jerusalem. Day after day the churches grew stronger in faith and increased in number.

They traveled through the Phrygian and Galatian territory because they had been prevented by the Holy Spirit from preaching the message in the province of Asia. When they came to Mysia, they tried to go on into Bithynia, but the Spirit of Jesus did not allow them, so they crossed through Mysia and came down to Troas. During the night Paul had a vision. A Macedonian stood before him and implored him with these words, "Come over to Macedonia and help us." When he had seen the vision, we sought passage to Macedonia at once, concluding that God had called us to proclaim the Good News to them.

Responsorial Psalm   **Psalm 100:1b-2, 3, 5**

R. (2a) Let all the earth cry out to God with joy.

Or:

R. Alleluia.

Sing joyfully to the LORD, all you lands; serve the LORD with
gladness; come before him with joyful song. **R.**

Know that the LORD is God; he made us, his we are; his people,
the flock he tends. **R.**

The LORD is good: his kindness endures forever, and his
faithfulness, to all generations. **R.**

Alleluia   **Colossians 3:1**

R. Alleluia, alleluia.

If then you were raised with Christ, seek what is above, where
Christ is seated at the right hand of God. **R.**

Gospel   **John 15:18-21**

Jesus said to his disciples:

"If the world hates you, realize that it hated me first. If you
belonged to the world, the world would love its own; but because
you do not belong to the world, and I have chosen you out of the
world, the world hates you. Remember the word I spoke to you,
'No slave is greater than his master.' If they persecuted me, they
will also persecute you. If they kept my word, they will also keep
yours. And they will do all these things to you on account of my
name, because they do not know the one who sent me."

SIXTH SUNDAY OF EASTER

First Reading   **Acts 10:25-26, 34-35, 44-48**

When Peter entered, Cornelius met him and, falling at his feet, paid him homage. Peter, however, raised him up, saying, "Get up. I myself am also a human being." Then Peter proceeded to speak and said, "In truth, I see that God shows no partiality. Rather, in every nation whoever fears him and acts uprightly is acceptable to him."

While Peter was still speaking these things, the Holy Spirit fell upon all who were listening to the word. The circumcised believers who had accompanied Peter were astounded that the gift of the Holy Spirit should have been poured out on the Gentiles also, for they could hear them speaking in tongues and glorifying God. Then Peter responded, "Can anyone withhold the water for baptizing these people, who have received the Holy Spirit even as we have?" He ordered them to be baptized in the name of Jesus Christ.

Responsorial Psalm   **Psalm 98:1, 2-3, 3-4**

R. (2b) The Lord has revealed to the nations his saving power.

Or:

R. Alleluia.

Sing to the LORD a new song, for he has done wondrous deeds;
His right hand has won victory for him, his holy arm. **R.**
The LORD has made his salvation known: in the sight of the nations he has revealed his justice. He has remembered his kindness and his faithfulness toward the house of Israel. **R.**

All the ends of the earth have seen the salvation by our God. Sing joyfully to the LORD, all you lands; break into song; sing praise. **R.**

Second Reading   1 John 4:7-10

Beloved, let us love one another, because love is of God; everyone who loves is begotten by God and knows God. Whoever is without love does not know God, for God is love. In this way the love of God was revealed to us: God sent his only Son into the world so that we might have life through him. In this is love: not that we have loved God, but that he loved us and sent his Son as expiation for our sins.

Alleluia   John 14:23

R. Alleluia, alleluia.

Whoever loves me will keep my word, says the Lord, and my Father will love him and we will come to him. **R.**

Gospel   John 15:9-17

Jesus said to his disciples:

"As the Father loves me, so I also love you. Remain in my love. If you keep my commandments, you will remain in my love, just as I have kept my Father's commandments and remain in his love.

"I have told you this so that my joy may be in you and your joy might be complete. This is my commandment: love one another as I love you. No one has greater love than this, to lay down one's life for one's friends. You are my friends if you do what I command you. I no longer call you slaves, because a slave does not know what his master is doing. I have called you friends, because I have told you everything I have heard from my Father. It was not you who chose me, but I who chose you and appointed you to go and bear fruit that will remain, so that whatever you ask the Father in my name he may give you. This I command you: love one another."

MONDAY OF THE SIXTH WEEK OF EASTER

First Reading   **Acts 16:11-15**

We set sail from Troas, making a straight run for Samothrace, and on the next day to Neapolis, and from there to Philippi, a leading city in that district of Macedonia and a Roman colony. We spent some time in that city. On the Sabbath we went outside the city gate along the river where we thought there would be a place of prayer. We sat and spoke with the women who had gathered there. One of them, a woman named Lydia, a dealer in purple cloth, from the city of Thyatira, a worshiper of God, listened, and the Lord opened her heart to pay attention to what Paul was saying. After she and her household had been baptized, she offered us an invitation, "If you consider me a believer in the Lord, come and stay at my home," and she prevailed on us.

Responsorial Psalm   **Psalm 149:1b-2, 3-4, 5-6a and 9b**

R. (4a) The Lord takes delight in his people.

Or:

R. Alleluia.

Sing to the LORD a new song of praise in the assembly of the faithful. Let Israel be glad in their maker, let the children of Zion rejoice in their king. **R.**

Let them praise his name in the festive dance, let them sing praise to him with timbrel and harp. For the LORD loves his people, and he adorns the lowly with victory. **R.**

Let the faithful exult in glory; let them sing for joy upon their couches. Let the high praises of God be in their throats. This is the glory of all his faithful. Alleluia. **R.**

Alleluia   John 15:26b, 27a

R. Alleluia, alleluia.

The Spirit of truth will testify to me, says the Lord, and you also will testify. **R.**

Gospel   John 15:26-16:4a

Jesus said to his disciples:

"When the Advocate comes whom I will send you from the Father, the Spirit of truth who proceeds from the Father, he will testify to me. And you also testify, because you have been with me from the beginning. "I have told you this so that you may not fall away. They will expel you from the synagogues; in fact, the hour is coming when everyone who kills you will think he is offering worship to God. They will do this because they have not known either the Father or me. I have told you this so that when their hour comes you may remember that I told you."

TUESDAY OF THE SIXTH WEEK OF EASTER

First Reading   **Acts 16:22-34**

The crowd in Philippi joined in the attack on Paul and Silas, and the magistrates had them stripped and ordered them to be beaten with rods. After inflicting many blows on them, they threw them into prison and instructed the jailer to guard them securely. When he received these instructions, he put them in the innermost cell and secured their feet to a stake.

About midnight, while Paul and Silas were praying and singing hymns to God as the prisoners listened, there was suddenly such a severe earthquake that the foundations of the jail shook; all the doors flew open, and the chains of all were pulled loose. When the jailer woke up and saw the prison doors wide open, he drew his sword and was about to kill himself, thinking that the prisoners had escaped. But Paul shouted out in a loud voice, "Do no harm to yourself; we are all here." He asked for a light and rushed in and, trembling with fear, he fell down before Paul and Silas. Then he brought them out and said, "Sirs, what must I do to be saved?" And they said, "Believe in the Lord Jesus and you and your household will be saved." So they spoke the word of the Lord to him and to everyone in his house. He took them in at that hour of the night and bathed their wounds; then he and all his family were baptized at once. He brought them up into his house and provided a meal and with his household rejoiced at having come to faith in God.

Responsorial Psalm   **Psalm 138:1-2ab, 2cde-3, 7c-8**

R. (7c) Your right hand saves me, O Lord.

Or:

R. Alleluia.

I will give thanks to you, O LORD, with all my heart, for you have heard the words of my mouth; in the presence of the angels I will sing your praise; I will worship at your holy temple, and give thanks to your name. **R.**

Because of your kindness and your truth, you have made great above all things your name and your promise. When I called, you answered me; you built up strength within me. **R.**

Your right hand saves me. The LORD will complete what he has done for me; your kindness, O LORD, endures forever; forsake not the work of your hands. **R.**

Alleluia   John 16:7, 13

R. Alleluia, alleluia.

I will send to you the Spirit of truth, says the Lord; he will guide you to all truth. **R.**

Gospel   John 16:5-11

Jesus said to his disciples:

"Now I am going to the one who sent me, and not one of you asks me, 'Where are you going?' But because I told you this, grief has filled your hearts. But I tell you the truth, it is better for you that I go. For if I do not go, the Advocate will not come to you. But if I go, I will send him to you. And when he comes he will convict the world in regard to sin and righteousness and condemnation: sin, because they do not believe in me; righteousness, because I am going to the Father and you will no longer see me; condemnation, because the ruler of this world has been condemned."

WEDNESDAY OF THE SIXTH WEEK OF EASTER

First Reading   **Acts 17:15, 22-18:1**

After Paul's escorts had taken him to Athens, they came away with instructions for Silas and Timothy to join him as soon as possible.

Then Paul stood up at the Areopagus and said: "You Athenians, I see that in every respect you are very religious. For as I walked around looking carefully at your shrines, I even discovered an altar inscribed, 'To an Unknown God.' What therefore you unknowingly worship, I proclaim to you. The God who made the world and all that is in it, the Lord of heaven and earth, does not dwell in sanctuaries made by human hands, nor is he served by human hands because he needs anything. Rather it is he who gives to everyone life and breath and everything. He made from one the whole human race to dwell on the entire surface of the earth, and he fixed the ordered seasons and the boundaries of their regions, so that people might seek God, even perhaps grope for him and find him, though indeed he is not far from any one of us. For 'In him we live and move and have our being,' as even some of your poets have said, 'for we too are his offspring.' Since therefore we are the offspring of God, we ought not to think that the divinity is like an image fashioned from gold, silver, or stone by human art and imagination. God has overlooked the times of ignorance, but now he demands that all people everywhere repent because he has established a day on which he will 'judge the world with justice' through a man he has appointed, and he has provided confirmation for all by raising him from the dead." When they heard about resurrection of the dead, some began to scoff, but

409

others said, "We should like to hear you on this some other time."
And so Paul left them. But some did join him, and became
believers. Among them were Dionysius, a member of the Court of
the Areopagus, a woman named Damaris, and others with them.
After this he left Athens and went to Corinth.

Responsorial Psalm   **Psalm 148:1-2, 11-12, 13, 14**
R. Heaven and earth are full of your glory.
Or:
R. Alleluia.
Praise the LORD from the heavens; praise him in the heights.
Praise him, all you his angels; praise him, all you his hosts. **R.**
Let the kings of the earth and all peoples, the princes and all the
judges of the earth, Young men too, and maidens, old men and
boys. **R.**
Praise the name of the LORD, for his name alone is exalted; His
majesty is above earth and heaven. **R.**
He has lifted up the horn of his people; be this his praise from all
his faithful ones, from the children of Israel, the people close to
him. Alleluia. **R.**

Alleluia   **John 14:16**
R. Alleluia, alleluia.
I will ask the Father and he will give you another Advocate to be
with you always. **R.**

Gospel   **John 16:12-15**
Jesus said to his disciples:
"I have much more to tell you, but you cannot bear it now. But
when he comes, the Spirit of truth, he will guide you to all truth.

He will not speak on his own, but he will speak what he hears, and will declare to you the things that are coming. He will glorify me, because he will take from what is mine and declare it to you. Everything that the Father has is mine; for this reason I told you that he will take from what is mine and declare it to you."

SOLEMNITY OF THE ASCENSION OF THE LORD OR THURSDAY OF THE SIXTH WEEK OF EASTER

SOLEMNITY OF THE ASCENSION OF THE LORD

First Reading   **Acts 1:1-11**

In the first book, Theophilus, I dealt with all that Jesus did and taught until the day he was taken up, after giving instructions through the Holy Spirit to the apostles whom he had chosen. He presented himself alive to them by many proofs after he had suffered, appearing to them during forty days and speaking about the kingdom of God. While meeting with them, he enjoined them not to depart from Jerusalem, but to wait for "the promise of the Father about which you have heard me speak; for John baptized with water, but in a few days you will be baptized with the Holy Spirit."

When they had gathered together they asked him, "Lord, are you at this time going to restore the kingdom to Israel?" He answered them, "It is not for you to know the times or seasons that the Father has established by his own authority. But you will receive power when the Holy Spirit comes upon you, and you will be my witnesses in Jerusalem, throughout Judea and Samaria, and to the ends of the earth." When he had said this, as they were looking on, he was lifted up, and a cloud took him from their sight. While they were looking intently at the sky as he was going, suddenly two men dressed in white garments stood beside them. They said, "Men of Galilee, why are you standing there looking at the sky? This Jesus who has been taken up from you into heaven will return in the same way as you have seen him going into heaven."

Responsorial Psalm   Psalm 47:2-3, 6-7, 8-9

R. (6) God mounts his throne to shouts of joy: a blare of trumpets for the Lord.

Or:

R. Alleluia.

All you peoples, clap your hands, shout to God with cries of gladness, For the LORD, the Most High, the awesome, is the great king over all the earth. **R.**

God mounts his throne amid shouts of joy; the LORD, amid trumpet blasts. Sing praise to God, sing praise; sing praise to our king, sing praise. **R.**

For king of all the earth is God; sing hymns of praise. God reigns over the nations,

God sits upon his holy throne. **R.**

Second Reading   Ephesians 1:17-23 or
                                        4:1-13 or 4:1-7, 11-13

Ephesians 1:17-23

Brothers and sisters:

May the God of our Lord Jesus Christ, the Father of glory, give you a Spirit of wisdom and revelation resulting in knowledge of him. May the eyes of your hearts be enlightened, that you may know what is the hope that belongs to his call, what are the riches of glory in his inheritance among the holy ones, and what is the surpassing greatness of his power for us who believe, in accord with the exercise of his great might, which he worked in Christ, raising him from the dead and seating him at his right hand in the heavens, far above every principality, authority, power, and dominion, and every name that is named not only in this age but also in the one to come. And he put all things beneath his feet and gave him as head over all things to the church, which is his body, the fullness of the one who fills all things in every way.

Or:

Ephesians 4:1-13

Brothers and sisters, I, a prisoner for the Lord, urge you to live in a manner worthy of the call you have received, with all humility and gentleness, with patience, bearing with one another through love, striving to preserve the unity of the spirit through the bond of peace: one body and one Spirit, as you were also called to the one hope of your call; one Lord, one faith, one baptism; one God and Father of all, who is over all and through all and in all.

But grace was given to each of us according to the measure of Christ's gift. Therefore, it says:

He ascended on high and took prisoners captive; he gave gifts to men.

What does "he ascended" mean except that he also descended into the lower regions of the earth? The one who descended is also the one who ascended far above all the heavens, that he might fill all things. And he gave some as apostles, others as prophets, others as evangelists, others as pastors and teachers, to equip the holy ones for the work of ministry, for building up the body of Christ, until we all attain to the unity of faith and knowledge of the Son of God, to mature to manhood, to the extent of the full stature of Christ.

Or

Ephesians 4:1-7, 11-13

Brothers and sisters,

I, a prisoner for the Lord, urge you to live in a manner worthy of the calling you have received, with all humility and gentleness, with patience, bearing with one another through love, striving to preserve the unity of the Spirit through the bond of peace: one body and one Spirit, as you were also called to the one hope of your calling; one Lord, one faith, one baptism; one God and Father of all, who is over all and through all and in all.

But grace was given to each of us according to the measure of Christ's gift.

And he gave some as apostles, others as prophets, others as evangelists, others as pastors and teachers, to equip the holy ones for the work of ministry, for building up the body of Christ, until we all attain to the unity of faith and knowledge of the Son of God, to mature to manhood, to the extent of the full stature of Christ.

Alleluia   **Matthew 28:19ab, 20b**

R. Alleluia, alleluia.

Go and teach all nations, says the Lord; I am with you always, until the end of the world. **R.**

Gospel   **Mark 16:15-20**

Jesus said to his disciples:

"Go into the whole world and proclaim the gospel to every creature. Whoever believes and is baptized will be saved; whoever does not believe will be condemned. These signs will accompany those who believe: in my name they will drive out demons, they will speak new languages. They will pick up serpents with their hands, and if they drink any deadly thing, it will not harm them. They will lay hands on the sick, and they will recover."

So then the Lord Jesus, after he spoke to them, was taken up into heaven and took his seat at the right hand of God. But they went forth and preached everywhere, while the Lord worked with them and confirmed the word through accompanying signs.

THURSDAY OF THE SIXTH WEEK OF EASTER

(The following readings are used on this Thursday if the celebration of Ascension is transferred to the Seventh Sunday of Easter)

First Reading   **Acts 18:1-8**

Paul left Athens and went to Corinth.

There he met a Jew named Aquila, a native of Pontus, who had recently come from Italy with his wife Priscilla because Claudius had ordered all the Jews to leave Rome. He went to visit them and, because he practiced the same trade, stayed with them and worked, for they were tentmakers by trade. Every Sabbath, he entered into discussions in the synagogue, attempting to convince both Jews and Greeks.

When Silas and Timothy came down from Macedonia, Paul began to occupy himself totally with preaching the word, testifying to the Jews that the Christ was Jesus. When they opposed him and reviled him, he shook out his garments and said to them, "Your blood be on your heads! I am clear of responsibility. From now on I will go to the Gentiles." So he left there and went to a house belonging to a man named Titus Justus, a worshiper of God; his house was next to a synagogue. Crispus, the synagogue official, came to believe in the Lord along with his entire household, and many of the Corinthians who heard believed and were baptized.

Responsorial Psalm   Psalm 98:1, 2-3ab, 3cd-4

R. (2b) The Lord has revealed to the nations his saving power.

Or:

R. Alleluia.

Sing to the LORD a new song, for he has done wondrous deeds;
His right hand has won victory for him, his holy arm. **R.**
The LORD has made his salvation known: in the sight of the
nations he has revealed his justice. He has remembered his
kindness and his faithfulness toward the house of Israel. **R.**
All the ends of the earth have seen the salvation by our God. Sing
joyfully to the LORD, all you lands; break into song; sing praise. **R.**

Alleluia   John 14:18

R. Alleluia, alleluia.

I will not leave you orphans, says the Lord; I will come back to you, and your hearts will rejoice. **R.**

Gospel   John 16:16-20

Jesus said to his disciples:

"A little while and you will no longer see me, and again a little while later and you will see me." So some of his disciples said to one another, "What does this mean that he is saying to us, 'A little while and you will not see me, and again a little while and you will see me,' and 'Because I am going to the Father'?" So they said, "What is this 'little while' of which he speaks? We do not know what he means." Jesus knew that they wanted to ask him, so he said to them, "Are you discussing with one another what I said, 'A little while and you will not see me, and again a little while and you will see me'? Amen, amen, I say to you, you will weep and mourn, while the world rejoices; you will grieve, but your grief will become joy."

FRIDAY, MAY 14, 2021
FEAST OF SAINT MATTHIAS, APOSTLE

First Reading   **Acts 1:15-17, 20-26**

Peter stood up in the midst of the brothers and sisters (there was a group of about one hundred and twenty persons in the one place). He said, "My brothers and sisters, the Scripture had to be fulfilled which the Holy Spirit spoke beforehand through the mouth of David, concerning Judas, who was the guide for those who arrested Jesus. Judas was numbered among us and was allotted a share in this ministry. For it is written in the Book of Psalms:
Let his encampment become desolate, and may no one dwell in it.
And: *May another take his office.* Therefore, it is necessary that one of the men who accompanied us the whole time the Lord Jesus came and went among us, beginning from the baptism of John until the day on which he was taken up from us, become with us a witness to his resurrection." So they proposed two, Joseph called Barsabbas, who was also known as Justus, and Matthias. Then they prayed, "You, Lord, who know the hearts of all, show

which one of these two you have chosen to take the place in this apostolic ministry from which Judas turned away to go to his own place." Then they gave lots to them, and the lot fell upon Matthias, and he was counted with the Eleven Apostles.

Responsorial Psalm   Psalm 113:1-2, 3-4, 5-6, 7-8
R. (8) The Lord will give him a seat with the leaders of his people.
Or:
R. Alleluia.
Praise, you servants of the LORD, praise the name of the LORD.
Blessed be the name of the LORD both now and forever. **R.**
From the rising to the setting of the sun is the name of the LORD
to be praised. High above all nations is the LORD; above the
heavens is his glory. **R.**
Who is like the LORD, our God, who is enthroned on high and
looks upon the heavens and the earth below? **R.**

He raises up the lowly from the dust; from the dunghill he lifts up
the poor to seat them with princes, with the princes of his own
people. **R.**

Alleluia   John 15:16
R. Alleluia, alleluia.
I chose you from the world, to go and bear fruit that will last, says
the Lord. **R.**

Gospel   John 15:9-17
Jesus said to his disciples:

"As the Father loves me, so I also love you. Remain in my love. If you keep my commandments, you will remain in my love, just as I have kept my Father's commandments and remain in his love.

"I have told you this so that my joy might be in you and your joy might be complete. This is my commandment: love one another as I love you. No one has greater love than this, to lay down one's life for one's friends. You are my friends if you do what I command you. I no longer call you slaves, because a slave does not know what his master is doing. I have called you friends, because I have told you everything I have heard from my Father. It was not you who chose me, but I who chose you and appointed you to go and bear fruit that will remain, so that whatever you ask the Father in my name he may give you. This I command you: love one another."

SATURDAY OF THE SIXTH WEEK OF EASTER

First Reading   **Acts 18:23-28**

After staying in Antioch some time, Paul left and traveled in orderly sequence through the Galatian country and Phrygia, bringing strength to all the disciples. A Jew named Apollos, a native of Alexandria, an eloquent speaker, arrived in Ephesus. He was an authority on the Scriptures. He had been instructed in the Way of the Lord and, with ardent spirit, spoke and taught accurately about Jesus, although he knew only the baptism of John. He began to speak boldly in the synagogue; but when Priscilla and Aquila heard him, they took him aside and explained to him the Way of God more accurately. And when he wanted to cross to Achaia, the brothers encouraged him and wrote to the disciples there to welcome him. After his arrival he gave great assistance to those who had come to believe through grace. He vigorously refuted the Jews in public, establishing from the Scriptures that the Christ is Jesus.

Responsorial Psalm   Psalm 47:2-3, 8-9, 10

R. (8a) God is king of all the earth.

Or:

R. Alleluia.

All you peoples, clap your hands; shout to God with cries of gladness. For the LORD, the Most High, the awesome, is the great king over all the earth. **R.**

For king of all the earth is God; sing hymns of praise. God reigns over the nations, God sits upon his holy throne. **R.**

The princes of the peoples are gathered together with the people of the God of Abraham. For God's are the guardians of the earth; he is supreme. **R.**

Alleluia   John 16:28

R. Alleluia, alleluia.

I came from the Father and have come into the world; now I am leaving the world and going back to the Father. **R.**

Gospel   John 16:23b-28

Jesus said to his disciples:

"Amen, amen, I say to you, whatever you ask the Father in my name he will give you. Until now you have not asked anything in my name; ask and you will receive, so that your joy may be complete.

"I have told you this in figures of speech. The hour is coming when I will no longer speak to you in figures but I will tell you clearly about the Father.

On that day you will ask in my name, and I do not tell you that I will ask the Father for you. For the Father himself loves you, because you have loved me and have come to believe that I came from God. I came from the Father and have come into the world. Now I am leaving the world and going back to the Father."

SUNDAY, MAY 16, 2021

SOLEMNITY OF THE ASCENSION OF THE LORD OR SEVENTH SUNDAY OF EASTER

SOLEMNITY OF THE ASCENSION OF THE LORD

First Reading   **Acts 1:1-11**

In the first book, Theophilus, I dealt with all that Jesus did and taught until the day he was taken up, after giving instructions through the Holy Spirit to the apostles whom he had chosen. He presented himself alive to them by many proofs after he had suffered, appearing to them during forty days and speaking about the kingdom of God. While meeting with them, he enjoined them not to depart from Jerusalem, but to wait for "the promise of the Father about which you have heard me speak; for John baptized with water, but in a few days you will be baptized with the Holy Spirit."

When they had gathered together they asked him, "Lord, are you at this time going to restore the kingdom to Israel?" He answered them, "It is not for you to know the times or seasons that the Father has established by his own authority. But you will receive power when the Holy Spirit comes upon you, and you will be my witnesses in Jerusalem, throughout Judea and Samaria, and to the ends of the earth." When he had said this, as they were looking on, he was lifted up, and a cloud took him from their sight. While they were looking intently at the sky as he was going, suddenly two men dressed in white garments stood beside them. They said, "Men of Galilee, why are you standing there looking at the sky? This Jesus who has been taken up from you into heaven will return in the same way as you have seen him going into heaven."

Responsorial Psalm **Psalm 47:2-3, 6-7, 8-9**

R. (6) God mounts his throne to shouts of joy: a blare of trumpets for the Lord.

Or:

R. Alleluia.

All you peoples, clap your hands, shout to God with cries of gladness, For the LORD, the Most High, the awesome, is the great king over all the earth. **R.**

God mounts his throne amid shouts of joy; the LORD, amid trumpet blasts. Sing praise to God, sing praise; sing praise to our king, sing praise. **R.**

For king of all the earth is God; sing hymns of praise. God reigns over the nations,

God sits upon his holy throne. **R.**

Second Reading **Ephesians 1:17-23 or**

4:1-13 or 4:1-7, 11-13

Ephesians 1:17-23

422

Brothers and sisters:

May the God of our Lord Jesus Christ, the Father of glory, give you a Spirit of wisdom and revelation resulting in knowledge of him. May the eyes of your hearts be enlightened, that you may know what is the hope that belongs to his call, what are the riches of glory in his inheritance among the holy ones, and what is the surpassing greatness of his power for us who believe, in accord with the exercise of his great might, which he worked in Christ, raising him from the dead and seating him at his right hand in the heavens, far above every principality, authority, power, and dominion, and every name that is named not only in this age but also in the one to come. And he put all things beneath his feet and gave him as head over all things to the church, which is his body, the fullness of the one who fills all things in every way.

Or:

Ephesians 4:1-13

Brothers and sisters, I, a prisoner for the Lord, urge you to live in a manner worthy of the call you have received, with all humility and gentleness, with patience, bearing with one another through love, striving to preserve the unity of the spirit through the bond of peace: one body and one Spirit, as you were also called to the one hope of your call; one Lord, one faith, one baptism; one God and Father of all, who is over all and through all and in all.

But grace was given to each of us according to the measure of Christ's gift. Therefore, it says:

He ascended on high and took prisoners captive; he gave gifts to men.

What does "he ascended" mean except that he also descended into the lower regions of the earth? The one who descended is also the one who ascended far above all the heavens, that he might fill all things. And he gave some as apostles, others as prophets, others as evangelists, others as pastors and teachers, to equip the holy ones for the work of ministry, for building up the body of Christ, until we all attain to the unity of faith and knowledge of the Son of God, to mature to manhood, to the extent of the full stature of Christ.

Or
Ephesians 4:1-7, 11-13

Brothers and sisters,

I, a prisoner for the Lord, urge you to live in a manner worthy of the calling you have received, with all humility and gentleness, with patience, bearing with one another through love, striving to preserve the unity of the Spirit through the bond of peace: one body and one Spirit, as you were also called to the one hope of your calling; one Lord, one faith, one baptism; one God and Father of all, who is over all and through all and in all.

But grace was given to each of us according to the measure of Christ's gift.

And he gave some as apostles, others as prophets, others as evangelists, others as pastors and teachers, to equip the holy ones for the work of ministry, for building up the body of Christ, until we all attain to the unity of faith and knowledge of the Son of God, to mature to manhood, to the extent of the full stature of Christ.

Alleluia   **Matthew 28:19ab, 20b**
R. Alleluia, alleluia.

Go and teach all nations, says the Lord; I am with you always, until the end of the world. **R.**

Gospel   Mark 16:15-20

Jesus said to his disciples:

"Go into the whole world and proclaim the gospel to every creature. Whoever believes and is baptized will be saved; whoever does not believe will be condemned. These signs will accompany those who believe: in my name they will drive out demons, they will speak new languages. They will pick up serpents with their hands, and if they drink any deadly thing, it will not harm them. They will lay hands on the sick, and they will recover."

So then the Lord Jesus, after he spoke to them, was taken up into heaven and took his seat at the right hand of God. But they went forth and preached everywhere, while the Lord worked with them and confirmed the word through accompanying signs.

SEVENTH SUNDAY OF EASTER

(The following readings are used on this Seventh Sunday of Easter if Ascension of the Lord was celebrated on Thursday)

First Reading   Acts 1:15-17, 20a, 20c-26

Peter stood up in the midst of the brothers —there was a group of about one hundred and twenty persons in the one place —.He said, "My brothers, the Scripture had to be fulfilled which the Holy Spirit spoke beforehand through the mouth of David, concerning Judas, who was the guide for those who arrested Jesus. He was numbered among us and was allotted a share in this ministry.

"For it is written in the Book of Psalms: *May another take his office.*

"Therefore, it is necessary that one of the men who accompanied us the whole time the Lord Jesus came and went among us, beginning from the baptism of John until the day on which he was taken up from us, become with us a witness to his resurrection."

So they proposed two, Judas called Barsabbas, who was also known as Justus, and Matthias. Then they prayed, "You, Lord, who know the hearts of all, show which one of these two you have chosen to take the place in this apostolic ministry from which Judas turned away to go to his own place." Then they gave lots to them, and the lot fell upon Matthias, and he was counted with the eleven apostles.

Responsorial Psalm   Psalm 103:1-2, 11-12, 19-20

R. (19a) The Lord has set his throne in heaven.

Or:

R. Alleluia.

Bless the LORD, O my soul; and all my being, bless his holy name. Bless the LORD, O my soul, and forget not all his benefits. **R.**

For as the heavens are high above the earth, so surpassing is his kindness toward those who fear him. As far as the east is from the west, so far has he put our transgressions from us. **R.**

The LORD has established his throne in heaven, and his kingdom rules over all. Bless the LORD, all you his angels, you mighty in strength, who do his bidding. **R.**

Second Reading   1 John 4:11-16

Beloved, if God so loved us, we also must love one another. No one has ever seen God. Yet, if we love one another, God remains in us, and his love is brought to perfection in us.

This is how we know that we remain in him and he in us, that he has given us of his Spirit. Moreover, we have seen and testify that the Father sent his Son as savior of the world. Whoever acknowledges that Jesus is the Son of God, God remains in him and he in God. We have come to know and to believe in the love God has for us. God is love, and whoever remains in love remains in God and God in him.

Alleluia   John 14:18

R. Alleluia, alleluia.

I will not leave you orphans, says the Lord. I will come back to you, and your hearts will rejoice. **R.**

Gospel   John 17:11b-19

Lifting up his eyes to heaven, Jesus prayed saying:

"Holy Father, keep them in your name that you have given me, so that they may be one just as we are one. When I was with them I protected them in your name that you gave me, and I guarded them, and none of them was lost except the son of destruction, in order that the Scripture might be fulfilled. But now I am coming to you. I speak this in the world so that they may share my joy completely. I gave them your word, and the world hated them, because they do not belong to the world any more than I belong to the world. I do not ask that you take them out of the world but that you keep them from the evil one. They do not belong to the world any more than I belong to the world. Consecrate them in the truth. Your word is truth. As you sent me into the world, so I sent them into the world. And I consecrate myself for them, so that they also may be consecrated in truth."

MONDAY OF THE SEVENTH WEEK OF EASTER

First Reading   **Acts 19:1-8**

While Apollos was in Corinth, Paul traveled through the interior of the country and down to Ephesus where he found some disciples. He said to them, "Did you receive the Holy Spirit when you became believers?" They answered him, "We have never even heard that there is a Holy Spirit." He said, "How were you baptized?" They replied, "With the baptism of John." Paul then said, "John baptized with a baptism of repentance, telling the people to believe in the one who was to come after him, that is, in Jesus." When they heard this, they were baptized in the name of the Lord Jesus. And when Paul laid his hands on them, the Holy Spirit came upon them, and they spoke in tongues and prophesied. Altogether there were about twelve men. He entered the synagogue, and for three months debated boldly with persuasive arguments about the Kingdom of God.

Responsorial Psalm   **Psalm 68:2-3ab, 4-5acd, 6-7ab**

R. (33a) Sing to God, O kingdoms of the earth.

Or:

R. Alleluia.

God arises; his enemies are scattered, and those who hate him flee before him. As smoke is driven away, so are they driven; as wax melts before the fire. **R.**

But the just rejoice and exult before God; they are glad and rejoice. Sing to God, chant praise to his name; whose name is the LORD. **R.**

The father of orphans and the defender of widows is God in his holy dwelling. God gives a home to the forsaken; he leads forth prisoners to prosperity. **R.**

Alleluia   Colossians 3:1

R. Alleluia, alleluia.

If then you were raised with Christ, seek what is above, where Christ is seated at the right hand of God. **R.**

Gospel   John 16:29-33

The disciples said to Jesus,

"Now you are talking plainly, and not in any figure of speech. Now we realize that you know everything and that you do not need to have anyone question you. Because of this we believe that you came from God." Jesus answered them, "Do you believe now? Behold, the hour is coming and has arrived when each of you will be scattered to his own home and you will leave me alone. But I am not alone, because the Father is with me. I have told you this so that you might have peace in me. In the world you will have trouble, but take courage, I have conquered the world."

TUESDAY, MAY 18, 2021

TUESDAY OF THE SEVENTH WEEK OF EASTER

From Miletus Paul had the presbyters of the Church at Ephesus summoned. When they came to him, he addressed them, "You know how I lived among you the whole time from the day I first came to the province of Asia. I served the Lord with all humility and with the tears and trials that came to me because of the plots of the Jews, and I did not at all shrink from telling you what was for your benefit, or from teaching you in public or in your homes. I earnestly bore witness for both Jews and Greeks to repentance before God and to faith in our Lord Jesus. But now, compelled by the Spirit, I am going to Jerusalem. What will happen to me there I do not know, except that in one city after another the Holy Spirit has been warning me that imprisonment and hardships await me. Yet I consider life of no importance to me, if only I may finish my course and the ministry that I received from the Lord Jesus, to bear witness to the Gospel of God's grace. "But now I know that none of you to whom I preached the kingdom during my travels will ever see my face again. And so I solemnly declare to you this day that I am not responsible for the blood of any of you, for I did not shrink from proclaiming to you the entire plan of God."

Responsorial Psalm   **Psalm 68:10-11, 20-21**

R. (33a) Sing to God, O kingdoms of the earth.
Or:
R. Alleluia.
A bountiful rain you showered down, O God, upon your
inheritance; you restored the land when it languished; your flock
settled in it; in your goodness, O God, you provided it for the
needy. **R.**

Blessed day by day be the Lord, who bears our burdens; God, who is our salvation. God is a saving God for us; the LORD, my Lord, controls the passageways of death. **R.**

Alleluia   **John 14:16**
R. Alleluia, alleluia.
I will ask the father and he will give you another Advocate to be with you always. **R.**

Gospel   **John 17:1-11a**
Jesus raised his eyes to heaven and said,
"Father, the hour has come. Give glory to your son, so that your son may glorify you, just as you gave him authority over all people, so that your son may give eternal life to all you gave him. Now this is eternal life, that they should know you, the only true God, and the one whom you sent, Jesus Christ. I glorified you on earth by accomplishing the work that you gave me to do. Now glorify me, Father, with you, with the glory that I had with you before the world began.

"I revealed your name to those whom you gave me out of the world. They belonged to you, and you gave them to me, and they have kept your word. Now they know that everything you gave me is from you, because the words you gave to me I have given to them, and they accepted them and truly understood that I came from you, and they have believed that you sent me. I pray for them. I do not pray for the world but for the ones you have given me, because they are yours, and everything of mine is yours and everything of yours is mine, and I have been glorified in them. And now I will no longer be in the world, but they are in the world, while I am coming to you."

WEDNESDAY OF THE SEVENTH WEEK OF EASTER

First Reading   **Acts 20:28-38**

At Miletus, Paul spoke to the presbyters of the Church of Ephesus: "Keep watch over yourselves and over the whole flock of which the Holy Spirit has appointed you overseers, in which you tend the Church of God that he acquired with his own Blood. I know that after my departure savage wolves will come among you, and they will not spare the flock. And from your own group, men will come forward perverting the truth to draw the disciples away after them. So be vigilant and remember that for three years, night and day, I unceasingly admonished each of you with tears. And now I commend you to God and to that gracious word of his that can build you up and give you the inheritance among all who are consecrated. I have never wanted anyone's silver or gold or clothing. You know well that these very hands have served my needs and my companions. In every way I have shown you that by hard work of that sort we must help the weak, and keep in mind the words of the Lord Jesus who himself said, 'It is more blessed to give than to receive.'"

When he had finished speaking he knelt down and prayed with them all. They were all weeping loudly as they threw their arms around Paul and kissed him, for they were deeply distressed that he had said that they would never see his face again. Then they escorted him to the ship.

Responsorial Psalm — Psalm 68:29-30, 33-35a, 35bc-36ab

R. (33a) Sing to God, O kingdoms of the earth.

Or:

R. Alleluia.

Show forth, O God, your power, the power, O God, with which you took our part; for your temple in Jerusalem let the kings bring you gifts. **R.**

You kingdoms of the earth, sing to God, chant praise to the Lord who rides on the heights of the ancient heavens. Behold, his voice resounds, the voice of power: "Confess the power of God!" **R.**

Over Israel is his majesty; his power is in the skies. Awesome in his sanctuary is God, the God of Israel; he gives power and strength to his people. **R.**

Alleluia — John 17:17b, 17a

R. Alleluia, alleluia.

Your word, O Lord, is truth; consecrate us in the truth. **R.**

Gospel — John 17:11b-19

Lifting up his eyes to heaven, Jesus prayed, saying:

"Holy Father, keep them in your name that you have given me, so that they may be one just as we are one. When I was with them I protected them in your name that you gave me, and I guarded them, and none of them was lost except the son of destruction, in order that the Scripture might be fulfilled. But now I am coming to you. I speak this in the world so that they may share my joy completely. I gave them your word, and the world hated them, because they do not belong to the world any more than I belong to the world. I do not ask that you take them out of the world but that you keep them from the Evil One. They do not belong to the world any more than I belong to the world. Consecrate them in the truth. Your word is truth. As you sent me into the world, so I sent them into the world. And I consecrate myself for them, so that they also may be consecrated in truth."

THURSDAY OF THE SEVENTH WEEK OF EASTER

First Reading   **Acts 22:30; 23:6-11**

Wishing to determine the truth about why Paul was being accused by the Jews, the commander freed him and ordered the chief priests and the whole Sanhedrin to convene. Then he brought Paul down and made him stand before them.

Paul was aware that some were Sadducees and some Pharisees, so he called out before the Sanhedrin, "My brothers, I am a Pharisee, the son of Pharisees; I am on trial for hope in the resurrection of the dead." When he said this, a dispute broke out between the Pharisees and Sadducees, and the group became divided. For the Sadducees say that there is no resurrection or angels or spirits, while the Pharisees acknowledge all three. A great uproar occurred, and some scribes belonging to the Pharisee party stood up and sharply argued, "We find nothing wrong with this man. Suppose a spirit or an angel has spoken to him?" The dispute was so serious that the commander, afraid that Paul would be torn to pieces by them, ordered his troops to go down and rescue Paul from their midst and take him into the compound.

The following night the Lord stood by him and said, "Take courage. For just as you have borne witness to my cause in Jerusalem, so you must also bear witness in Rome."

Responsorial Psalm   **Psalm 16:1-2a and 5, 7-8, 9-10, 11**

R. (1) Keep me safe, O God; you are my hope.

Or:

R. Alleluia.

Keep me, O God, for in you I take refuge; I say to the LORD, "My Lord are you." O LORD, my allotted portion and my cup, you it is who hold fast my lot. **R.**

I bless the LORD who counsels me; even in the night my heart exhorts me. I set the LORD ever before me; with him at my right hand I shall not be disturbed. **R.**

Therefore my heart is glad and my soul rejoices, my body, too, abides in confidence; because you will not abandon my soul to the nether world, nor will you suffer your faithful one to undergo corruption. **R.**

You will show me the path to life, fullness of joys in your presence, the delights at your right hand forever. **R.**

Alleluia   **John 17:21**

R. Alleluia, alleluia.

May they all be one as you, Father, are in me and I in you, that the world may believe that you sent me, says the Lord. **R.**

Gospel   **John 17:20-26**

Lifting up his eyes to heaven, Jesus prayed saying:

"I pray not only for these, but also for those who will believe in me through their word, so that they may all be one, as you, Father, are in me and I in you, that they also may be in us, that the world may believe that you sent me. And I have given them the glory you gave me, so that they may be one, as we are one, I in them and you in me, that they may be brought to perfection as one, that the world may know that you sent me, and that you loved them even as you loved me. Father, they are your gift to me. I wish that where I am they also may be with me, that they may see my glory that you gave me, because you loved me before the foundation of the world. Righteous Father, the world also does not know you, but I know you, and they know that you sent me. I made known to them your name and I will make it known, that the love with which you loved me may be in them and I in them."

FRIDAY OF THE SEVENTH WEEK OF EASTER

First Reading   **Acts 25:13b-21**

King Agrippa and Bernice arrived in Caesarea on a visit to Festus. Since they spent several days there, Festus referred Paul's case to the king, saying, "There is a man here left in custody by Felix. When I was in Jerusalem the chief priests and the elders of the Jews brought charges against him and demanded his condemnation. I answered them that it was not Roman practice to hand over an accused person before he has faced his accusers and had the opportunity to defend himself against their charge. So when they came together here, I made no delay; the next day I took my seat on the tribunal and ordered the man to be brought in. His accusers stood around him, but did not charge him with any of the crimes I suspected. Instead they had some issues with him about their own religion and about a certain Jesus who had died but who Paul claimed was alive. Since I was at a loss how to investigate this controversy, I asked if he were willing to go to Jerusalem and there stand trial on these charges. And when Paul appealed that he be held in custody for the Emperor's decision, I ordered him held until I could send him to Caesar."

Responsorial Psalm   Psalm 103:1-2, 11-12, 19-20ab
R. (19a) The Lord has established his throne in heaven.
Or:
R. Alleluia.
Bless the LORD, O my soul; and all my being, bless his holy name. Bless the LORD, O my soul, and forget not all his benefits. **R.**
For as the heavens are high above the earth, so surpassing is his kindness toward those who fear him. As far as the east is from the west, so far has he put our transgressions from us. **R.**
The LORD has established his throne in heaven, and his kingdom rules over all. Bless the LORD, all you his angels, you mighty in strength, who do his bidding. **R.**

Alleluia   John 14:26
R. Alleluia, alleluia.
The Holy Spirit will teach you everything and remind you of all I told you. **R.**

Gospel   John 21:15-19
After Jesus had revealed himself to his disciples and eaten breakfast with them, he said to Simon Peter, "Simon, son of John,

do you love me more than these?" Simon Peter answered him, "Yes, Lord, you know that I love you." Jesus said to him, "Feed my lambs." He then said to Simon Peter a second time, "Simon, son of John, do you love me?" Simon Peter answered him, "Yes, Lord, you know that I love you." He said to him, "Tend my sheep." He said to him the third time, "Simon, son of John, do you love me?" Peter was distressed that he had said to him a third time, "Do you love me?" and he said to him, "Lord, you know everything; you know that I love you." Jesus said to him, "Feed my sheep. Amen, amen, I say to you, when you were younger, you used to dress yourself and go where you wanted; but when you grow old, you will stretch out your hands, and someone else will dress you and lead you where you do not want to go." He said this signifying by what kind of death he would glorify God. And when he had said this, he said to him, "Follow me."

SATURDAY, MAY 22, 2021

SATURDAY OF THE SEVENTH WEEK OF EASTER

(Mass in the Morning)

First Reading   **Acts 28:16-20, 30-31**

When he entered Rome, Paul was allowed to live by himself, with the soldier who was guarding him.

Three days later he called together the leaders of the Jews. When they had gathered he said to them, "My brothers, although I had done nothing against our people or our ancestral customs, I was handed over to the Romans as a prisoner from Jerusalem. After trying my case the Romans wanted to release me, because they found nothing against me deserving the death penalty. But when the Jews objected, I was obliged to appeal to Caesar, even though I had no accusation to make against my own nation. This is the reason, then, I have requested to see you and to speak with you, for it is on account of the hope of Israel that I wear these chains."

He remained for two full years in his lodgings. He received all who came to him, and with complete assurance and without hindrance he proclaimed the Kingdom of God and taught about the Lord Jesus Christ.

Responsorial Psalm   Psalm 11:4, 5 and 7

R. (7b) The just will gaze on your face, O Lord.

Or:

R. Alleluia.

The LORD is in his holy temple; the LORD's throne is in heaven.
His eyes behold, his searching glance is on mankind. **R.**
The LORD searches the just and the wicked; the lover of violence
he hates. For the LORD is just, he loves just deeds; the upright
shall see his face. **R.**

Alleluia   John 16:7, 13

R. Alleluia, alleluia.

I will send to you the Spirit of truth, says the Lord; he will guide you to all truth. **R.**

Gospel   John 21:20-25

Peter turned and saw the disciple following whom Jesus loved, the one who had also reclined upon his chest during the supper and had said, "Master, who is the one who will betray you?" When Peter saw him, he said to Jesus, "Lord, what about him?" Jesus said to him, "What if I want him to remain until I come? What concern is it of yours? You follow me."

So the word spread among the brothers that that disciple would not die. But Jesus had not told him that he would not die, just "What if I want him to remain until I come? What concern is it of yours?" It is this disciple who testifies to these things and has written them, and we know that his testimony is true. There are also many other things that Jesus did, but if these were to be described individually, I do not think the whole world would contain the books that would be written.

PENTECOST SUNDAY

(At the Vigil Mass)

First Reading   Genesis 11:1-9 or Exodus 19:3-8a, 16-20b or Ezekiel 37:1-14 or Joel 3:1-5

Genesis 11:1-9

The whole world spoke the same language, using the same words. While the people were migrating in the east, they came upon a valley in the land of Shinar and settled there. They said to one another, "Come, let us mold bricks and harden them with fire." They used bricks for stone, and bitumen for mortar. Then they said, "Come, let us build ourselves a city and a tower with its top in the sky, and so make a name for ourselves; otherwise we shall be scattered all over the earth."

The LORD came down to see the city and the tower that the people had built. Then the LORD said: "If now, while they are one people, all speaking the same language, they have started to do this, nothing will later stop them from doing whatever they presume to do. Let us then go down there and confuse their language, so that one will not understand what another says." Thus the LORD scattered them from there all over the earth, and they stopped building the city. That is why it was called Babel, because there the LORD confused the speech of all the world. It was from that place that he scattered them all over the earth.

Or:

Exodus 19:3-8a, 16-20b

Moses went up the mountain to God. Then the LORD called to him and said, "Thus shall you say to the house of Jacob; tell the Israelites: You have seen for yourselves how I treated the Egyptians and how I bore you up on eagle wings and brought you here to myself. Therefore, if you hearken to my voice and keep my covenant, you shall be my special possession, dearer to me than all other people, though all the earth is mine. You shall be to me a kingdom of priests, a holy nation. That is what you must tell the Israelites." So Moses went and summoned the elders of the people. When he set before them all that the LORD had ordered him to tell them, the people all answered together, "Everything the LORD has said, we will do."

On the morning of the third day there were peals of thunder and lightning, and a heavy cloud over the mountain, and a very loud trumpet blast, so that all the people in the camp trembled. But Moses led the people out of the camp to meet God, and they stationed themselves at the foot of the mountain. Mount Sinai was all wrapped in smoke, for the LORD came down upon it in fire. The smoke rose from it as though from a furnace, and the whole mountain trembled violently. The trumpet blast grew louder and louder, while Moses was speaking, and God answering him with thunder. When the LORD came down to the top of Mount Sinai, he summoned Moses to the top of the mountain.

Or:

Ezekiel 37:1-14

The hand of the LORD came upon me, and he led me out in the spirit of the LORD and set me in the center of the plain, which was now filled with bones. He made me walk among the bones in every direction so that I saw how many they were on the surface of the plain. How dry they were! He asked me: Son of man, can these bones come to life? I answered, "Lord GOD, you alone know that." Then he said to me: Prophesy over these bones, and say to them: Dry bones, hear the word of the LORD! Thus says the Lord GOD to these bones: See! I will bring spirit into you, that you may come to life. I will put sinews upon you, make flesh grow over you, cover you with skin, and put spirit in you so that you may come to life and know that I am the LORD.

I, Ezekiel, prophesied as I had been told, and even as I was prophesying I heard a noise; it was a rattling as the bones came together, bone joining bone. I saw the sinews and the flesh come upon them, and the skin cover them, but there was no spirit in them. Then the LORD said to me: Prophesy to the spirit, prophesy, son of man, and say to the spirit: Thus says the Lord GOD: From the four winds come, O spirit, and breathe into these slain that they may come to life. I prophesied as he told me, and the spirit came into them; they came alive and stood upright, a vast army. Then he said to me: Son of man, these bones are the whole house of Israel. They have been saying, "Our bones are dried up, our hope is lost, and we are cut off."

Therefore, prophesy and say to them: Thus says the Lord GOD: O my people, I will open your graves and have you rise from them, and bring you back to the land of Israel. Then you shall know that I am the LORD, when I open your graves and have you rise from them, O my people! I will put my spirit in you that you may live, and I will settle you upon your land; thus you shall know that I am the LORD. I have promised, and I will do it, says the LORD.

Or:

Joel 3:1-5

Thus says the LORD:

I will pour out my spirit upon all flesh. Your sons and daughters shall prophesy, your old men shall dream dreams, your young men shall see visions; even upon the servants and the handmaids, in those days, I will pour out my spirit. And I will work wonders in the heavens and on the earth, blood, fire, and columns of smoke; the sun will be turned to darkness, and the moon to blood, at the coming of the day of the LORD, the great and terrible day. Then everyone shall be rescued who calls on the name of the LORD; for on Mount Zion there shall be a remnant, as the LORD has said, and in Jerusalem survivors whom the LORD shall call.

Responsorial Psalm   **Psalm 104:1-2, 24, 35, 27-28, 29, 30**

R. (30) Lord, send out your Spirit, and renew the face of the earth.

Or:

R. Alleluia.

Bless the LORD, O my soul! O LORD, my God, you are great indeed! You are clothed with majesty and glory, robed in light as with a cloak. **R.**

How manifold are your works, O LORD! In wisdom you have wrought them all the earth is full of your creatures; bless the LORD, O my soul! Alleluia. **R.**

Creatures all look to you to give them food in due time. When you give it to them, they gather it; when you open your hand, they are filled with good things. **R.**

If you take away their breath, they perish and return to their dust. When you send forth your spirit, they are created, and you renew the face of the earth. **R.**

Second Reading   Romans 8:22-27

Brothers and sisters:

We know that all creation is groaning in labor pains even until now; and not only that, but we ourselves, who have the first fruits of the Spirit, we also groan within ourselves as we wait for adoption, the redemption of our bodies. For in hope we were saved. Now hope that sees is not hope. For who hopes for what one sees? But if we hope for what we do not see, we wait with endurance.

In the same way, the Spirit too comes to the aid of our weakness; for we do not know how to pray as we ought, but the Spirit himself intercedes with inexpressible groanings. And the one who searches hearts knows what is the intention of the Spirit, because he intercedes for the holy ones according to God's will.

Alleluia

R. Alleluia, alleluia.

Come, Holy Spirit, fill the hearts of the faithful and kindle in them the fire of your love. **R.**

Gospel   John 7:37-39

On the last and greatest day of the feast, Jesus stood up and exclaimed, "Let anyone who thirsts come to me and drink. As Scripture says:

Rivers of living water will flow from within him who believes in me." He said this in reference to the Spirit that those who came to believe in him were to receive. There was, of course, no Spirit yet, because Jesus had not yet been glorified.

PENTECOST SUNDAY

(Mass during the Day)

First Reading   Acts 2:1-11

When the time for Pentecost was fulfilled, they were all in one place together. And suddenly there came from the sky a noise like a strong driving wind, and it filled the entire house in which they were. Then there appeared to them tongues as of fire, which parted and came to rest on each one of them. And they were all filled with the Holy Spirit and began to speak in different tongues, as the Spirit enabled them to proclaim. Now there were devout Jews from every nation under heaven staying in Jerusalem. At this sound, they gathered in a large crowd, but they were confused because each one heard them speaking in his own language. They were astounded, and in amazement they asked, "Are not all these people who are speaking Galileans? Then how does each of us hear them in his native language? We are Parthians, Medes, and Elamites, inhabitants of Mesopotamia, Judea and Cappadocia, Pontus and Asia, Phrygia and Pamphylia, Egypt and the districts of Libya near Cyrene, as well as travelers from Rome, both Jews and converts to Judaism, Cretans and Arabs, yet we hear them speaking in our own tongues of the mighty acts of God."

Responsorial Psalm   Psalm 104:1, 24, 29-30, 31, 34

R. (30) Lord, send out your Spirit, and renew the face of the earth.

Or:

R. Alleluia.

Bless the LORD, O my soul! O LORD, my God, you are great indeed! How manifold are your works, O Lord! The earth is full of your creatures; **R.**

May the glory of the LORD endure forever; may the LORD be glad in his works! Pleasing to him be my theme; I will be glad in the LORD. **R.**

If you take away their breath, they perish and return to their dust. When you send forth your spirit, they are created, and you renew the face of the earth. **R.**

Second Reading   1 Cor 12:3b-7, 12-13 or Gal 5:16-25

1 Corinthians 12:3b-7, 12-13

Brothers and sisters:

No one can say, "Jesus is Lord," except by the Holy Spirit. There are different kinds of spiritual gifts but the same Spirit; there are different forms of service but the same Lord; there are different workings but the same God who produces all of them in everyone.

To each individual the manifestation of the Spirit is given for some benefit.

As a body is one though it has many parts, and all the parts of the body, though many, are one body, so also Christ. For in one Spirit we were all baptized into one body, whether Jews or Greeks, slaves or free persons, and we were all given to drink of one Spirit.

Or:

Galatians 5:16-25

Brothers and sisters, live by the Spirit and you will certainly not gratify the desire of the flesh. For the flesh has desires against the Spirit, and the Spirit against the flesh; these are opposed to each other, so that you may not do what you want. But if you are guided by the Spirit, you are not under the law. Now the works of the flesh are obvious: immorality, impurity, lust, idolatry, sorcery, hatreds, rivalry, jealousy, outbursts of fury, acts of selfishness, dissensions, factions, occasions of envy, drinking bouts, orgies, and the like. I warn you, as I warned you before, that those who do such things will not inherit the kingdom of God. In contrast, the fruit of the Spirit is love, joy, peace, patience, kindness, generosity, faithfulness, gentleness, self-control. Against such there is no law. Now those who belong to Christ Jesus have crucified their flesh with its passions and desires. If we live in the Spirit, let us also follow the Spirit.

Sequence   *Veni, Sancte Spiritus*

Come, Holy Spirit, come!
And from your celestial home
Shed a ray of light divine!

Come, Father of the poor!
Come, source of all our store!
Come, within our bosoms shine.
You, of comforters the best;
You, the soul's most welcome guest;
Sweet refreshment here below;
In our labor, rest most sweet;
Grateful coolness in the heat;
Solace in the midst of woe.
O most blessed Light divine,
Shine within these hearts of yours,
And our inmost being fill!
Where you are not, we have naught,
Nothing good in deed or thought,
Nothing free from taint of ill.
Heal our wounds, our strength renew;
On our dryness pour your dew;
Wash the stains of guilt away:
Bend the stubborn heart and will;
Melt the frozen, warm the chill;
Guide the steps that go astray.
On the faithful, who adore
And confess you, evermore
In your sevenfold gift descend;
Give them virtue's sure reward;
Give them your salvation, Lord;
Give them joys that never end. Amen.
Alleluia.

Alleluia

R. Alleluia, alleluia.

Come, Holy Spirit, fill the hearts of your faithful and kindle in them the fire of your love. **R.**

Gospel   John 20:19-23 or 15:26-27; 16:12-15

John 20:19-23

On the evening of that first day of the week, when the doors were locked, where the disciples were, for fear of the Jews, Jesus came and stood in their midst and said to them, "Peace be with you." When he had said this, he showed them his hands and his side. The disciples rejoiced when they saw the Lord. Jesus said to them again, "Peace be with you. As the Father has sent me, so I send you." And when he had said this, he breathed on them and said to them, "Receive the Holy Spirit. Whose sins you forgive are forgiven them, and whose sins you retain are retained."

Or:

John 15:26-27; 16:12-15

Jesus said to his disciples:

"When the Advocate comes whom I will send you from the Father, the Spirit of truth that proceeds from the Father, he will testify to me. And you also testify, because you have been with me from the beginning.

"I have much more to tell you, but you cannot bear it now. But when he comes, the Spirit of truth, he will guide you to all truth. He will not speak on his own, but he will speak what he hears, and will declare to you the things that are coming. He will glorify me, because he will take from what is mine and declare it to you.

449

Everything that the Father has is mine; for this reason I told you that he will take from what is mine and declare it to you."

MEMORIAL OF THE BLESSED VIRGIN MARY, MOTHER OF THE CHURCH

First Reading   **Genesis 3:9-15, 20 or**

Acts 1:12-14

Genesis 3:9-15

After Adam had eaten of the tree, the LORD God called to him and asked him, "Where are you?" He answered, "I heard you in the garden; but I was afraid, because I was naked, so I hid myself." Then he asked, "Who told you that you were naked? You have eaten, then, from the tree of which I had forbidden you to eat!" The man replied, "The woman whom you put here with me—she gave me fruit from the tree, and so I ate it." The LORD God then asked the woman, "Why did you do such a thing?" The woman answered, "The serpent tricked me into it, so I ate it." Then the LORD God said to the serpent: "Because you have done this, you shall be banned from all the animals and from all the wild creatures; on your belly shall you crawl, and dirt shall you eat all the days of your life. I will put enmity between you and the woman, and between your offspring and hers; He will strike at your head, while you strike at his heel." The man called his wife Eve, because she became the mother of all the living.

Or:

Acts 1:12-14

After Jesus had been taken up to heaven, the Apostles returned to Jerusalem from the mount called Olivet, which is near Jerusalem, a Sabbath day's journey away.

When they entered the city they went to the upper room where they were staying, Peter and John and James and Andrew, Philip and Thomas, Bartholomew and Matthew, James son of Alphaeus, Simon the Zealot, and Judas son of James.

All these devoted themselves with one accord to prayer, together with some women, and Mary the mother of Jesus, and his brothers.

Responsorial Psalm   Psalm 87:1-2, 3 and 5, 6-7

R. (3) Glorious things are told of you, O city of God.

His foundation upon the holy mountains the LORD loves: The gates of Zion, more than any dwelling of Jacob. **R.**

Glorious things are said of you, O city of God! And of Zion they shall say: "One and all were born in her; and he who has established her is the Most High LORD." **R.**

They shall note, when the peoples are enrolled: "This man was born there." And all shall sing, in their festive dance: "My home is within you." **R.**

Alleluia

R. Alleluia, alleluia.

O happy Virgin, you gave birth to the Lord; O blessed mother of the Church, you warm our hearts with the Spirit of your Son Jesus Christ. **R.**

Gospel   John 19:25-34

Standing by the cross of Jesus were his mother and his mother's sister, Mary the wife of Clopas, and Mary of Magdala. When Jesus saw his mother and the disciple there whom he loved, he said to his mother, "Woman, behold, your son."

Then he said to the disciple, "Behold, your mother." And from that hour the disciple took her into his home. After this, aware that everything was now finished, in order that the Scripture might be fulfilled, Jesus said, "I thirst." There was a vessel filled with common wine. So they put a sponge soaked in wine on a sprig of hyssop and put it up to his mouth. When Jesus had taken the wine, he said, "It is finished." And bowing his head, he handed over the spirit.

Now since it was preparation day, in order that the bodies might not remain on the cross on the sabbath, for the sabbath day of that week was a solemn one, the Jews asked Pilate that their legs be broken and they be taken down. So the soldiers came and broke the legs of the first and then of the other one who was crucified with Jesus. But when they came to Jesus and saw that he was already dead, they did not break his legs, but one soldier thrust his lance into his side, and immediately Blood and water flowed out.

TUESDAY OF THE EIGHTH WEEK IN ORDINARY TIME

First Reading   **Sirach 35:1-12**

To keep the law is a great oblation, and he who observes the commandments sacrifices a peace offering. In works of charity one offers fine flour, and when he gives alms he presents his sacrifice of praise. To refrain from evil pleases the LORD, and to avoid injustice is an atonement. Appear not before the LORD empty-handed, for all that you offer is in fulfillment of the precepts. The just one's offering enriches the altar and rises as a sweet odor before the Most High. The just one's sacrifice is most pleasing, nor will it ever be forgotten. In a generous spirit pay homage to the LORD, be not sparing of freewill gifts. With each contribution show a cheerful countenance, and pay your tithes in a spirit of joy. Give to the Most High as he has given to you, generously, according to your means.

For the LORD is one who always repays, and he will give back to you sevenfold. But offer no bribes, these he does not accept! Trust not in sacrifice of the fruits of extortion. For he is a God of justice, who knows no favorites.

Responsorial Psalm   Psalm 50:5-6, 7-8, 14 and 23
R. (23b) To the upright I will show the saving power of God.

"Gather my faithful ones before me, those who have made a covenant with me by sacrifice." And the heavens proclaim his justice; for God himself is the judge. **R.**

"Hear, my people, and I will speak; Israel, I will testify against you; God, your God, am I. Not for your sacrifices do I rebuke you, for your burnt offerings are before me always." **R.**

"Offer to God praise as your sacrifice and fulfill your vows to the Most High. He that offers praise as a sacrifice glorifies me; and to him that goes the right way I will show the salvation of God." **R.**

Alleluia   Matthew 11:25
R. Alleluia, alleluia.

Blessed are you, Father, Lord of heaven and earth; you have revealed to little ones the mysteries of the Kingdom. **R.**

Gospel   Mark 10:28-31

Peter began to say to Jesus, 'We have given up everything and followed you." Jesus said, "Amen, I say to you, there is no one who has given up house or brothers or sisters or mother or father or children or lands for my sake and for the sake of the Gospel who will not receive a hundred times more now in this present age: houses and brothers and sisters and mothers and children and lands, with persecutions, and eternal life in the age to come. But many that are first will be last, and the last will be first."

WEDNESDAY, MAY 26, 2021

MEMORIAL OF SAINT PHILIP NERI, PRIEST

First Reading   Sirach 36:1, 4-5a, 10-17

Come to our aid, O God of the universe, look upon us, show us the light of your mercies, and put all the nations in dread of you! Thus they will know, as we know, that there is no God but you, O Lord. Give new signs and work new wonders. Gather all the tribes of Jacob, that they may inherit the land as of old, Show mercy to the people called by your name; Israel, whom you named your firstborn. Take pity on your holy city, Jerusalem, your dwelling place. Fill Zion with your majesty, your temple with your glory.

Give evidence of your deeds of old; fulfill the prophecies spoken in your name, Reward those who have hoped in you, and let your prophets be proved true. Hear the prayer of your servants, for you are ever gracious to your people; and lead us in the way of justice.

Thus it will be known to the very ends of the earth that you are the eternal God.

Responsorial Psalm   Psalm 79:8, 9, 11 and 13

R. (Sirach 36:1b) Show us, O Lord, the light of your kindness.

Remember not against us the iniquities of the past; may your compassion quickly come to us, for we are brought very low. **R.**

Help us, O God our savior, because of the glory of your name; Deliver us and pardon our sins for your name's sake. **R.**

Let the prisoners' sighing come before you; with your great power free those doomed to death. Then we, your people and the sheep of your pasture, will give thanks to you forever; through all generations we will declare your praise. **R.**

Alleluia   Mark 10:45

R. Alleluia, alleluia.

The Son of Man came to serve, and to give his life as a ransom for many. **R.**

Gospel   Mark 10:32-45

The disciples were on the way, going up to Jerusalem, and Jesus went ahead of them. They were amazed, and those who followed were afraid. Taking the Twelve aside again, he began to tell them what was going to happen to him. "Behold, we are going up to Jerusalem, and the Son of Man will be handed over to the chief priests and the scribes, and they will condemn him to death and hand him over to the Gentiles who will mock him, spit upon him, scourge him, and put him to death, but after three days he will rise."

Then James and John, the sons of Zebedee, came to Jesus and said to him, 'Teacher, we want you to do for us whatever we ask of you.' He replied, 'What do you wish me to do for you?' They answered him, "Grant that in your glory we may sit one at your right and the other at your left." Jesus said to them, "You do not know what you are asking. Can you drink the chalice that I drink or be baptized with the baptism with which I am baptized?" They said to him, 'We can.' Jesus said to them, "The chalice that I drink, you will drink, and with the baptism with which I am baptized, you will be baptized; but to sit at my right or at my left is not mine to give but is for those for whom it has been prepared."

When the ten heard this, they became indignant at James and John. Jesus summoned them and said to them, "You know that those who are recognized as rulers over the Gentiles lord it over them, and their great ones make their authority over them felt. But it shall not be so among you. Rather, whoever wishes to be great among you will be your servant; whoever wishes to be first among you will be the slave of all. For the Son of Man did not come to be served but to serve and to give his life as a ransom for many."

THURSDAY OF THE EIGHTH WEEK IN ORDINARY TIME

First Reading   **Sirach 42:15-25**

Now will I recall God's works; what I have seen, I will describe. At God's word were his works brought into being; they do his will as he has ordained for them. As the rising sun is clear to all, so the glory of the LORD fills all his works; yet even God's holy ones must fail in recounting the wonders of the LORD, Though God has given these, his hosts, the strength to stand firm before his glory. He plumbs the depths and penetrates the heart; their innermost being he understands. The Most High possesses all knowledge, and sees from of old the things that are to come: He makes known the past and the future, and reveals the deepest secrets. No understanding does he lack; no single thing escapes him. Perennial is his almighty wisdom; he is from all eternity one and the same, With nothing added, nothing taken away; no need of a counselor for him! How beautiful are all his works! Even to the spark and fleeting vision! The universe lives and abides forever; to meet each need, each creature is preserved. All of them differ, one from another, yet none of them has he made in vain, for each in turn, as it comes, is good; can one ever see enough of their splendor?

<u>Responsorial Psalm</u>   Psalm 33:2-3, 4-5, 6-7, 8-9

R. (6a) By the word of the Lord the heavens were made.

Give thanks to the LORD on the harp; with the ten-stringed lyre chant his praises. Sing to him a new song; pluck the strings skillfully, with shouts of gladness. **R.**

For upright is the word of the LORD and all his works are trustworthy. He loves justice and right; of the kindness of the LORD the earth is full. **R.**

By the word of the Lord the heavens were made; by the breath of his mouth all their host. He gathers the waters of the sea as in a flask; in cellars he confines the deep. **R.**

Let all the earth fear the Lord; let all who dwell in the world revere him. For he spoke, and it was made; he commanded, and it stood forth. **R.**

Alleluia   John 8:12

R. Alleluia, alleluia.

I am the light of the world, says the Lord; whoever follows me will have the light of life. **R.**

Gospel   Mark 10:46-52

As Jesus was leaving Jericho with his disciples and a sizable crowd, Bartimaeus, a blind man, the son of Timaeus, sat by the roadside begging. On hearing that it was Jesus of Nazareth, he began to cry out and say, "Jesus, son of David, have pity on me." And many rebuked him, telling him to be silent. But he kept calling out all the more, "Son of David, have pity on me." Jesus stopped and said, "Call him." So they called the blind man, saying to him, "Take courage; get up, Jesus is calling you." He threw aside his cloak, sprang up, and came to Jesus. Jesus said to him in reply, "What do you want me to do for you?" The blind man replied to him, "Master, I want to see." Jesus told him, 'Go your way; your faith has saved you." Immediately he received his sight and followed him on the way.

FRIDAY OF THE EIGHTH WEEK IN ORDINARY TIME

First Reading   **Sirach 44:1, 9-13**

Now will I praise those godly men, our ancestors, each in his own time. But of others there is no memory, for when they ceased, they ceased. And they are as though they had not lived, they and their children after them. Yet these also were godly men whose virtues have not been forgotten; their wealth remains in their families, their heritage with their descendants; Through God's covenant with them their family endures, their posterity, for their sake. And for all time their progeny will endure, their glory will never be blotted out.

Responsorial Psalm   **Psalm 149:1b-2, 3-4, 5-6a and 9b**

R. (4a) The Lord takes delight in his people.
Or:
R. Alleluia

Sing to the LORD a new song of praise in the assembly of the faithful. Let Israel be glad in their maker, let the children of Zion rejoice in their king. **R.**

Let them praise his name in the festive dance, let them sing praise to him with timbrel and harp. For the LORD loves his people, and he adorns the lowly with victory. **R.**

Let the faithful exult in glory; let them sing for joy upon their couches; Let the high praises of God be in their throats. This is the glory of all his faithful. Alleluia. **R.**

Alleluia   **John 15:16**

R. Alleluia, alleluia.

I chose you from the world, to go and bear fruit that will last, says the Lord. **R.**

Gospel   Mark 11:11-26

Jesus entered Jerusalem and went into the temple area. He looked around at everything and, since it was already late, went out to Bethany with the Twelve.

The next day as they were leaving Bethany he was hungry. Seeing from a distance a fig tree in leaf, he went over to see if he could find anything on it. When he reached it he found nothing but leaves; it was not the time for figs. And he said to it in reply, "May no one ever eat of your fruit again!" And his disciples heard it.

They came to Jerusalem, and on entering the temple area he began to drive out those selling and buying there. He overturned the tables of the money changers and the seats of those who were selling doves. He did not permit anyone to carry anything through the temple area. Then he taught them saying, "Is it not written:

My house shall be called a house of prayer for all peoples? But you have made it a den of thieves."

The chief priests and the scribes came to hear of it and were seeking a way to put him to death, yet they feared him because the whole crowd was astonished at his teaching. When evening came, they went out of the city.

Early in the morning, as they were walking along, they saw the fig tree withered to its roots. Peter remembered and said to him, "Rabbi, look! The fig tree that you cursed has withered." Jesus said to them in reply, "Have faith in God. Amen, I say to you, whoever says to this mountain, 'Be lifted up and thrown into the sea,' and does not doubt in his heart but believes that what he says will happen, it shall be done for him. Therefore I tell you, all that you ask for in prayer, believe that you will receive it and it shall be yours. When you stand to pray, forgive anyone against whom you have a grievance, so that your heavenly Father may in turn forgive you your transgressions."

SATURDAY OF THE EIGHTH WEEK IN ORDINARY TIME

First Reading   **Sirach 51:12cd-20**

I thank the LORD and I praise him; I bless the name of the LORD. When I was young and innocent, I sought wisdom openly in my prayer I prayed for her before the temple, and I will seek her until the end, and she flourished as a grape soon ripe. My heart delighted in her, my feet kept to the level path because from earliest youth I was familiar with her. In the short time I paid heed, I met with great instruction. Since in this way I have profited, I will give my teacher grateful praise. I became resolutely devoted to her — the good I persistently strove for. My soul was tormented in seeking her, my hand opened her gate and I came to know her secrets. I directed my soul to her, and in cleanness I attained to her.

Responsorial Psalm   **Psalm 19:8, 9, 10, 11**

R. (9ab) **The precepts of the Lord give joy to the heart.**

The law of the LORD is perfect, refreshing the soul. The decree of the LORD is trustworthy, giving wisdom to the simple. **R.**

The precepts of the LORD are right, rejoicing the heart. The command of the LORD is clear, enlightening the eye. **R.**

The fear of the LORD is pure, enduring forever; the ordinances of the LORD are true, all of them just. **R.**

They are more precious than gold, than a heap of purest gold; Sweeter also than syrup or honey from the comb. **R.**

Alleluia   Colossians 3:16a, 17c

R. Alleluia, alleluia.

Let the word of Christ dwell in you richly; giving thanks to God the Father through him. **R.**

Gospel   Mark 11:27-33

Jesus and his disciples returned once more to Jerusalem. As he was walking in the temple area, the chief priests, the scribes, and the elders approached him and said to him, "By what authority are you doing these things? Or who gave you this authority to do them?" Jesus said to them, "I shall ask you one question. Answer me, and I will tell you by what authority I do these things. Was John's baptism of heavenly or of human origin? Answer me." They discussed this among themselves and said, "If we say, 'Of heavenly origin,' he will say, 'then why did you not believe him?' But shall we say, 'Of human origin'?"– They feared the crowd, for they all thought John really was a prophet. So they said to Jesus in reply, "We do not know." Then Jesus said to them, "Neither shall I tell you by what authority I do these things."

THE SOLEMNITY OF THE MOST HOLY TRINITY

First Reading   **Deuteronomy 4:32-34, 39-40**

Moses said to the people:

"Ask now of the days of old, before your time, ever since God created man upon the earth; ask from one end of the sky to the other: Did anything so great ever happen before? Was it ever heard of? Did a people ever hear the voice of God speaking from the midst of fire, as you did, and live? Or did any god venture to go and take a nation for himself from the midst of another nation, by testings, by signs and wonders, by war, with strong hand and outstretched arm, and by great terrors, all of which the LORD, your God, did for you in Egypt before your very eyes?

This is why you must now know, and fix in your heart, that the LORD is God in the heavens above and on earth below, and that there is no other. You must keep his statutes and commandments that I enjoin on you today, that you and your children after you may prosper, and that you may have long life on the land which the LORD, your God, is giving you forever."

Responsorial Psalm   **Psalm 33:4-5, 6, 9, 18-19, 20, 22**

R. (12b) Blessed the people the Lord has chosen to be his own.

Upright is the word of the LORD, and all his works are trustworthy. He loves justice and right; of the kindness of the Lord the earth is full. **R.**

By the word of the LORD the heavens were made; by the breath of his mouth all their host. For he spoke, and it was made; he commanded, and it stood forth. **R.**

See, the eyes of the LORD are upon those who fear him, upon those who hope for his kindness, to deliver them from death and preserve them in spite of famine. **R.**

Our soul waits for the LORD, who is our help and our shield. May your kindness, O LORD, be upon us who have put our hope in you. **R.**

Second Reading   Romans 8:14-17

Brothers and sisters:

For those who are led by the Spirit of God are sons of God. For you did not receive a spirit of slavery to fall back into fear, but you received a Spirit of adoption, through whom we cry, "Abba, Father!" The Spirit himself bears witness with our spirit that we are children of God, and if children, then heirs, heirs of God and joint heirs with Christ, if only we suffer with him so that we may also be glorified with him.

Alleluia   Revelation 1:8

R. Alleluia, alleluia.

Glory to the Father, the Son, and the Holy Spirit; to God who is, who was, and who is to come. **R.**

Gospel   Matthew 28:16-20

The eleven disciples went to Galilee, to the mountain to which Jesus had ordered them. When they all saw him, they worshiped, but they doubted. Then Jesus approached and said to them, "All power in heaven and on earth has been given to me. Go, therefore, and make disciples of all nations, baptizing them in the name of the Father, and of the Son, and of the Holy Spirit, teaching them to observe all that I have commanded you. And behold, I am with you always, until the end of the age."

FEAST OF THE VISITATION OF THE BLESSED VIRGIN MARY

First Reading   **Zeph 3:14-18a or Rom 12:9-16**

Zephaniah 3:14-18a

Shout for joy, O daughter Zion! Sing joyfully, O Israel! Be glad and exult with all your heart, O daughter Jerusalem! The LORD has removed the judgment against you, he has turned away your enemies; The King of Israel, the LORD, is in your midst, you have no further misfortune to fear. On that day, it shall be said to Jerusalem: Fear not, O Zion, be not discouraged! The LORD, your God, is in your midst, a mighty savior; He will rejoice over you with gladness, and renew you in his love, He will sing joyfully because of you, as one sings at festivals.

Or:

Romans 12:9-16

Brothers and sisters:

Let love be sincere; hate what is evil, hold on to what is good; love one another with mutual affection; anticipate one another in showing honor. Do not grow slack in zeal, be fervent in spirit, serve the Lord. Rejoice in hope, endure in affliction, persevere in prayer. Contribute to the needs of the holy ones, exercise hospitality. Bless those who persecute you, bless and do not curse them. Rejoice with those who rejoice, weep with those who weep.

Have the same regard for one another; do not be haughty but associate with the lowly; do not be wise in your own estimation.

Responsorial Psalm   Isaiah 12:2-3, 4bcd, 5-6
R. (6) Among you is the great and Holy One of Israel.
God indeed is my savior; I am confident and unafraid. My strength and my courage is the LORD, and he has been my savior. With joy you will draw water at the fountain of salvation. **R.**
Give thanks to the LORD, acclaim his name; among the nations make known his deeds, proclaim how exalted is his name. **R.**
Sing praise to the LORD for his glorious achievement; let this be known throughout all the earth. Shout with exultation, O city of Zion, for great in your midst is the Holy One of Israel! **R.**

Alleluia   Luke 1:45
R. Alleluia, alleluia.
Blessed are you, O Virgin Mary, who believed that what was spoken to you by the Lord would be fulfilled. **R.**

Gospel   Luke 1:39-56
Mary set out and traveled to the hill country in haste to a town of Judah, where she entered the house of Zechariah and greeted Elizabeth. When Elizabeth heard Mary's greeting, the infant leaped in her womb, and Elizabeth, filled with the Holy Spirit, cried out in a loud voice and said, "Most blessed are you among women, and blessed is the fruit of your womb. And how does this happen to me, that the mother of my Lord should come to me? For at the moment the sound of your greeting reached my ears, the

infant in my womb leaped for joy. Blessed are you who believed that what was spoken to you by the Lord would be fulfilled."

And Mary said:

"My soul proclaims the greatness of the Lord; my spirit rejoices in God my Savior, for he has looked with favor on his lowly servant. From this day all generations will call me blessed: the Almighty has done great things for me, and holy is his Name.

He has mercy on those who fear him in every generation. He has shown the strength of his arm, he has scattered the proud in their conceit. He has cast down the mighty from their thrones, and has lifted up the lowly. He has filled the hungry with good things, and the rich he has sent away empty. He has come to the help of his servant Israel for he has remembered his promise of mercy, the promise he made to our fathers, to Abraham and his children for ever."

Mary remained with her about three months and then returned to her home.

Made in the USA
Middletown, DE
13 December 2020